Governing through Globalised Crime

Governing through Globalised Crime
Futures for international criminal justice

Mark Findlay

WILLAN
PUBLISHING

Published by

Willan Publishing
Culmcott House
Mill Street, Uffculme
Cullompton, Devon
EX15 3AT, UK
Tel: +44(0)1884 840337
Fax: +44(0)1884 840251
e-mail: info@willanpublishing.co.uk
website: www.willanpublishing.co.uk

Published simultaneously in the USA and Canada by

Willan Publishing
c/o ISBS, 920 NE 58th Ave, Suite 300,
Portland, Oregon 97213-3786, USA
Tel: +001(0)503 287 3093
Fax: +001(0)503 280 8832
e-mail: info@isbs.com
website: www.isbs.com

First published 2008

ISBN   978-1-84392-308-4 paperback
       978-1-84392-309-1 hardback

British Library Cataloguing-in-Publication Data

A catalogue record for this book is available from the British Library

Cover image
'Winterreise' by James Gleeson, courtesy University of Sydney Art Collection

Project managed by Deer Park Productions, Tavistock, Devon
Typeset by GCS, Leighton Buzzard, Bedfordshire
Printed and bound by T.J. International Ltd., Padstow, Cornwall

Contents

Acknowledgements

I recognise the assistance of the Legal Scholarship Support Fund, and the Staff Development Fund, Law School, University of Sydney. These sources enabled much of the travel and critical engagement essential for the experience of a book about globalisation. In addition, the excellent and creative research assistance from Rachel Miller would not have been possible without this support. My faculty has demonstrated through this generous and structured commitment to monograph writing not just the value it places on socio-legal scholarship, but also on internationalisation and comparativism as research priorities.

I am an Associate Senior Research Fellow at the Institute of Advanced Legal Studies, London University. The Institute's library and research facilities were important in accessing the rich case-study resources on which several of the chapters are based.

Recently I was awarded a fractional chair in International Criminal Justice at the Centre for Criminal Justice Studies, University of Leeds. I recognise the interest and support of colleagues at the centre, Adam Crawford in particular.

Several of the central themes in the book have been tested against critical student audiences in my classes on Advanced Criminal Law, and Policing Australian Society. I also had the pleasure of exposing some of my more contentious ideas to a sharp group of doctoral students at the Max Planck Institute for Foreign and International Criminal Law in Freiburg, as well as at the Leuven Centre for Global Governance, Catholic University of Leuven. My own doctoral students, Edwin Bikundo in particular have offered insights into the development of my thinking.

Much earlier versions of components in Chapters 3, 4, 5, 7 and 9 have been presented at conferences in Hong Kong, Singapore, Melbourne, Sydney, London and Canberra. To the conference organisers and my audiences, many thanks for the opportunity to fly a few kites.

Short excerpts have been redeveloped, expanded and reconfigured from publications in *Crime, Law and Social Change*, *Current Issues in Criminal Justice* and *The Asian Journal of Criminology*. I am particularly indebted to the critical comments of anonymous reviewers for those publications and for the editorial opportunities that these journals provide. Much thanks also to Wayne for his careful eye.

My colleague and co-author Ralph Henham as always has given me wise counsel and commented in detail on earlier drafts. Chris Cunneen, Jonathan Simon, James Cockayne, Clare McLean, Pat O'Malley and other colleagues at the Institute of Criminology have to differing extents looked over the work and kindly offered critical direction. Even so, I retain responsibility for the arguments that follow in all their fragility.

The intriguing cover graphic is courtesy of the University of Sydney Art Collection and the generous permission of the celebrated Australian artist James Gleeson.

I dedicate this book to James, Nicholas, Alice and Lucy with the hope that some of what I do here, and daily through my social commentary, might in some small way contribute to a more just world order. My efforts are for your world and your futures, with much love.

Introduction

The most visible and discussed features of governing through crime involve practices of punishing, repressing and confining people. But much of the work of governing through crime involves equipping and guiding subjects in the socially valorised pursuit of justice. Here we are no longer talking primarily about the work of imposing the discipline of punishment over a resentful mind and resistant body. (Simon 2007: 20–1)

Aspirations

We are well into an age where crime and punishment are constructed and employed to govern the globe. Criminal law once associated with sovereignty and the state's monopoly over the legitimate means of violence (Simon 2007: 21) has outreached into the management of international relations (Zahar and Sluiter 2007). International criminal justice is applied via formal instrumentalities and community-centred engagement to advance political dominion through *peacemaking* in post-conflict states (Findlay and Henham 2005).

Analysing the relationship between crime and governance is not new. In *Discipline and Punish*, Foucault (1975) explored the transition in governing individuals from controlling the body to constraining the mind. Before him, Rusche and Kirchheimer (1939) in *Punishment and Social Structure* traced the historical development of criminal sanctions as mechanisms for the subjugation of labour. Garland argued the relationship between punishment and styles of social cohesion in *Punishment and Modern Society* (1990). The following discussion moves out from this tradition in employing the contemporary context of globalisation to chart the critical nexus between crime/risk and control/security. From here the challenge is to appreciate international criminal justice as a central tool for global governance, as well as the social conditions under which this has arisen. Finally, in exploring the dependency of global governance on crime and control, projections can be made about the changing face of international criminal justice. Fundamental transformation is required to hold *unjust* global dominion to account.

The relationship between crime, control and modernisation in transitional cultures has been sketched out in *The Globalisation of Crime: Understanding Transitional Relationships in Context* (Findlay 1999b). Since writing that book it can be said that globalisation has entered a new risk and security focus.[1] Risk and security responses have become tools for global governance wherein crime/risk and control/security are essentially conflated in the context of international criminal justice.[2] Governance is now reliant on risk and security balances (O'Malley 2007). The *risk society* has joined modernity as the organising framework of a globalised world. Security is the aspiration for global governance, while globalised crime and control have become key ingredients in the risk/security nexus.

My interest in the role of criminal justice within global governance has its links back to *The Globalisation of Crime* in its cultural focus. Global governance is intended, theoretically at least, for a *global community*. What today takes that community beyond the 'pastoral' notions of Stan Cohen's critique (1985: ch. 4) is the *nostalgia* for order and harmony. One side of the globalisation paradox is the move to a single culture (Findlay 1999: ch. 1). The disorder that attaches to the reality of cultural diversity and the dynamics of transformation is read in the risk/security regime as justification for a *war* on pluralism (discussed in Chapter 9). Cohen's identification of the 'quest for community' in social control, when translated to the global level, relies on imagining cultural ascription to a uniform world order. Resistance is risky. Violent resistance endangers security. The cultural contexts of resistance require governance to conformity. The *global community* which will remain as a consequence of contemporary globalisation becomes a sectarian but profoundly symbolic vision for the new world order. The governance ideologies now directed towards securing *global community*:

... are sustained by, and owe their public appeal to, the rhetorical quest for community. It would be difficult to exaggerate how this ideology – or more accurately this single word – has come to dominate Western crime control discourse ... (Cohen 1985: 116)

If those who claim a privileged place in the global community are threatened by terrorist violence, then this is a call to war. International criminal justice (ICJ) provides the 'legal shadow' (Cohen 1985: ch. 4) in the wake of administrative sanctions and military intervention. Globalisation in the risk/security phase moves on from modernisation as the modus for world order. Global governance is tending to transform criminal justice into a mechanism for conflict resolution and state restoration (Findlay and Henham 2005).

International political discourse speaks to this shift through the *war on terror*. The post-9/11 (7/7) *war on terror* as a foundation of (or a justification for) dominant global political alliances, has coincidently rejuvenated the governance potential of criminal justice in post-military-intervention, state regeneration contexts. This transition has come at a price for international criminal justice. What later will be examined as *para-justice* distortions are a disturbing by-product of the emerging justice/governance synthesis. Even legitimate mechanisms and processes of justice have had their legitimacy compromised by drawing too close to the governance demands of dominant political alliances.[3]

In the domestic setting Simon suggests that the terror attacks of 9/11 have created:

a kind of amnesia wherein the quarter century of fearing crime and securing social spaces has been suddenly recognised, but misidentified as a response to an outstanding act of terrorism rather than a generation long pattern of political and social change. (2007: 11)

Driven by considerations of global risk and security awakening, the crime and governance relationship has been reformulated internationally. The *war on terror* is reshaping the governance priorities of many modern nation states. However, terrorism and violent security responses are critically constructing the possibility of global governance wherein ICJ is taking a regulatory presence. The manner in which global governance is being defined by crimes of terror and ICJ as security is a central analytical concern for what follows.

This book proposes a way forward for the governance capacity of international criminal justice. The values of freedom, equality, communitarian harmony and personal integrity which the prosecution of crimes against humanity are said to advance need not be sacrificed in a new *world order* obsessed with partial security and secularised risk.

Crime is central to the exercise of state authority (and now to the legitimacy of global institutions), but its control need not be deployed only to reinforce and reposition political dominion. The technologies, discourses and layered styles of international criminal justice are open to developing inclusive governance opportunities (Findlay and Henham, forthcoming). Genuine peacemaking can and will be the outcome of justice interventions internationally (Braithwaite 2002), provided that these locate their legitimacy in a new justice morality wherein humanity rather than political dominion prevails.

The book's policy perspective challenges international criminal justice to return to the more critical position justice has exercised in the *separation of powers* constitutional legality. For liberal democratic theory at least, judicial authority and its institutions have ensured constitutional legality by requiring the legislature and the executive to operate accountably against a higher normative order. This is not a predominant function of judges and courts in the international context despite their statutory invocation to this task (see Cryer *et al.* 2007: pt. C).

Case studies of global crime and control reveal contexts in which the co-opted governance of institutional ICJ in particular has a politicised motivation which too often advances the authority and interests of one world order against the sometimes legitimate resistance of criminalised communities. When the analysis moves to the consideration of victim community interests (see Chapter 7 in particular), and from there to the appropriate global constituencies of ICJ, the nature and limitations of ICJ supporting governance in the risk/security model will be made apparent.

Re-imagining victim communities

Global crime problems – and international terrorism in particular – have come to dominate the way victim communities are defined and given (or denied) status and standing. The valorisation of the victim citizen and the simultaneous alienation of resistant communities have justified the exploitation of violent justice responses (Findlay 2007). As Garland observes (2001: 11–12), crime victims are in a real sense the representative subjects of our time. The analysis of these themes will critically evaluate the determination of victim/global citizenship, in order to reveal how the criminalisation of violent contexts internationally has diminished the legitimacy of regressive criminal justice interventions.

The authority to distinguish victim citizens has also enabled dominant political alliances to claim to represent the legitimate needs of a *global community*. A closer examination of the communitarian forms and directions of international criminal justice will challenge these assertions and the authority which they claim.

The international fault lines of difference between victim and resistant communities provide rich case studies of crime/governance dilemmas (see Chapter 9). With international terrorism in particular, the negotiation of violence around selective victim representation reveals the partiality of global governance motivations. Crime victims, their loved ones and the communities which fear terror, while justifying violent justice interventions, are more idealised political subjects (Simon 2007: 110) whose circumstances stand for good. In reality, the flip-side of this political modelling is that international criminal justice risks dangerous co-option into the powers of political alienation. The monopoly possessed by criminal justice to award and impose violent discrimination on those it deems liable is an all too attractive capacity for dominant political alliances.

Entangling violence and justice

Better understanding of the mutuality of global risk and security, violence and justice will enable a dialectical analysis to develop. Crime and state violence in response are conventionally viewed as a last and unwanted reaction against violent challenges to individual integrity or lawful governance. In the *new age of globalisation* violent crime and violent responses have moved forward as predictable behaviours of resistance and retaliation (Chapter 5). Violence is seen as a challenge to styles of legitimate governance. In response, violence or the threat of violence within and beyond the law, confirms political dominion (through military might and then justice sanction).

This book interrogates these violent relationships (see particularly Chapter 4). It also unmasks the utility of sectarian violence (terror and responses to it) for the construction of global governance.

The forms of knowledge that tend to interpret violence and its legitimacy through the prism of crime and control are another important analytical theme. The rationality of global governance aligned with violent dominion reveals the pressure for victors to move quickly to courtroom justice and away from battlefield contest. In this imperative reside essential risks to, and the compromise of, international criminal justice in making global governance more accountable to critical community stakeholders.

Rights or justice?

This book will also consider the significance of human rights as a measure of legitimate governance through crime and control. The current global order values autonomy and stresses personal responsibility. At the same time its preferred construction of *human rights* rejects opposing cultural interests that advance communitarian considerations and through these the sharing and spreading of collective risk (see Chapter 8).

A consequentialist measure of justice limited to individualised rights sits within the political ideology of the dominant political alliance which also contains minimum economic and social protections. In the *war on terror*, recent practice within global regulatory institutions that complement the dominant political alliance (such as international criminal tribunals) tends to deny individual rights to the *enemy*. In addition, these institutions exhibit a radical and sectarian regulatory *morality* where the dangerousness of crime risks (terrorism in particular) demands further sacrificing of rights protections.

Paradoxically it is conceded that the world is in a dangerous security free-fall despite the severity of these *unavoidable* emergency control measures. International criminal justice is proposed as a modification for militarist controls, while offering legitimacy to preceding violent phases of governance.

The structural and procedural legitimacy afforded by formal and institutional justice at the international level has rarely percolated down to conflict communities and their *alternative* justice experiences. Because communitarian rights do not feature in formal ICJ (see Chapter 8) germane and meaningful victim engagement has been relegated to these *alternative* options. The analysis to follow will argue for a repositioning of international justice paradigms so that access for victim communities to justice in both its formal and less formal manifestations is a condition of the justice-rights focus of ICJ. The extent to which professionalised justice has a capacity to better police the rights of victim communities before whatever justice process will be argued through a critique of discretion and accountability (Chapter 9).

If the rights of victim communities are to be endorsed, ensured and protected through ICJ, then its role in determining the legitimate and *worthy* global community must disengage from its present political patronage. Justice as a discriminator of the valorised victim and global citizen is currently crucial in determining whose rights have value and currency. The result is that international criminal justice divides rather than reconciles communities, and not just on the basis of criminal liability.

Humanity and justice?

The risk and security tension which I argue is driving the present phase of globalisation will not be effectively controlled through international criminal justice as it presently operates. In fact, the collusion of ICJ in the legitimation of violent response to terror may exacerbate the medium-term risks to global security. Certainly, the determination by justice institutions of what constitutes a risk and what is an appropriate and humane security response should not consistently be governed by dominant political considerations, if ICJ is to offer a credible accountability function in global governance (Chapter 9).

This book argues that the power to discriminate between risk and security globally needs to be exercised against a *humanitarian* justice morality above and beyond dominant political pre-conditions. This morality is enunciated more fully in our other work (Findlay and Henham, forthcoming) but in summary it involves:

- a moral focus on the justice process as a *good*;
- a *new morality* critically informing justice pathways of influence[4] as they determine justice decision-making in a more communitarian context;

- the new morality focused on *humanitarianism*;

- the normative framework for the new morality concerned to elaborate on the principles of *humanity* as justice, determined through measures of access, inclusion and integration;

- recipient *communities of justice* representing collectivist liability and communitarian reintegration more than individualised rights and responsibilities;

- humanitarian morality linked to an important victim focus for justice;

- both in determining liability on behalf of humanity and the peacemaking which flows from this, the importance of *truth* within new moralities of ICJ;

- therefore, legitimate outcomes for transformed ICJ endorse and expand retributive punishment paradigms;

- the new morality accepts that all forms of justice are open to abuse if they do not allow truth to emerge, not just the case to be proved;

- the new moralities of justice determine the nature and coexistence of current alternative ICJ paradigms to benefit legitimate victim community interests;

- *humanitarian justice* (as a *good*) directed towards restoring and strengthening those relationships essential for resolving rather than creating and sustaining conflict;

- the outcomes of *humanitarian justice* being multipurpose in order to reflect complex and sometimes competing legitimate victim interests;

- transformed international criminal process providing the rationale and the structure for determining *truth*. By being moral rather than essentially legal, *truth* is legitimated as justice, and provides the key to the peaceful resolution of conflict from a victim perspective;

- *humanitarian justice*, while being apolitical, exposing the politicised *governance* imperatives of ICJ as they presently operate; and

- *humanitarian justice*, while countering the excessive utilitarian purposes of retributive justice, is interested in governing disputes within and between innocent victim communities.

The new morality is not just a case for ideological reordering. The creation and sustaining of *humanity* rather than risk/security as the moral and operational concern of ICJ on behalf of victim communities will magnify the peacemaking and peacekeeping potential of ICJ. The consequences of this shift for social harmony and global order more inclusively conceived will decrease both the risks from terrorist violence and the requirement to govern confrontationally in the name of security.

Structure of analysis

The structure of the book progresses from exploring the analytical context of globalisation and concludes with speculation on the transformation of international criminal justice:

Chapter 1: The new globalisation – modernity to risk societies

The evolving analysis of crime and global governance develops from my earlier interrogations of the crime/globalisation nexus in the context of modernisation to a more particular recognition of globalised cultures as *risk societies*. The place of crime and control in this transition is suggested with crime conflated as *risk* and the imperative for control is explored as *security*. *Globalisation* is both a paradigm for international relations and an analytical tool with which to understand global governance and international criminal justice. Globalisation is a transitional process, a political priority and a consequence of contemporary international relations. As such it can explain the shifting dynamics of global governance along with the relationships crucial for order's achievement and maintenance. The chapter examines a series of key feature of *new globalisation* and its explanation. The intention is to understand how these features construct the risk/security foundations for global governance.

Chapter 2: Crime and risk – nexus between crime and globalisation

The need to reduce a discussion of crime problems down to particular risk potentials in order to reveal its political moment is recognised in this chapter. The nexus between crime and globalisation is given a contemporary location within risk societies. Crime prioritising, ruled by global governance concerns, is critically analysed so as to appreciate the creation of risk/security control agendas. The discussion commences with a look at *risk societies* and their analytical utility in a global context. The risks contingent on risk responses in the risk society are highlighted. The conditionality and contextualisation of risk is analysed before raising the question, why has the risk of terror come to dominate crime/risk priorities in the *new globalisation*? Next, the connection between terror risks and criminal justice (local and global) is fleshed out in order to test the crime/globalisation nexus.

Chapter 3: A review of global crime problems – studies of crime as global risk

The case studies of global terrorism and organised crime reveal how both citizen and resistant cultures, interfacing with dominant political/security alliances, demonstrate the importance of violence for contemporary global governance. Violence here is considered as terrorist resistance and justice responses. The theme of *misrepresentation* emerges when exploring the contextual locations of violence and their interpretation. The thesis of this chapter is that a central risk paradigm in the risk/security/globalisation nexus is terrorism, providing as it does a unique foundation for security responses. Law enforcement agencies in particular are persuaded by material connections between organised crime and global terrorism. This has the consequence of heightening the risk posed by both crime types, and through association their challenge to world order. These offences and their control provide a powerful but deeply problematic platform for radical criminal justice intervention in the name of global governance. The consequence is a reordering of global crime and control priorities which gain presence and significance from perpetual misunderstandings about the governance challenges posed by organised crime. The case studies chart the connection between corruption and modernisation, organised crime and corrupt opportunities, and terrorist enterprise and organised crime as threats to world order.

Chapter 4: Risk and security – studies of global crime control responses in the context of international security

From the particularities of global crime problems and their justification for security responses to *new* risks comes the need to investigate the nature of global crime control. Violent justice responses are related to the continued case study of international terrorism. The impact of new security players internationally has significance for the nature of conventional governance arrangements. The essential accountability of the nation state or the international organisation reliant on structures of democracy may have little purchase over the commercial imperatives which engage and direct private security provisions. The problematic place of violence in the risk/security nexus undermines *humanitarian space* as a location for accountable global regulation. In the name of securing global order, by meeting terrorism with violence (military, mercenary or penal) the legitimacy of global governance is at risk. The issue here is who should and does have legitimate access to the provision of violence for governance sake. The better recognition and regulation of violence in challenging or ensuring global governance for security's sake is the focus of this chapter.

Chapter 5: International criminal justice and governance

Whither international criminal justice processes and institutions as the pressure for security to confront risk becomes the dominant political paradigm? How will ICJ regulate terror-based resistance on the retreat of militarism and what might be the outcome of this struggle for international governance concerns? The current problematic synthesis between international criminal justice and governance is exposed, and the impact on legitimacy without accountability is made clear. The chapter contrasts the pervasive but arguably less politically potent *alternative* incarnations of international criminal justice. Truth and reconciliation commissions, for instance, are said to have ensured the relevance of international criminal justice to a host of victim communities otherwise excluded from the formal institutions. The international criminal trial, on the other hand, will require transformation if its conflict resolution potential is to be realised and if victim community interests are to reflect its legitimacy. In its concluding sections the chapter details the connections between global governance and ICJ. From this relationship is drawn initial speculation on the future development of ICJ, then taken up in the chapter to follow in the context of governing through globalised crime.

Chapter 6: Governing through globalised crime

This chapter moves beyond the suggestion that crime is a problem for global governance. Instead it advances crime and terrorism in particular as instrumental in the promotion of the *new globalisation* and *para-justice* control regimes. Along with the argued utility of crime in global governance, the fear of crime and the valorisation of crime victims are identified as vital forces within the crime/governance nexus. As we explored in Chapter 5, international terrorism enables and validates the risk/security configuration of global governance, wherein criminal justice is both relied upon and contorted in the achievement of often violent control agendas. This chapter takes the relationship between crime and governance to the level of international relations and globalisation. It argues that as important as crime and control may now be to domestic governance, in a global age of crime/risk and control/security the interconnection between crime and governance can direct the future of international criminal justice.

Chapter 7: Tensions between globalised governance and internationalised justice

How will international criminal justice emerge as a power in global governance while remaining captured by security imperatives? Hybrid justice traditions and alternative justice developments are seen as challenging the notion of risk societies essential in constructing the security centre of global governance. In particular, considerations of victim communities and communities of resistance reveal tensions in the application of violent governance resolutions, thereby qualifying their legitimacy. This chapter starts out by discussing some of the contextual realities that challenge both international criminal justice and global governance. But the analysis does not remain stuck in specific tensions or even strategies for their resolution. Rather it develops into an argument for a communitarian justice model as an affective foundation for global governance. To achieve this will require regulatory strategies with an inclusive victim community direction rather than an exclusive valorised victim focus.

Chapter 8: The crucial place of crime and control within the transformation of globalised cultures

The structural and process requirements for transformed processes of crime control and governance are explored. The limitations inherent in an individualised *rights framework* covering control and governance are considered in terms of more communitarian cultures. The case study of China's engagement (or current lack of it) with international criminal justice is advanced in order to speculate on the progressive relationship between international criminal justice and cultural transformation. Transitional legal cultures and the alternative justice resolutions they practise should have greater impact on the face of international criminal justice into the future. The interpretation of rights and justice in these transitional cultures will have a significant influence on the development of global governance when engagement across cultures is more affective. To break ICJ free from its current political patronage, those currently marginalised criminal justice traditions will need to have a more practical engagement with the justice dimensions of global governance.

Chapter 9: Global governance and the future of international criminal justice transformed

Earlier work on *communities of justice* and the internalisation of risk and security are developed here. Concluding reflections will position international criminal justice within a framework of global governance and peacemaking to promote inclusion rather than alienation though deterrence and resistance. The separation of global governance from political dominion is assured if international criminal justice provides an accountability framework where cultural inclusion and humanity are the foundation for conflict resolution. International criminal justice may then gain legitimacy from community engagement rather than political allegiance. To conclude, a reinvigorated *separation of powers* model is proposed wherein criminal justice accountability is the mirror against which the other major arms of global governance may be measured. A return to pluralism and a tolerance of cultural diversity may challenge the central security pre-occupation of the new globalisation as presently envisaged. On the other hand it will invigorate ICJ to better protect a global community representative of a wider humanity. The *paths yet to be taken* by ICJ as a crucial governance mechanism will rely on the development and declaration of a new morality foreshadowed in the book's beginning. An inclusive and tolerant global community will not, in this context, only or even emerge from the denial of pluralism and the aversion to cultural transformation.

Notes

1 *The Globalisation of Crime* examined crime as a feature of modernisation and the consequent strains of socio-economic development on transitional cultures. While modernisation remains a strong foundation for globalisation, this new book will particularise the connection between risk societies and governance, around terror risks and violent security responses.
2 The concept of justice here goes well beyond the institutions and processes of the international criminal tribunals. See Findlay and Henham (2005) *Transforming International Criminal Justice: Retributive and Restorative Justice in the Trial Process.*

3 This is a recurrent generic in the text to follow which loosely refers to the coalition of Western states supporting the US neo-liberal position on economic development and world order.

4 See Findlay and Henham (2005: ch. 7).

Chapter I

The new globalisation – modernity to risk societies

Globalisation is like a three-fold prism or a three-fold figure. Globalisation, especially the global marketplace, takes certain powers away from the state ... nations are not as much in command of their economic futures as they used to be. On the other hand, globalisation has an opposite connotation and force. As it pushes down it creates new possibilities and motivations for local cultural autonomy and identities. If you represent it visually it pushes upwards but also pushes downwards, and the push down effect of globalisation is the reason for the revival of local nationalism, local forms of cultural identity and, even ... for the kind of events which happened in ex-Yugoslavia and other areas of the world. (Giddens 1999: 7)

Introduction

Brian Tamanaha envisions globalisation in a full sweep, against the background of cultural, economic and legal pluralism (Tamanaha 2007). For him globalisation is a cluster of characteristics (economic, social, political, legal and custom-centred) that demonstrate growing human interrelationships.

In his work *Global Transformations – Politics, Economics, and Culture*, David Held (1999) and his colleagues[1] divide the debate over globalisation between:

- The globalisation sceptics who suggest it is just a new term for old knowledge. They challenge that the world is becoming more integrated. Globalisation for them is a myth created in politics which promotes autonomy and the opportunity for competition in the marketplace. What is taken for globalisation, they say, was largely set in Europe at the end of the Industrial Revolution.

- The 'hyper-globalisers' who embrace the borderless world and the end of the nation state. They argue not only is globalisation real, but that it is ever present and changing everything. It is transforming the structure of states, the nature of economies and our basic institutions. Intensified economic interdependence and competition require economic engagement globally. The knowledge and information economies are the grease for this interdependency.

Scepticism or advocacy over globalisation aside, there can be little doubt that the image of globalisation has a potent political resonance. It demands that the analysis of international relations and global institutions focus on change.

As Giddens puts it:

> ... globalisation is about the transformation of our basic institutions. It's not just dominated by economic forces. It's much more closely connected with communication. It affects the state. It affects nations. It affects our personal lives.
>
> (Giddens 1999: 3)

The state and the citizen within globalisation cannot be removed from analysis which encompasses the international. Through influencing the state and the citizen, globalisation is a story of governance and order (see Chapter 7).

The title to this book suggests that crime, control and governance progress uniquely in the context of globalisation. If this is to be established, globalisation requires appreciation in its contemporary form. As an age of risk and security, globalisation today:

- explains the predominant governance concerns for international relations;

- foreshadows the need to replace military might with criminal justice resolutions if the risk posed by global terrorism in particular is to be re-envisaged as crime rather than war;

- identifies the manner in which crime as risk and crime control for the sake of security have been elevated internationally to global governance priorities; and

- locates the problematic features of international criminal justice as a governance strategy so closely aligned to prominent political considerations of security and world order.

This book argues that formal international criminal justice (ICJ) is integral to post-military global governance. This is a consequence of the current phase of globalisation and to appreciate such a relationship, globalisation must first be interrogated from the perspective of criminal justice regulation. Unfortunately for the evolution of criminal justice as an effective accountability mechanism within global governance, the current phase of globalisation, with its risk/security focus, has over politicised ICJ in the governance spectrum. The legitimacy of ICJ in conflict resolution, beyond the narrow administration of retributive justice, is undermined from the perspective of victim communities (see Chapter 7). The challenge I propose in the conclusion is through radical transformation to return ICJ to a more communitarian, inclusive and accountable practice of justice for the sake of good global governance.

But conclusions are a long way off, as is the promise of radical justice transformation. The more modest, but no less demanding, intention of this chapter is to understand globalisation as it works through the *war on terror*, to determine global citizenship and its place in an exclusive global hegemony. Along the way it is useful to consider whether globalisation accelerates the demise of the nation state, assisted in the process by a dominant neo-liberal global ethic. Evidence of the significant shift from national to global governance in the new globalisation is the place of international criminal justice as a key regulatory strategy in the *war on terror*. As Simon suggests in the domestic state setting (2007) crime concerns have become crucial to a style of governance where sovereignty, territoriality and political power rest on the achievement and maintenance of security in shifting climates of risk. The new globalisation reflects this focus and the *war on terror* has given criminal justice and crime control a new relevance in the struggle for global security. In the new globalisation the risk security nexus is confronted on behalf of a valorised citizenry and against communities and cultures which violently resist and oppose the modernisation project of the West. In the chapters that follow this

3

interpretation of globalisation and its application of crime, control and criminal justice is tested in specific crime and community contexts.

Imagining globalisation

Globalisation is both a paradigm for international relations and an analytical tool with which to understand global governance and international criminal justice. The contextual relativity of globalisation has been criticised as limiting its utility in contemporary political science (Heinz-Ladeur 2004). It is just that relativity which I argue enables globalisation to represent crucial agendas and directions for the transition of ICJ.

Globalisation is a transitional process, a political priority and a consequence of contemporary international relations. As such it can explain the shifting dynamics of world order along with the relationships crucial for order's achievement and maintenance.

In *The Globalisation of Crime* (1999b) I discussed a stage of globalisation where time and space were collapsing, a single culture was the aspiration of dominant political and commercial alliances, and modernisation was the driver for socio-economic development. As with the mercantile age that saw the discovery of the Americas and the industrial revolution in Western Europe, globalisation appears in changing forms aligned with political dominion (Held 2004b).

The contemporary phase of globalisation that interests this book is constructed on a risk/security nexus. International relations have been redefined since 11 September around who is for or against the *war on terror*. Global governance has regressed to a militarist emphasis on protecting preferred ways of life against the threats from alien cultures. International relations are becoming polarised around the enemy without and the fear within.

Violence is a binding theme in this *war* discourse. Violence initially features in some crucial governance encounters internationally. I will argue later that the nature and legitimacy of such violence represent a challenge for formal criminal justice interventions and the authority upon which international criminal justice institutions and processes rely. This chapter recognises the importance of globalisation for the critique of governance which will evolve.

The risk/security nexus, the foundation for globalisation today,[2] has produced a formula for violent conflict against which recurrent and regressive military intervention is short-lived as a convincing governance strategy (see Chapter 5). For international criminal justice to take over from military violence and hold accountable both sides of the conflict will not be easy. This book considers successfully negotiating such challenges a key to the credible evolution of global governance from a victim community perspective.[3]

Societies, faiths, cultures, communities and individuals are divided for the sake of risk and security. Realities concerning both are contested. From the perspective of global governance, the legitimacy to determine risk and protect security is reliant on dominant political and economic authorities, more than the justice and majority of any cause. Criminal justice at an international level is being conscripted into the governance framework in order to relieve the alienating consequences of military intervention and to resolve conflict in terms which accommodate the prevailing politics of world order.

To test these assumptions it is necessary to become familiar with the potential and problems associated with globalisation as a framework for global governance.[4] The discussion to follow works to identify the *new era* of globalisation in contrast with modernisation and materialism in particular. The tensions posed for transitional cultures and their violent confrontations are a central part of this reflection. The features of justice and governance which enable globalisation are rehearsed so that globalisation can be more convincingly displayed in its context mode.

Understanding the impact of globalisation on contesting cultures (and their communities) is essential if the implication of justice in governance culture to culture is to be revealed (also see Findlay 1999b). The chapter's provocative theme is that only when communitarian obligations help remove international criminal justice from the political obligations which globalisation requires will justice resume its role in protecting the community from the excesses of politicised global authority. How to achieve such a transformation will concern the remainder of the text.

The central elements of risk and security are examined as particular pre-conditions for the role of criminal justice in governance. The nexus between risk and security is then advanced as the dynamic underpinning this phase of globalisation, to be expanded against the case studies in later chapters. Crime and control, particular manifestations of the risk/security nexus, are introduced to indicate the conventional role of criminal justice in governance, along with international concerns for conflict resolution and legitimacy building.

Globalisation is a space for international relations. In risk/security terms the *global covenants* which prop up world order are in turn endorsed through the new globalisation. Globalisation is associated with a transformation or unbundling of the relationship between sovereignty, territoriality and political power. Moving down from international governance, the state, if not under challenge in the present phase of globalisation, at least is no longer the dominant jurisdiction in which crime, control and criminal justice should be viewed as crucial constituents of governance. What has replaced considerations of state jurisdiction and law enforcement in the transition to international criminal justice is also best understood, I argue, in the context of globalisation.

Globalisation dynamics

In the *Globalisation of Crime* (Findlay 1999b) I envisaged globalisation in a political age where modernisation and materialism promoted common culturation through economic development. The *new globalisation* considered throughout this work takes mass communication as a given and modernisation as the medium for the advancement of international political hegemony.

The world remains divided over more than just levels of economic development. Even the economic powerhouses of India and China are consigned beyond the dominant political alliance in part because the affluence of their citizens has not reached the consumerist *sophistication* of the modernised West. Likewise, the cultures whose ideologies have not embraced liberal democracy or in which the secular defers to the religious lie beyond the reach of the globalisation project, except as its adversaries.

The risk/security nexus which determines the new globalisation is itself determined through the domination of (and violent challenges to) the prevailing political/economic hegemony, and as such provides a focus for global order. Risk and security are essentially relative determinations. However, the current phase of globalisation represents the nexus in the context of a *war on terror* where the security warriors are a powerful if marginalised Western political alliance, and the threat is an often violent challenge to the cultural, religious, materialist and imperial predispositions of that alliance.

Another influential discriminator of globalisation in its present phase is the move away from bilateralism in international relations. While not directly compatible or consistent with the US approach to autonomy and constitutional integrity (Simon 2007), the US international relations push contrarily invokes the protection of the global community as one justification for recent US militarism. Further, the *coalition of the willing* is directed through complex regional and strategic multilateral alliances to advance the interests of Western world order. These form a relatively exclusive club of modernised states, ranged against opponents who are resistant to modernisation and the political and cultural influence of Western values.

Activist, fundamentalist and extremist cells within these opponent states and cultures have not triggered the war on terror simply as a consequence of the extent and effect of their violent incursions. International terrorism at the behest of political and ideological extremism is hardly new. Yet in recent years the attacks have been at the heart of the dominant power and designed to destabilise its domestic security. The risk has been brought home, and more than national pride is at stake.

The push to restore and maintain security in the present era of globalisation is paradoxical. On the one hand it invokes the authority and legitimacy of international organisations, international law and supportive multilateral legislative and procedural confirmation. On the other hand, at critical junctures of violent intervention it rejects as impotent and compromised the authority of international consensus and seeks to stamp alliance authority through militarism and dominion. The latter course has been at a cost to claims for the integrity of the cause. There is no doubt that the commitment of the suicide bombers (and their proliferation), for instance, is steeled by the savage consequences of waging war against the innocent as well as the guilty.

Enter international criminal justice as a platform for global governance.

With the present (somewhat limited) legitimating potential of international criminal justice above military intervention in post-conflict states (Findlay and Henham 2005: esp. ch. 7) the connection between criminalisation and governance in a world where legitimacy is violently contested is culturally contingent. As such, violence breeds violence, reaction and response in cultural settings moving further apart.

Terror triggers

Terrorism presents a recipe for disorder, and all this in a susceptible, fundamentalist and regressive age of risk and security. From the perspective of *liberal* Western democracies vying for global hegemony,

9/11 was the crunch point, the apocalypse now. In such *showpiece* scenarios of terrorism, be they in the UK, Spain and the USA rather than the Congo or the Sudan, lie the seeds of the new globalisation. The radical conflation which was 9/11 complemented long-standing antipathies and ushered in a regime of *war* against ideology and dominion and a redefinition of global citizenship.

It would be a misrepresentation for this analysis to assume that terrorist triggers in a risk/security age are calibrated by their violence or the havoc they wreak. In the case of state-sponsored terror, or where the aggressor is otherwise politically or economically aligned to the West, savage terrorist incursions pass either unrecognised for what they are or only receive mild administrative sanction. The recent civilian losses in Lebanon, the Sudan, Chechnya and Palestine rate much less attention from international organisations or the Western alliance than challenges to the homeland security of alliance members. The nature and evolution of the new globalisation can help explain this seemingly unbalanced prioritisation.

In this respect even the *imagining* of terror within globalisation is dependent on a prevailing cultural location (Findlay 2007c). Baxi (2007) identifies the interactive nature of terrorist enterprise in his discussion of the war *of* terror and the war *on* terror. He impugns its potential neutrality from either perspective of the terror enterprise. Even the nature and impact of violence is not unequivocal:

> The term 'terror', as philosopher Alian Badiou maintains, has no 'neutral readability'. Precisely because of this, we need to understand the many histories of the noun (terror) and the adjective (terrorism) which have always and abundantly pre-existed prior to 9/11 and its aftermaths.
>
> The notion of 'terror' as a way of achieving human emancipation has always been contested, both in terms of the ends to be achieved and the means deployed, if by terror we mean the deployment of asymmetrical collective insurgent political violence directed at civilian and military targets to achieve a stated political purpose. (2007: 13)

It is the politicality of that purpose which recently has invited the dominant Western alliance to respond with violence to deny claims for emancipation, in terms of a civilising mission. The restructuring of jurisdiction, standing, citizenship, humanity, community and exclusion, essential for the new age of globalisation (and its *us and them*, risk/security resonance), have their justifications and projections in 9/11. Global governance through reaction to terror and fear became the reluctant priority. Battle lines were redrawn. Global crime agendas were reordered. Wars went from drugs to terror in an instant. Security priorities realigned.

Western cultural values are endorsed through military superiority. Violent challenges to those values contextualise any measure of terror and responses to it. Risk and security in globalisation are, therefore, distinctly relative to the political and economic frameworks against which global order is established.

War discourse and citizenship

War discourse is no novelty as a language of international crime control. Whether it is a *war on drugs, war on vice* or *war on child abuse* the conflictual discourse resounds through the political representation of law enforcement. This is particularly so in places such as China, where criminality is considered to undermine social harmony and state authority (see Chapter 8).

Now we are immersed in the *war on terror*. What distinguishes this discourse from, say, that which relates to the war on drugs is its justification for actual and extensive military interventions. This state of war is more universalised.

In the context of the *war on terror* crime victimisation and the legitimate claims to global citizenship are conflated. The fissures of exclusion and inclusion are drawn against criminality and victimisation across global communities. Governance becomes defined by criminalisation and the restoration of global security through a battery of control institutions (see Simon 2007).

Along with this, the *risk society* has surpassed modernisation as the organising framework for globalisation. *Victim communities* identified at risk and valorised as without blame require the intercession and security proffered by the dominant political *culture* (see Chapter 5). With modernisation the underdeveloped and transitional cultures required material advancement through the dominant economy (Findlay 1999b: ch. 2). If in the process these cultures move into the terror orbit of the enemy, then that advancement is denied. The destruction of the Danube infrastructure as part of the recent NATO war against Serbia, is evidence of this.

Achieving the *international* through new globalisation

The common push to a monoculture in globalisation similar to earlier mercantile and colonial epochs currently has had to defer its economic modernisation priorities in order to address the violent challenges of contesting cultures.[5] The *cultures of dominance and repression* that result from the victor's justice eschew the values of the enemy and embrace the moral and political supremacy of Western secular materialism. Rather than engage with the complexity of resistance to these imperatives, a control methodology of criminalisation is now being employed by the dominant political hegemony internationally, and the immediate motivations for globalisation have become redefined in response to the multinational crime risk as security/control (see Chapter 9).

Cross-border politics and the institutions which they foster have proliferated during the last phase of globalisation as a consequence of the collapsing of space and the contraction of time (der Derian 1990). The temporal limitations which gave reality to state jurisdictions and the autonomy of their political frameworks are of diminishing consequence as globalisation makes the achievement of international organisations and global communities more possible, practical and relevant. Even so, the limitations and failings of the international political project have been manipulated by the dominant political alliance to justify its unilateralism when progressing the *war on terror*. The most recent invasion of Iraq and its justification is a case in point.

While the spatial/temporal location of state and social entities is central to post modern theorising about governance, it is becoming less significant in terms of international relations in the present phase of globalisation. The speed over space and the suspension of time has influenced the progress of the state to the globe as vital governance arenas, and it is not difficult to anticipate the impact on international relations and the nature of global order as a result. Those political alliances with the strongest reach within and beyond the jurisdictional boundaries of the temporal state are setting the global governance models and priorities. This is in the face of violent resistance, which in turn confirms the risk/security focus of emerging globalisation.

It could be said that the violent resistance represented in global terrorism has inadvertently promoted a new *internationalism* not possible during the Cold War era and not featuring in other recent phases of terrorist enterprise. This can be explained in part by the nature and direction of contemporary terrorism. Unlike the terrorism practised by the Shining Path, or by Farq in Peru and Columbia, or even Hammas in southern Lebanon, which are distinctly directed against state opponents and towards national sovereignty, the terror exported by al Qaeda fights Western ideologies and sectarian lifestyles. While the new terrorism may be no more dangerous and damaging than that exercised in the context of national integrity, it poses a broader challenge to the preferred politic and economic entity of the Western world and its satellites. Normative and ideological terrorism requires otherwise reluctant political superpowers like the US and economic powerhouses like the EU to engage beyond their traditional spheres of interest and influence in order to confront violent representations of an *alternative world religion* and opposing world views on hegemony.

The hegemonic project

The hegemonic project of global governance in the current phase of globalisation contradicts what Gramsci saw as:

> ... the maintenance and reproduction of a hegemonic order, able to reach compliance without having to resort to force.
>
> (Massicotte 1999: 136)

The hegemony of the dominant political alliance under the threat of terrorist resistance appears incapable of restoring world order without violent responses. Violent governance is a characteristic of the current hegemonic project.

Hegemony is fragile when confirmed through terror and violent resistance. The formation and reformation of hegemonic orders in the context of wars of any type gives disproportionate and dangerous precedence to violence in challenging or confirming order. Hegemony over the *war on terror* is no different.

Constructive political configurations are less possible or sustainable where oppositional forces are determined through violent risks and countered with more violence rather than by grounded diplomacy. Security becomes the overriding aspiration for hegemony where order is contested and violence is the language of hegemonic dominion.

Security prioritisation features in the governance of the dominant political alliance as it encounters terrorist resistance to its view of world order. Whether it is the ideology of liberal democracy, the social foundation of the nuclear family, a materialist economic ethic or ecumenism, the central characteristics of this hegemonic order are currently and unequivocally threatened by violent resistance. The nature of the hegemony, reliant as it is on military might and economic domination, results in other conditions for order and cohesion becoming unavailable or undervalued. This hegemonic style defends itself against pressures to modify and transform, as the forces for change are more threatening of its core values. The usual cycles of hegemonic transformation become distorted by *wars* of regulation and resistance.

The global political and economic dominance of the United States of America (and its allies) is clear both in the modernisation and the risk/security phases of globalisation. It follows then that US political ideologies and alliances are crucial to the definition and maintenance of world ordering (Devetak and True 2006). In a sense of labelling theory, the US is the *significant other* against which concepts of risk and security will be determined within globalisation. The domestic and foreign policy of those states which come within the US sphere of influence will be inextricably aligned to the US case for global order. Risk and security concerns are at the centre of that order and challenges to it. Risk is largely determined against Western interests and security is in their restoration.

If internationalism is seen as complementing that notion of Westernised world order then it too is embraced by the current hegemony. In such a setting hegemony tolerates and works with other political forces within global institutions which may peacefully oppose Western values. If hegemonic order is contested then the return to the alliance-based security is apparent.

I argue in chapters to follow that *security* in the current phase of globalisation is primarily concerned with order maintenance. Representative international institutions have not always been seen by the dominant political alliance as working to a common and acceptable world order. In such instances, the tension between representative international governance institutions and the dominant alliance is not always negotiated within democratic governance frameworks. The recent unilateral invasion of Iraq without UN endorsement confirms the supremacy of the alliance above the international where US risk/security determinations prevail. The paradox is the rejection of democratic order resolution in the name of global democracy.

For the lesser members of the alliance their pathway to internationalism is inextricably bound to the American risk/security interpretation. Take Australia for example:

Since 9/11 the threat of global terrorism has dominated Australian foreign and defence policy agendas (MacDonald 2005). It has been used to frame Australia's policy response to a range of issues, including nuclear proliferation, global poverty, and people movement. Moreover, it has reshaped Australia's relations to international law and the United Nations as well as relations with regional neighbours and old allies. At the core of Australia's insecurity is the fear that rogue states like Iraq will align with transnational terrorist groups like al-Qaeda, a fear echoing the US National Security Strategy (2002).

   This led the Australian government, unlike New Zealand, enthusiastically to endorse President Bush's calls for the invasion of Iraq, even in the absence of a UN mandate. Though Howard (the then Australian Prime Minister) declined to publicly endorse Bush's policy of 'regime change', he clearly subscribes to the world view underpinning it – namely, that international order is not the product of international organisations and multilateral institutions but the product of states acting unilaterally or in a coalition to enforce order. (Devetak and True 2006: 251–2)

The dominance of Western values as the ideology of globalisation is compatible with the profit motive of globalisation just past and the risk security focus of the current phase. Multinational corporations and their profit, capitalist production, international trade and finance are at risk from terrorism, as much as is the safety of the citizen market. The perspective of Western global ideals determines risk/security concerns for world trade and commerce as integral to globalisation of the present.

Internationalism has also been achieved more effectively in recent times through deregulating trade and commerce. Despite protracted negotiations and the prevailing influence of domestic, bilateral and regional self-interest, the new economic tigers like China have driven deep into the markets of the South World. Foreign policy, as history regularly reveals, has opened up pathways of economic expansion and reflected its priorities. Therefore, if there are risks to the market and to the consumer, then shared commercial concerns for security will proliferate.

International laws and conventions have also appreciated rejuvenation in this age of risk and security (Cryer *et al*. 2007). But strains across international relations arise if the statute, the court or the convention challenge the autonomy of the dominant alliance. The current US position on the International Criminal Court (ICC) (see

Chapter 5) reveals that tension, where formal involvement is denied yet still the US is active in persuading the ICC to take up the conflict in Sudan as one of its earliest investigation briefs (Bantekas and Nash 2007: 219–20).

International legality in this sense faces at least three challenges from globalisation:

- the challenge of failing to achieve security and minimise risk in a governance environment where the expectations for legality are unrealistic;

- the challenge from the dominant alliance where, through self-interest, it limits the potential impact of laws and conventions, or where the alliance rejects the authority of international legality and works outside it;

- the challenge of violent resistance to an international legality which is viewed by its opponents as compromised and illegitimate.

At base, global hegemony is a political construct. Friedrichs (2005) suggests that global politics are not the same as international politics or relations. Rather, global politics is a meta concept encompassing political relations among governments in a process of selection and mutual self-interest. Global governance, at the same time, can exclude and include international politics.

> This apparent contradiction becomes less confusing as soon as global governance is understood as a hegemonic project.
>
> (2005: 61)

As Friedrich determines, to provide the glue for world capitalism and an ordered global community, global governance is sometimes construed as beyond and sometimes above politics.

Neo-liberalism

The dominant Western political ideology which accompanies the new phase of globalisation is neo-liberalism. Winding down the nation-state as it was known during the welfare and early modernisation phases is an aspiration of neo-liberal governance. At the same time, neo-liberal philosophy seeks in parallel strong domestic regulation of welfarest or oppositional political references. Another paradox is the neo-liberal interest in autonomy and individualised responsibility, *and* community locations for regulation.

Neo-liberal international relations tend to favour bilateral arrangements, limited regional economic mutuality and specific and binding military alliances. Neo-liberalism complements the normative framework of the new globalisation and the governance strategies it prefers, insofar as they advance the interests of the dominant political alliance away from egalitarian and inclusive internationalism.

Neo-liberalism broadly demonstrates:

- an attack on state-centred governance, the large state and the expansion of state enterprise and intervention;

- in particular, an assault on welfarism as a central state policy and the major motivation for state enterprise;

- the centrality of a market model and profit motivation as the most valuable frameworks for social order;

- a denial of cultural values which stand outside or contest this market model of social relations;

- the promotion of commercial/business relationships in the design of state responsibilities, and along with this a commitment to managerialism in the delivery of state services;

- an apparent emphasis on evidence or results-based government service delivery, made accountable through reference to productivity. This is often contrary to actual measures of cost-effectiveness, particular in the criminal justice area;

- the individualisation of rights and responsibility, autonomy and family and community-centred regulation;

- a normative ascription to individual freedoms and a belief in free and rational choice which spills over into the construction of criminal liability and punishment models.

These neo-liberal values have had a significant effect on how risk is imagined and the manner in which it influences social regulation strategies, particularly crime control. For instance, the recent emphasis in policing on crime prevention has seen a return to community-centred policing responsibilities and away from the conventional emphasis on more reactionary policing styles. That said, police cultural resistance to crime prevention and community policing has clashed with the neo-liberal imperative to make state-sponsored police more receptive to community and business demands. Paradoxically, the current resurgence of force-based policing to meet the risk of terror has removed policing from community imperatives and locations and returned it to the criminal investigation, intelligence and technology focus for state policing.

Another paradoxical neo-liberal influence on crime control is the explosion in private-sector policing and commercial security services. These contractual services have satisfied new markets of risk and security which emerge as a consequence of the ever growing socio-economic gulf in modernised societies, and the associated *user pays* ethic. In this respect, neo-liberalism has challenged state monopolies over crime control while at the same time sponsoring the growth in commercial security provision as a *market enterprise* feature of governance and social order. The commercialisation of regulatory governance service is in line with neo-liberal minimisation strategies for the state and for its public domain. The new globalisation comfortably accommodates the commercialisation of regulation and moves away nation-state control.

In many respects contemporary politics within the dominant global alliance demonstrates a merging of neo-liberal and neo-conservative agendas. Both support the economic modernisation project. Both, perhaps for different reasons, identify the integrity of the nation-state as of paramount importance in the quest for security over risk. Neither accommodates cultural diversity as a natural moderator of state identity. In these respects, the terrorist and the defender of the dominant alliance would find much to commend neo-liberal, neo-conservative fundamentalism.

New globalisation and domestic states

It has been argued that despite the risk/security emphasis, globalisation has weakened the nation-state and thereby made the world more susceptible to transnational crime (Herbert 1999). Even so dominant nation-states like the USA have strengthened their domestic and international commitment to counter crime in the name of good governance (Simon 2007). The US administration has recently endeavoured to enhance its legitimacy and international presence by focusing on domestic *and* international security, primarily through alliance and bilateral relations. The rhetoric at home is that a secure globe makes for homeland security. At the international level at least this has transpired as a risky strategy.

The difficulty even in generalist terms with employing the state as a definitive concept when analysing contemporary global governance lies in the illusory notion of *pure state*. It matters little what theory of the state is preferred on which to base this analysis, the diversity of state forms and the transitional forces at work on state construction and maintenance make anything more than a modelling exercise problematic.

However, I am not at liberty here to simply sideline the state in considerations of global governance, as a consequence of its dynamic and diverse entity. Credible globalisation literature continues to comparatively construct the existence and influence of globalisation against notions of liberal-democratic states in particular (der Derian 1990). And state transformation, state withering and state reconstruction are readily (if often simplistically) explained in terms of globalisation (Newman 2006).

Further, a distinct motivation for terrorist violence worldwide is the condition of nationhood. This can produce the under-recognised but potent arenas of state-sponsored terrorism (Bantekas and Nash 2007: 218–22; Reno 2006).

To confront the likely criticism that naive and universalist state analysis will tend to confirm or confound globalisation phases inextricable from model states I present two problematic assertions which propose a dynamic relationship between globalisation and the state – that:

- the state is a natural casualty of globalisation (Johnson 2005); and
- globalisation means a borderless world (Agnew 2003).

Both assertions I suggest demonstrate a fundamental misunderstanding of the role of the nation-state in global hegemony and challenges to it. From the perspective of international criminal justice and its institutional processes, the nation-state is built-in as a jurisdiction of first resort. This means that state governance is a natural starting point for the development and consideration of governance (and governability) internationally (Krasner 2001).

The transaction of legitimacy in governance terms from the local to the global is another reason for considering nation-states and their regulatory regimes. The state has long rested much of its legitimacy on its role in creating and enforcing the law. Crime is a more potent political issue than ever and thus states must address it to retain legitimacy (Simon 2007).

In the United States case especially, state responses to crime take a predominantly *get tough* form which employs an ever growing criminal justice system to enable more numerous arrests, detentions and executions. The continued significance of the state in crime control thus rests upon its bureaucratic dynamics and its need to remain legitimate in the eyes of the public. In the case of crime control, at least, rumors of the death of the territorially-sovereign state are premature.

(Herbert 1999: 153)

Are these rumours of state demise premature? In his analysis of crime control, Garland identifies the state as abdicating its role in crime control (Garland 2001). O'Malley (1992) refers to this as a 'responsibilisation' strategy where autonomy is paramount and where crime control is devolved to citizen groups or private agencies. Shearing (1992) supports this view of state devolution, using the rise of private security and policing agencies that he sees as taking over the state's monopoly of lawful force in the realm of civil policing. If these instances do reveal a recent and recurrent surrendering of responsibility by the state for crime control while at the same time confirming crime control as a crucial governance tool, then are we really witnessing at the domestic level a withering away of the state in governance commitment?

Krasner (2001) disputes the death of the nation-state as a consequence of globalisation. Instead he offers the view that globalisation is changing the scope of state control. Globalisation, he argues, has blurred distinctions of citizenship through the massive exploitation of migrant and *guest* worker underclasses which move and exist without the benefits of citizen rights and protections. These underclasses have become crucial to the modernisation project in Western and transitional states. The globalisation of labour, as I suggest in Chapter 9, is also paradoxical by drawing on many cultures to resource an economic *monoculture*.

The middle ground may be that while states remain powerful actors in domestic governance, their energies are rooted within their jurisdiction. Even in transitional states, where legitimacy and authority are fought for, the prize is defined nationhood and redefined state borders. Such spatial and temporal constriction is no longer a feature of global governance and its sponsoring politic, as it was in the mercantile, colonial and industrial phases.

Tamanaha (2007) prefers to see the impact of globalisation on nation-states in a more interactive plane. States have been losing power up and down as they break up into smaller communities of shared interest. I will talk of these later as *communities of justice* (Chapter 7) wherein justice is achieved and denied. States have certainly lost their individual and separate capacity to shape and guide their own economies. More significant perhaps to the concerns of this book, states have either lost or conceded their monopoly to control and regulate the space and existence of their people.

The break-up of state control monopolies has been stimulated by free market economics and by communitarian developments in social relations which are filling the spaces left as the state retreats from grassroots regulation. These developments are apparent in domestic, regional and international governance trends. The recent language of international relations is distinctly communitarian. The *global community* is of necessity stateless.

In the past, the jurisdiction over crime and its control was an essential identifier of the nation-state. More recently, regional and international political alliances have claimed an interest in criminalisation and crime control. For instance, the EU, while recognising the idiosyncratic jurisdictions of member states, is keen to make work a European arrest warrant regime to better control transnational and cross-border crime.

Both international and state-based community concerns about crime, safety and disorder are unlikely to abate. As communities globalise, for victim communities in particular their frameworks of obligation and dependence no longer remain exclusively within the domestic state. This is particularly the case where states are in transition and the community victimisation arises as a consequence of intra-state conflict. The question becomes whether in the face of this transition the ill-formed mechanics of global governance can be responsible for community security, particularly where the threat is exacerbated by its international presence.

The reaction to community victimisation within and beyond the state is also paradoxical. At the level of international communities, the UN, for instance, selectively intervenes with peacekeeping missions and war crimes tribunals. This is only insofar as the dominant political alliance has not pre-empted the international response by laying claim, usually militarily, to protect its patron victims and to punish its enemies. Similar to the response directed against terrorism, the choice of intervention style will have more to do with the strategic nature of the conflict than simply the nature of the violence or victimisation involved.

Globalising crime concerns

As suggested previously, it is not necessarily the case that with global crime a central concern for international criminal justice, then the seriousness, scope and harm of instances of crime, will determine the impact of any international crime type on risk, security and control. Were this so, then illegal arms trade, people trafficking, child pornography, illicit drug marketing and money-laundering (to name a few important global crime types) would be the focus of the international criminal tribunals. They are not. The explanation for this contradiction lies within the present risk/security focus of globalisation.

I have indicated that today the risk posed by crime and the security potential of crime control are important constituents of globalisation and of global governance. There are essential qualifications that must be recognised within these relationships, evidenced as they are in the current *war on terror* politics. The International Criminal Court, for instance, has its mandate largely restricted to crimes against humanity and genocide. These offence types are determined as arising from illegitimate national and transnational conflict. The inclusion of enterprises and collectives within this criminality is in large measure prohibited from the consideration of the ICC (see Chapter 7). And unless other important transnational and international crime types result in crimes against humanity or genocide they as yet will not be the concern of tribunal-based international criminal justice.

Certain pre-conditions for international crimes are evidenced in all these crime types:

- they are not bound by geography or jurisdiction;
- they defy traditional notions of legal sovereignty;
- they selectively experience government regulation against legitimate and illegitimate market forces;
- they pit domestic control bureaucracies against international enterprise networks; and
- they have the capacity to victimise whole communities.

Yet some international crimes and not others are designated in the present phase of globalisation as the real and present risk to security, and as such a priority for international criminal justice resolution. In addition, the *global order* outcomes of ICJ are prioritised above other crime control concerns as ensuring security.

An explanation for the prioritisation of international crime types, and control outcomes may be found in the challenge posed by particular crimes to the nation-state, its authority, and its reflection of dominant economic and political values. International terrorism, ethnic cleansing, treasonous military uprisings and crimes against state integrity are branded (by the UN Security Council and by the dominant political alliance) as the principal dangers to global governance. The indictments before international criminal tribunals and special criminal courts under the authority of the Security Council confirm this concentration. Decades ago drug trafficking was accorded a similar status if not offered a similar global response (Chambliss 1989). Yet with the onset of the *war on terror*, risk/security globalisation has justified the shift away from more conventional and sustained global criminal enterprise as the focus for international criminal justice.

A natural consequence of this narrow *terror risk* focus is to equate security with global order. Terrorism as the global crime of highest risk is a direct threat to that order. Economic sanctions and military intervention have featured in the regulatory responses of the dominant political alliance directed at bringing down political orders which challenge global hegemony. Disorder and regime change come first, then follows reordering through the trial of key figures in the regime and the imposition of external justice regimes to resolve conflict and make peace. Even the alternative ICJ paradigms are promoted for their state reconstruction and community reordering capacities.

The risk involved and the security preferred, however, are now measured by the proximity of terror to core world economies. Global terror as an assault on economic order as well as an attack on humanity moves beyond considerations of violence to endanger the hegemony of globalisation (McCulloch 2003).

Globalisation and world systems theory

Arguing that commercial imperatives and economic considerations are central to the risk/security focus of the current globalisation phase sounds like world systems theory (WST). In this context, world systems theory might be expected to enlighten the development of globalisation and its connection to governance. Without significant elaboration WST does not achieve this outcome. Rather, WST is useful for explaining the battle lines dividing what is risk and how it is to be made secure.

However, the introduction of criminal justice into the global

21

governance mix is not, I suggest, only predetermined through economic realities. If WST is to inform an appreciation of global governance through economic configurations alone then it will not help us understand how and why international criminal justice has assumed a central standing in that governance framework.

World systems theory in broadest measure declares that a nation's development depends on the configuration of the world economy and the place of that nation-state within it (Onwudiwe 2001b). WST, as developed by Wallerstein (1979), Evans (1979) and Chirot (1977), is now being applied to the understanding of terrorism (Onwudiwe 2001a). Rather than seeing the terrorist as a criminal or a freedom fighter, it is argued that WST offers an explanation of terrorism as a consequence of global economic order. That order is said to have a concentric form:

1 *The core.* Core nations are France, the US and the UK. They dominate through ownership of the primary means of production.

2 *The periphery.* These countries are said to have a dualistic domestic structure: traditional and modern. The modern sectors of these societies link with core countries. These countries are often exploited by core countries as a cheap source of labour. Nations of the periphery are the weakest economically and governments are often militaristic.

3 *The semi-periphery.* Countries so located are intermediate because of their internal structures. These countries engage in business with core countries but do not have the same degree of influence over the economic order as do core countries. These countries may provide an essential conduit through which pass the resources of the periphery on to the enterprises of the core.

The core exploits the semi-periphery and it in turn exploits the periphery. Through the process of economic development nations can progress closer to the core but in so doing they are still subject to exploitation.

In the weakened and exploited state, some nations or groups and communities within those states may rebel against the constraints imposed through world economic order. Violence directed against states in the core is just one form of that rebellion. It is more likely to occur through a subversion of the markets and financial structures on which the core relies for dominion.

In some respects the roots of this economic model of international relations are in structures of dependency. Such dependency can be maintained through cycles of development either sponsored through postcolonial aid delivery, or the proscriptive intervention of international financial agencies (see Findlay 1999b: ch. 2). Other associated dependency relationships might arise out of corporate domination (Cardoso 1979), technological and industrial dependence, capitalist financial relations and the structural components of world economic history (mercantilism, resource exploitation, slavery, etc.). Artificial divisions of labour which come with cash economies are also likely to discriminate against states where self-sufficiency is a central occupation and levels of industrialisation are low.

If global terrorism is primarily or even largely motivated by the desire to publicise the inequalities which arise from unfair and unequal frameworks of economic dependence then WST is potent in explaining the principal political *threat* in contemporary globalisation. But economic motivation is neither a consistent nor a paramount motivation for terror.

World systems theory does position the economic context in which terrorism is fostered and imbued with its sense of injustice. However, the fundamentalist ideologies which give some major terrorist movements much more ideological purchase than does economic deprivation are not consistent with economic ordering alone (Findlay 2007c).

Where WST does offer an important reflection on contemporary globalisation is by raising the question, why not economic inequality as the greatest risk to global security? In fact socio-economic inequality, the rich and the poor worlds, the growing affluence gaps and all the social dysfunctions which accompany these, are at the heart of much real and potential world disorder. Yet this realisation awaits a future and perhaps less polarised age of globalisation to find its prominence. At present, the states in the core will not out of crucial economic self-interest concede that economic exploitation and inequality, the product of world economic order, are significant causes for global insecurity. To do this would require the ancillary admission that modernisation and economic development strategies worldwide are at best unfair and at worst unjustly criminogenic. Unfortunately, the ideological and dogmatic divisions which are publicised as motivating global terror (from both sides) diminish the cruel reality of economic dependency and give the core at least the mask it needs for economic exploitation to prevail.

The myth of a borderless world?

The present stage of globalisation is the result of technological change, the spread of modernity, neo-liberal economics and more (Agnew 2003). However, there is no denying that the drive behind this globalising transition, politically and economically, can be sourced back to US domestic and foreign policy. And this has a deep history, as with the development of a *free-market capitalist* world economy.

The United States government set out in 1945–47 to sponsor a liberal international order in which military expenditure would provide a protective apparatus for increased trade (and, if less so, investment). Such an apparatus would, in turn, rebound to domestic American advantage. The logic behind this international relations perspective lay in the presumed transcendental identity of the American and world economies. The expansion of one was seen as inextricably beneficial for the other (Agnew 2003: 10).

Some may say that there is nothing new in this. The same economic self-interest can be seen in the mutuality of military and commercial expansion by great mercantile and colonial powers in centuries past. What is different, however, is that the American ideological and economic conquest did not require the seizing of physical territory or the military subjugation of states as a priority, although this has been a sporadic feature of this outreach.

The United States has colonised contemporary international relations through exporting a modernisation package, where capitalism and neo-liberal democratic government have changed the face of international order. In this respect it has been a project of internationalisation through Americanisation, as much as was the aspiration of the early Marxists with the 'internationale'.

Has this produced a borderless world? Yes and no. Perhaps the borders remaining are not an inflexible reflection of static nation-states. Statehood determined through jurisdiction, dominion and territory is currently as transitional in many parts of the globe as it has ever been. National borders are more bifurcated. Economic dividing lines are between rich and poor, industrialised and agrarian, capital wealthy and capital starved, modernised or not.

In a political sense the age of the Cold War was the clash of the two superpowers and their client states. Since the fall of the Soviet Union and the rise of successful regional alliances such as the EU, this polarisation of politics is less distinct but no less real. The divide is now between those political entities which embrace to whatever degree the Western economic or ideological project and those which don't.

Globalisation or Westernisation?

So, internationalism is a feature of contemporary globalisation insofar as it promotes or struggles to control resistance to the dominant political and economic hegemony. The place of states and alliances in global world ordering cannot escape reference to the Westernisation project (Keohane 2001).

America's 'Empire' (Ignatieff 2003) is centrally located within the current phase of globalisation and its crucial governance themes. The spread of Western ideologies, economies and *democratic* institutions into post-conflict states has seen to that. Even in transitional, conflict-ridden nation states like Afghanistan, Iraq and the Balkans, US military might is progressing imperial rule in a post-imperial age.

War, in the current phase of globalisation, acts significantly to accelerate Western imperial powers (McCulloch 2003). However, as argued earlier, global governance through warfare is unsustainable. Crime fighting is replacing warfare as the preferred control over international terrorism. *Homeland security* protected and prosecuted by police and courts is taking over the *war on terror* from the problematic maintenance of military presence.

Interestingly, the transposition of criminal justice over military force in the struggle for global security has tended to compromise many of the core rights of the individual, which justice is conventionally seen as championing. The perceived emergency which justified military incursions against terror has prevailed in order to necessitate this rejection of civil liberties (Findlay 2007c).

The dangers inherent in forcefully broadcasting Western ideals in many respects resemble the risks against which the war on terror is waged. The destabilisation of frail indigenous governance in post-conflict states (Jaber 1999) has been a risk consequence which now occupies the energies of international criminal justice. Spreading Western values which can contradict the morality, religion and authority of transitional states such as Lebanon has been vilified as sowing the seed for terrorist reaction.

Protecting the modernisation project has informed and been informed by globalisation. State boundaries are endorsed and fought for when they are seen as a bulwark against terror. Peacemaking through ICJ resolutions is also significantly designed to undermine community comfort for the politics and ideologies of the enemy. The dominant political alliance seeks economic and legal sanctions against the *axis of evil*. Through these regulatory mechanisms, as much as through militarism, the enemy is exiled from the global community. The integrity of their statehood is neutralised through criminalisation more effectively and long-lastingly than through military overthrow and contentious regime change. The benefit of *waging war through justice means* is in terms of legitimacy. In any case, communities fall foul of criminalisation through ICJ, as they would if treated as enemies in the victor's path. The Serbian side in Kosovo has been demonised through selective criminal prosecution for Albanian ethnic cleansing. Arguably this remains more effective in isolating *the enemy* of the West than NATO's destructive military energies.

Individuals and communities

Citizenship is protected through globalisation where it accords with the constructs of the global community, its market economies, liberal democratic styles of government and allegiance to the modernisation project. The nature and ramification of global citizenship is clearer in the context of ICJ than it may be in other global regulatory frameworks.

Humanity is represented and protected through the prosecutions before international criminal tribunals. The *global community*, through the enabling legislation of the international criminal tribunals, carries actionable responsibility for a limited range of harms caused to communities within its compass. In this regard it is not simply individual or nation-states that are the subjects of tribunal interest. The ICC prosecutor has already foreshadowed his preferred intention to investigate a wide range of collective and communal entities that could be seen as committing offences against humanity.

The challenge when conceptualising and actuating global citizenship is to avoid the political partiality demonstrated by the dominant international hegemonies. From the regulatory perspective of the dominant political alliance domestic citizens are cherished if they fall within the political allegiance and jurisdictional boundaries of alliance and supporter states. Outside those boundaries, the protection of the nation-state and the celebration of nationalism and citizenship are conditional on risk and security evaluation.

Resistance is sometimes violent to the partial recognition of citizenship within communities where the individualised rights are subservient to communitarianism and concerns for social harmony (see Chapter 9). Western governance models which promote individual autonomy over community responsibility have not received easy and general acceptance through globalisation. Levi (1997) argues that citizens are more likely to comply and give active consent to imposed democratic governance when the institutions and processes that evolve are perceived as fair in decision-making and implementation. Inclusivity and community collaboration are also conditions which affect the acceptance of imposed governance models. The same could be said about the response to international criminal justice as an introduced governance model from communities where justice is not primarily individualised.

Where citizenship is more dependent on the jurisdiction of the secular state than membership of a religious culture or a cohesive community, issues such as territoriality, sovereignty and political authority are central risk/security considerations.

Unbundling the relationship between sovereignty, territoriality and political power

Where globalisation is promoted through the collapsing of time and space, citizenship will become a more fluid and layered governance condition. Migration across regional alliances in particular is a feature of globalisation. The flow of regional citizens is a model for an emergent global community. However, the tension between protecting exclusionist domestic citizenship and encouraging a flexible labour market significantly challenges the reality of a global community.

The place of migration within global governance tests any communitarian, common-culture impetus in globalisation. Migration across a global community is increasingly problematic as links are drawn between the pathways from certain cultures and the threats they pose to the security of Western territoriality, sovereignty and political autonomy.

Global terrorism is seen by Western interests to reside within particular oppositional cultures. The terrorist risk is feared as a consequential export in the migration from within these cultures. The impact of *the war on terror* on the protection of refugees and on migration has heightened the paradox of globalisation and nationalism.

Sovereignty and territoriality are targets of terrorism. As mentioned above, the imperialism of Western modernisation projects is waged for culture, economic dominion and territorial gain. Like terrorism in its ideological motivations, modernisation is a quest for the minds as well as the markets of recipient cultures.

The repositioning of domestic and regional borders as part of globalisation takes on the appearance of cultural and territorial distinction. Against this perceived and actual cultural encroachment many terrorist enterprises are directed.

Certainly up until the modernisation phase of globalisation political power corresponded with territory and economic dominion (Held 2004b). As globalisation transforms through the risk/security focus, territoriality and sovereignty as temporal and spatial concepts have taken on an almost feudal significance. The events of 9/11 graphically demonstrated that territory and sovereignty will be attacked by the terrorist through assaults on domestic security, rather than on economic or international presence. The consequent *homeland security* consciousness, not seen since the Second World War, is a strong influence from national through regional and on to global governance.

Territoriality and its borders provide a target for terrorism and a motivation for violent responses. In the *war on terror* the dominant political alliance has attacked the physical and political integrity of states which it determines as impeding the prosecution of terrorism. More interesting from a global perspective is the manner in which globalised communication and information technology enables home-grown terrorism, physically removed from the territories that are the sites of struggle. Again, home-grown terror is neutralised through representation as a consequence of cultural infiltration and not domestic dissent. Narrow interpretations of citizenship (local and global) are not compatible with such a contrary interpretation.

> The trans-boundary cyber-dissemination of information among groups supporting the political cause of global terrorism enables inhabitants of a country to operate inside the country of their own citizenship without the need to physically cross the border and gain entry, as was the case with the suicide bombers in London in August 2005. (Newman 2006: 12)

So it is home-grown terrorism as well as the threat from beyond which closes borders to protect territory and dominion.

> Nowhere is this more blatant than in the USA, where crossing borders, even between two of the world's most friendly countries – the USA and Canada – has become more difficult in the post 9/11 era. (Newman 2006: 12)

Protection of culture at home, like the task to entrench that culture abroad, has created a globalisation dialectic between expansionist cultural imperialism and protectionist cultural isolation. In the political discourse of contemporary international relations this tension is unconvincingly neutralised through the representation of Western values as the global values worth fighting for. Terrorist violence contests any such assertion.

Globalised values and governance?

Governance is an exhausted term in contemporary criminology. Reference to governance provokes general confusion not only about the meaning of the term but also its application. In referring to governance is the analysis confined to theory? Will it move from governance as a regulatory technology on to applied considerations of governance in action?

In looking at global governance, these considerations demand greater acuity. Governance forms, frameworks and futures in a global context are as problematic as the conceptualisation of a global community to be governed. The institutions and processes of global governance fail many of the fundamental, mechanical tests of governance in the domestic, state or regional setting. The sands are shifting for global governance and even its binding ideology is contingent on a contested understanding of world order.

In talking of global governance I am interested in relationships and processes more than institutions and frameworks, if it is in fact possible to differentiate these. In Chapter 6 Foucault's concern for the 'reasoning' behind governability is explored in order to claim for governance a more explicable and integrated representation, the *logic* of which is open to interrogation. The progress from:

- theorising the regulation of crime as risk;
- determining security as global order;
- appreciating globalisation as a force for regulatory preference; and
- evaluating the place of criminal justice when determining international governance parameters.

is the style of analytical progression I am intending for the *governance* theme.

Rather than seeing global governance as some general form of social action I agree with Lederer and Muller that it is a hegemonic project (2005: ch. 1). More particularly I take a similar course to Friedrichs (2005) in arguing that global governance is the hegemonic project of transatlantic civil (and not so civil) society. Friedrichs posits 'five truths about global governance':

- global governance is an offspring of economic globalisation;
- one should be careful not to romaticise civil society;
- global governance has an Anglo-American imprint;
- global governance has a transatlantic organisational bias; and more often than not
- ideas about global governance are inherently economistic.

To this I would add:

- global governance is now disproportionately concerned with risk and security;
- as such the politics of risk and security as determined by whose side of the *war on terror* cultures and communities find themselves determine world order in the interests of modernisation.

Friedrich's critical interrogation of global governance as a hegemonic project:

> ... dampened some high-flown expectations with regard to the problem-solving capacity, universal applicability and value neutrality of global governance. In particular, it has become clear why the advent of global governance is neither political in the conventional meaning of the word, nor tantamount to the advent of politics in a morally higher sense. At the basis of global governance there is too much inequality and injustice to justify its representation as an arena for Habermasian 'domination free discourse'. (2005: 58–9)

Global governance and global politics are not contradictions in terms. As I see it later in this work, global governance is a style of *para-politics* beyond the organisational frameworks of the state, of regional alliances and of international representative institutions. It is clearly aligned to the 'lures of global corporatism' (Friedrichs 2005).

In interpreting and applying a workable image of global governance I concur with Matthias Finger's (2005) reflection that the political dimensions of globalisation deny the easy transfer of representative democracy from a state to an international context.

> The pressure on the UN system, resulting in particular from the various dimensions of globalization ... (leave the UN facing four main challenges): financial pressure, legitimacy problems, competition and instrumentalization. (2005: 145 154)

Testing the representative international organisations against the instrumentality measure of security and world order, the dominant political alliance has taken charge of global governance. Super-states and their domestic interests have now formed the politics of global governance.

Moving from the local to the global is a massive step when interpreting governance as regulation. At the local level, clear normative constraints on the operation of sovereign states are a consequence of risk/security globalisation. These are very culturally dependent. More particularly, forms of governance and community order foreign to the Westernisation project are compared pejoratively with the normative frameworks of world order.

> The process [of globalisation] naturally affects non-Western societies more than Western ones. For example, in some cases globalization has come about through imposition of Western values, norms, and standards on many states, especially the developing countries. These 'global' values, which include important issues such as justice, liberal democracy, individual liberties, free markets, and particular forms of environmental objectives, are not values that have been arrived at through reflection and consensus in the world community. They are the norms, rules and standards that have been promoted by the politically, technically and militarily more powerful Western countries. (Pendleton 1999: para. 25)

At the level of the global, normative frameworks are informed by state alliances and international priorities which may struggle for compatibility. It is not enough to dismiss globalised values as a simple surrogate for Western ideals. The focus of international criminal justice reflecting and protecting global values is squarely on *humanity*. As I will develop later in my analysis of the more appropriate relationship between ICJ and victim communities (see Chapters 7 and 9), a transforming morality for ICJ should recognise and promote access, inclusivity and integration. In the context of protecting humanity, the values of ICJ on behalf of the global community are concerned with the rights of central stakeholders, and these will not always essentially correspond with a Western individual rights paradigm (see Chapter 8).

The strain in the evolution of normative frameworks for global governance is caused by the propensity in globalisation to deny cultural pluralism (Findlay 1999c). This has led to contests within global governance between regulatory frameworks that benefit different constituencies and as such are invested with different moralities. Another paradox of globalisation is the plurality of regulation within a wider project for cultural dominion.

In examining the relationship between global values and governance in the context of legal pluralism Tamanaha (2007) sees influential styles of legality as having less to do with norms than achieving the purposes of governance. Tamanaha suggests six sources of normative ordering which mix into the global governance dynamic:

- official legal systems which have expanded their influence through the modern period;

- customary norms either as they have survived globalisation or as they are rediscovered and interpreted in a modern context;

- religious norm systems which cross over custom and contest official legal legitimacy;

- economic norm systems;

- functional norm systems which arise out of institutions and are process designed for a specified function and exist within their own authority and regulatory frameworks; and

- community cultural norm systems which are on the rise to challenge the intrusions and failings of other more formal and state-centred paradigms.

Tamanaha suggests that in the context of globalisation these normative systems have led to clashes which in turn become both the justification for preferring one framework over the other and the governance objective to diminish the significance of any particular normative system. This is developed in the context of international criminal justice in Chapter 5, to follow.

Communitarianism interestingly is on the rise as a grassroots governance phenomenon, despite its discriminatory interpretation in dominant Westernised strategies of global governance. Pendleton (1999) targets the tendency through nationalism to see cultures and communities focusing more on collective responsibility. The prosecution of crimes against humanity is currently constrained within the framework of individual liability. This will become indefensible if the ICC in particular is to bring to justice organisations, groups and corporations as much responsible for crimes against humanity and genocide as might be individual perpetrators. Along with the progress of collective liability will evolve a stronger recognition of the need to confirm and protect communitarian rights. A more prominent communitarian rights paradigm in global values will result, giving strength to the bonds of a global community and distinguishing the narrow, individualised value structure informing global governance.

New globalisation?

If there is a consistent theme in globalisation as an analytical concept it is its undeniable economic dimension (Held 2004a). Whether in mercantile, colonial, industrial or modernisation incarnations, a powerful justification for globalisation analysis is the power dynamics around economic dominion and diversification. The present phase of globalisation demonstrates, in its desire for a stable and secure global economy, more than an increasingly detached commitment to the security of humanity above economy.

It could also be convincingly argued that the *global community* is an economic convergence, rather than some new cultural entity. In conceding this, however, the place of dominant market relations in the conceptualisation of world order is only one important feature of governance regulatory frameworks internationally. Militarism, perhaps to protect economic security, recurs through global governance despite the recent reliance on ICJ as a more legitimate regulatory alternative.

Van Creveld (2004) argues that the *new globalisation* is distinguished by militarism and wars. How these might be extracted from the project of colonisation to capture and expand economic dominion is neither simple nor definitive. What is useful about highlighting relationships between globalisation and war is the importance of nationalism and emergent global alliances in progressing militarism and the victors' justice.

War-making for global conquest is nothing new. Wars over cultural domination or religious extinction go back beyond the Crusades. So how do wars and the talk of war add distinction to the present phase of globalisation?

- Wars over world order are currently steeped in the language of terrorism. The enemy is both ideological and visible. In this context wars against oppositional cultures can be justified in terms of threat and security.

- Theatres of war are not constrained within state borders. Rather, military incursions are regional and transient. War can be waged selectively to restore preferred state borders in the same way that it can advance *regime change*.

- The authority to go to war may not originate from representative international organisations. Indeed, it may be constructed in the context of alliances which reject the unwillingness or incapacity of such organisations to confer authority. The alliance led initiatives can be justified as a necessary consequence of the prevarication and indecisiveness that results from representative global governance.

- Wars on terror can be waged within domestic jurisdictions against cells and communities, without troubling the constitutional integrity of the nation-state. Wars as such need not be fought offshore in order to disable domestic attacks.

- While *regime change* is widely identified as justification for violent military incursion, once achieved the process of economic and cultural realignment will be backed up by armies of occupation. Attached to these forces will be the institutions of imposed democratic governance, compatible as they are with preferred models for domestic, if not global, governance.

- Some war tactics resemble the *hit-and-run* strikes common in terrorist strategies. Terror against terror ultimately claims its justification through the victors' justice.

- Whether the alliance/aggressor chooses war rather than other forms of intervention and regulation may have, in reality, more to do with ideological significance and regional positioning than the dangers of threats posed by the target.

It would be overrating their relative significance as world regulatory regimes to declare that militarism and war-making against global terror are what defines the present phase of globalisation as *new*. It is enough to observe that a military regulatory framework is an important if somewhat selective and transient option for the dominant global alliance in identifying and confronting the risk/security challenge. What follows in terms of preferred regulatory options will have a more long-lasting impact on the nature and evolution of global governance.

The internationalisation of prevailing governance paradigms, international criminal justice and militarism being important possibilities, is what determines the new phase of globalisation. It is the driving concern for world order and security through the lens of *risk* and determined by *terror* that influences the nature of governance regulatory options as well as their selection and when.

International organisations have bolstered a more global approach to the regulation of trade, commerce and thereby modernisation (through the WTO and GATT) (Finger 2005). In so doing there is recognition by the UN and international financial agencies such as the World Bank that nation-states are incapable on their own of maintaining economic environments compatible with world economic ordering. New mechanisms for governance, being essentially international in their frameworks and operations, are relied upon to advance global order.

Yet global governance and the world order it seeks is not simply a *top-down* enterprise. The discord and *risk* against which global governance is set are intensely local and particular grievances (Keohane 2001). The governance strategies directed against such discord move from persuasion and coercion. Where international criminal justice is placed in this control continuum and why will focus the analysis of later chapters.

What has become clear in the global governance priorities of the *new* globalisation is that they should incorporate (through themes of rights and justice) the individual and critical institutions of citizenship, sovereignty and dominion (Teixeira 2004). The *ordering* as such required by global governance is not only social or economic. It includes incursions into multinational corporations, multicultural ideologies and multistructural communities. An example of the latter is where grassroots community engagement, through truth commissions and other restorative frameworks, attempts to reconstruct state order from fragmented communities in post-conflict state settings. I will elaborate my interest in *bottom-up* governance options as a reaction to the limitations of imposed governance instrumentalities when discussing the nature and legitimacy of victim communities (see Chapter 7).

Demonstrating the unique coalescence of community need, non-governmental patronage, state facilitation and critical engagement with formal ICJ is the transitional justice movement. Some would argue that transitional justice has had a greater impact on conflict resolution and peacemaking than has formal ICJ (Gilligan and Pratt 2004). If this is so then transitional justice may also offer a unique characteristic of the criminal justice/governance nexus in the new globalisation.

Transitional justice is claimed to address gaps in state-centred or *top-down* international criminal justice imposition. In essence transitional justice:

- holds that post-conflict justice must go wider than retribution;
- sees truth commissions as importantly recognising the social, economic and political particularities of post-conflict situations;
- promotes reconciliation beyond religious connotations; and
- encourages reparations where they resolve rather than perpetuate the foundations of conflict (such as with blood money) (Boraine 2004).

Cockayne (2004) suggests that transitional justice does not go far enough to exploit the community context for conflict resolution. He argues that by not concerning itself sufficiently with the causes of conflict or its critical socio-political conditions, transitional justice is at risk of the same criticism of generality which it directs against formal ICJ.

A challenge for transitional and formal or transformed ICJ is to effectively engage and represent victim communities, rather than prioritising the prosecution of individual liability (see Chapter 7). Crimes against humanity and genocide are the mandate for the ICC and the international criminal tribunals. They reinforce the distinguishing significance of collective liability as the concern for ICJ. Yet, how *humanity* is treated by international criminal justice will be a vital indicator of its special place in global governance and the concerns of the new globalisation.

Patomaki (2005) argues that to specifically locate *humanity* at the centre of global governance requires a deeper consideration of more conventional political and economic frameworks of governance. He talks of a 'coming together of humanity' allowing for a better understanding of the ways in which humanity can be collectivised as a crime victim. In achieving this, the constituency of international criminal justice (and in turn global governance) can be rescued from the objectives of Westernised international relations and returned to the more humane intentions for both the ICC, and for transitional justice.

Conclusion

The new globalisation is an age of risk and security. The restructuring of jurisdiction, standing, citizenship, humanity, community and exclusion, essential for the new age of globalisation, have their justifications and projections in 9/11.

My interpretation of what's new in globalisation is open to the criticism that it distorts the significance of risk/security post 9/11. To some extent I will concede the charge. The over emphasis on risk/security as a dominant regulatory framework in achieving world order is self-serving for the associated contention that ICJ is now central in global governance. However, as the later chapters progress, the place of terror as risk and order as security gives way to wider considerations of violence and violent reaction in shaping global governance.

International criminal justice assumes a more potent position in the struggle for governability when violence is the crucial context for crimes against humanity. Further, formal ICJ mediates violent retributive justice to coercively regulate aggression against communities, cultures and even preferred normative orders.

The conclusion of the book reflects on a more balanced regulatory agenda for global governance in which other pluralist regulation regimes join ICJ in the protection of the global economy and the modernisation project. This lessening of the risk/security emphasis, however, does not deny the distorted significance of violent terror and violent reaction in determining key themes in global reordering.

Global governance through reaction to terror is certainly the reluctant strategy for world order following the 9/11 terror. Its employment of violence in confronting violent resistance to globalisation is a risky strategy for order maintenance and legitimate governance. The dominant political alliance has assumed its domestic challenge in the name of international liberal democratic values and those which claim citizenship in a *global community*. Battle lines are redrawn. Military intervention demands *regime change* in ways similar to how in decades past other alliances attacked the progress of Communism and the Central American drug trade.

Global crime agendas are now being reordered and security priorities realigned. Victims and citizens are valorised while terrorists and collaborators neutralised or criminalised. Governance is currently defined by criminalisation and the restoration of global security.

The place of international criminal justice in this phase of globalisation requires critical analysis against the influence of political patronage and compromise. The problematic nexus between crime and globalisation as a precursor to the application of ICJ to ensure security and restore order is the concern of the chapter to follow.

Notes

1 Anthony G. McGrew, David Goldblatt and Jonathan Perraton.
2 Another critique of globalisation is its 'Western-centric' focus. The developing or underdeveloped worlds, it is argued, are little concerned with the central indicators of globalisation marketed by the dominant political alliance. This may be so, but I would suggest that the *powerless* within world order considerations are more likely to be the victims of the risk/security fascination, and as such cannot be excluded from the consequences of this new era.
3 The nature and influence of victim communities in the emergence of international criminal justice, and its governance function are discussed in detail, in Chapters 8 and 9.
4 At this point I do not intend to detail my understanding of 'the global' or of 'governance'. These understandings will be made clearer through the case-study discussions in later chapters, and through the interrogation of relations between risk/security and crime/control. I will say something, however, about the applications of governance.
5 The similarities might be extended in contrast with the militaristic mercantile companies in Asia and the New World, chartered by their sponsoring states to make war, colonise and deliver criminal justice along with the predominant commitment of wealth creation. None of this, however, operated in the same atmosphere of internationalisation as we see it today.

Chapter 2

Crime and risk – nexus between crime and globalisation

... while risks grow, people become more conscious of the riskiness of life, and demand more information about the risks they face. Risk techniques develop in pace with this demand, but this only breeds more insecurity as new risks are discovered all the time ... this is the risk society. (O'Malley 2007: 2)

Introduction

The community's need to know about risk and its expectations for security, have changed significantly in the current phase of globalisation. We want more information on global warming, more open action against child pornography worldwide and greater accountability in global drug law enforcement. At the same time individuals and communities seem unquestioningly content to trust control agencies with the carriage and knowledge of the *war on terror*. Is the difference explained by the nature and extent of the threat? Comparatively this is difficult to establish at least against the degree and coverage of potential harm to the global community. Blind faith in security responses against terrorism seems satisfied with limited concrete understanding of the threat represented by terrorism. Graphic but sporadic and contained attacks, recurrent normative political pronouncements and occasional law enforcement warnings are enough to locate terrorism centre stage within risk/security globalisation.

The suspension of critique around global terror, somewhat

remarkably against recent decades of civil rights struggle in many Western states, has enabled radical compromises of individual liberties. Threats of future terror and undisclosed security capacities are sufficient justification (McCulloch 2003). Later chapters will explore the relationship between risk redefined and radical control as a feature of global governance. In this chapter connections between crime and risk in the context of *new* globalisation will be investigated in order that risks redefined against global imperatives can be seen for the influence they have on international criminal justice and its role in governance.

In this chapter's analysis crime is conflated with risk, thereby indicating the justification of *security* as the imperative for crime/ risk control. Where the consciousness of risk pervades society then risk management becomes central in the governance of all sorts of social problems. Global governance has adopted this risk/security paradigm particularly in the context of terror risks, as terror is considered globalised and beyond the responsibility and capacity of nation-states alone.

The discussion commences with a look at *risk societies* and their analytical utility in a global context. The risks contingent on risk responses in the risk society are highlighted. The conditionality and contextualisation of risk is analysed before addressing the question why the risk of terror has come to dominate crime/risk priorities in the new globalisation. Next, the connection between terror risks and criminal justice (local and global) is fleshed out, taking the analysis to the crime/globalisation nexus through risk and its reduction.

Risk societies

Risk is constantly identified across the essential responsibilities of the state, particularly in health provision, work safety, transportation, sport, financial management and family relations. In this the recent role of the state (and to a growing extent specialist private agencies) has been to identify risk factors and either regulate them or provide information to the citizen on how risks can be minimised from an individual and community perspective.

Ulrich Beck (1992) concludes that the risk society is a product of 'modernisation risks'. As I have suggested (Findlay 1999b) the previous phase of globalisation was largely motivated by modernisation. Shadowing modernisation was a range of risks to individuals, indigenous communities and transitional cultures in particular, with troubling (and risk-generating) crime and control outcomes (Findlay 1999b: ch. 2). The pressure on developing cultures to embrace global capitalism through unnatural technologies and economies has strained and reformulated essential social and community relations. Cultural integrity has been challenged through the development push and in many instances modernisation has failed to achieve the material promise which economic development strategies have promised (Findlay 1999b: ch. 5).

O'Malley (2007) challenges Beck's application of the *risk society* when interpreting current developments in crime control. He argues that as grand theory, Beck's approach 'reduces complex phenomena (well beyond the world of crime) to effects of one grand contradiction' (O'Malley 2007: 2). For the purposes of the present analysis O'Malley is right in observing that to change risk societies through crime control requires first addressing global order.

> This seems a rather massive and long-term process, when many criminologists are more concerned to consider and deal with specific changes in crime control associated with risk frameworks ... while the rise of risk may be vitally important, criminologists may be more concerned with particular ways in which risk is used ... increasing attention has been paid to the ways in which risk has been promoted and shaped by more immediate political processes. (2007: 3)

The purpose of interrogating the crime/risk, security/control nexus is to see its relevance for global governance in the present phase of globalisation. Global terror is broadcast within global governance regulatory frameworks as the primary politicised risk confronting world order, despite generations dying from famine, environmental degradation and neglect. No doubt the prominent position given to global terror risks above these other threats to the *global community* has to do with unequivocal terrorist representations compared with fiercely contested responsibilities for these other significant threats.

The *risk society* is here viewed as more than merely some chaotic or catastrophic collapse of world order. Communities which demonstrate the characteristics of a *risk society* are now caught up, in different ways and directions, within a notion of *global community*. Terror is directed against communities. The interconnected regulation (military and justice in particular) of global terror at a community level has produced unfortunate consequences of exacerbating the risk that it is determined to manage. For instance, a prime declared purpose for the dominant political alliance intervening militarily in Iraq was to confront the advance in global terror through the risk of weapons of mass destruction. The domestic consequences for already divided communities in Iraq have been an upsurge in terrorist attacks unseen in that country prior to regime change. Hence, consequential and exaggerated risk can build out from crime and control strategies. Security is not the predictable result of violent control responses. Governance, domestic and global, is threatened by a direct violent challenge and by violent responses to meet that challenge. The risk/ security balance remains a test for global governance as it advances and resists sectarian political interests.

Risk from risk

In the context of corruption regulation (Findlay 1994) and drug law enforcement (Findlay 1999b) I suggested that particular regulation strategies can have adverse consequences for crime control. A *crime-control nexus* is contingent on risk and regulation. Wise crime prevention and control policy therefore should reflect on and observe the criminogenic consequences of regulation and control if the latter is to be maximised. The recent experience of global governance tends not to indicate that reflection so as to modify regulation strategies beyond a retreat from militarism.

Largely within market settings and especially where these markets are oligopolistic, regulation will influence fundamental market relationships and advantage some interests over others. This influence holds for illegitimate as well as legitimate markets. As I will discuss later, the selection of a particular model of regulation can have a profound affect on whether risks of crime are reduced, merely shifted within market locations or exacerbated. Often the failure to appreciate the 'profitable market conditions of the criminal enterprise' (Findlay 1994: 276) when settling on and implementing a regulatory strategy can make legitimate markets more vulnerable through the risk of concentrating criminal opportunity in the hands of the strongest illegitimate market players. This is a common outcome when, for instance, inelastic drug markets are regulated rather than repressed.

Having appreciated the risks inherent in a regulation and control strategy advancing crime control in particular, it is important to attempt to resolve some perennial risk/control dilemmas. These dilemmas, if they go unrecognised and unaddressed, have the potential to produce security risks at least as serious as the risk against which the original control strategy might have been directed. For instance:

- *Independence* v. *accountability*. To what extent will the efficacy and resilience of control agencies be compromised or diminished if in the name of good governance the agency's independence (and hence legitimacy) is challenged through efforts to make its operations accountable? The risk here is that efficient but unaccountable crime control may generate risky law enforcement practice.

- *Responsibility* v. *indemnity*. Can control agencies advance their power and legitimacy if they rely on indemnity as a central control technique? The risk here is that some offenders and offence behaviours will be favoured over others which are controlled for governance priorities outside the control agenda.

- *Publicity* v. *secrecy*. How is the balance to be struck between the community interest in seeing crime risk controlled and the need to maximise investigative efficiency through secrecy? The risk here, again, is that criminality and risky law enforcement will be easier to justify for immediate control gains, removed beyond the gaze of other regulatory and governance checks.

- *Anonymity* v. *exposure*. From the perspective of the risky enterprise requiring regulation, to what extent should the punitive consequences of control accompany each stage of exposure through regulation? The risk here is not only in the clandestine relationships of crime control, but also in the selective negotiation of the rights of those under investigation.

- *Selectivity* v. *total enforcement*. Facing the reality that total prohibition is not a realistic crime control option, will selective law enforcement compromise the rule of law? The risk here is that stereotyping and discriminatory enforcement practices will undermine the impact of retribution and deterrence as credible principles of punishment.

Whether it is systemic or process based, the realisation that regulation can create risks which in turn require control should influence how risks are prioritised and security is incurred. As the recent risk-generating consequences of controlling global terror keenly evidence, this consequential risk/control relationship features little in domestic, regional or global governance regulatory decision-making.

Prediction

I have suggested in other parts of this chapter that, unlike similar risk issues for governance, risk prediction in crime and justice is problematic, if not downright wishful. We hear much today about evidence-based criminal justice policy and the extent to which expectations for justice can be validated. However, when cornerstone causation themes such as the impact prison has on reoffending and how policing influences crime rates cannot be convincingly or consistently established then what hope is there for a risk-based science of global terror?

Problems with predicting crime risk and justice security outcomes haven't stopped the irrepressible expansion of behaviour prediction as a justice policy motivator. In recent years, for instance, the Australian jurisdictions of Victoria, Queensland, Western Australia and Tasmania have legislated to impose indefinite sentences on offenders convicted of violent crimes. This sentencing practice runs counter to prevailing considerations of retribution, just deserts and proportionality which otherwise govern contemporary sentencing (Henham 2003). The reforms are speciously justified on the basis of the risk posed to the community by the offender if he were to be released. On the strength of this the public may believe:

- community risk is ascertained;
- the risk potential of the offender can be evaluated;
- the preventive sentence will counter this risk with further custody and hopefully on till after release; and if relevant;
- the sacrifice of the rights of the offender and the integrity of the sentencing process are outweighed by community protection, actual and perceived.

Proponents of these policy developments should be responsible for ascertaining and establishing these presumptions in some empirically predictable fashion. However, largely as a consequence of normative 'law and order' politics and a blindly receptive population otherwise dulled to the need for factual justification of justice policy, the legislative enactment alone can be seen as enough to satisfy community concern (Hogg and Brown 1998).

In the UK recent developments in sentencing legislation now enable judges to consider the dangerousness of the offender along with other more definitive offence and offender characteristics when imposing sentence (Floud and Young 1981; Henham 1997). As with indeterminate sentencing, the consideration of dangerousness presupposes a predictive science which removes dangerousness and community risk away from the level of allegory or case experience. Were it only so simple (Pratt 2000). If we reflect on the literature surrounding genetic predisposition and its influence on behaviour modification (McKay: forthcoming) right back to Lombroso and phrenology (Vold 2005) connections between crime risk, harm and sanctioning practice have been far from scientifically convincing.

Predictive risk, empirical or aspirational, is also influencing other areas of domestic crime and justice policy. Again in the UK, anti-social behaviour orders are now widely used as a preventative tool regardless of the evidence about whether they target the right individuals and effectively alter offending behaviour (Scratton 2007). At the other end of the justice process, the risk to communities is becoming a predominant consideration when administrators consider granting parole to an inmate approaching their release date. The behavioural and situational factors from which this risk potential is projected may include such questionable considerations as a failure to engage in rehabilitation programmes when access to such programmes in prison can be strictly limited.

Yet the fragile association between crime risk and predictive justice intervention seems to have little restraining influence over domestic criminal justice policy development. This parallels the way in which crime risks internationally have been prioritised in recent political contexts without a clear correlation to proportional or comparative harm measures. Obviously it is the nature of these contexts and the conditional representation of risks, rather than the empirical reality of risk/security relations which more significantly govern the regulatory positioning of particular crime risks and security responses.

Currently at a global level, international terrorism has achieved the highest risk rating, one which has justified tremendous military intervention. The same cannot be said for international environmental degradation, transnational people smuggling or occupational health and safety worldwide. If as I allege the determination of global risk priority is not essentially dependent on comparative harm to the global community, then security responses will also not require comparative or empirical grounding. More likely the significance of political and cultural contexts in which the crime is identified and represented, will determine the manner in which security is valued and protected.

From a global governance perspective the risk/security paradigm itself is risky. With risk prediction and security evaluation more reliant on political and cultural context than comprehensive and comparative harm measures, community safety gives way to political imperative as a primary governance obligation. It might be said that this is not unusual for governance frameworks which run to service political agendas. However, the difference for global governance is its declared commitment to the safety of humanity. That safety may be less likely to be achieved and even more likely to be endangered when terrorism and violent control responses exemplify the risk/security commitment for global governance. Further, with globalisation promoting preferred regulatory strategies to address risk/security concerns, governance against terror will become more polarised and essentially less tolerant of cultural diversity as it is deemed threatening.

The conditionality and contextualisation of risk

Despite what insurance actuaries and risk management consultants would have us believe otherwise, risk is not an empirically predictive phenomenon reliant entirely on objective and indicative correlations. On the other hand it is possible to estimate where risks have more often occurred, what is a risky situation and who or what presents risks. But even in the most recurrent risk scenarios popular wisdom can confound from our limited empirical knowledge. For instance, women perceive stranger-danger risk as that which they must principally guard against to maintain their physical safety. Yet the figures show a woman is more at risk of harm in the kitchen with her husband or the car with her boyfriend than she may be walking alone at night. And each of these situations have their wider risk potentials besides comparative measures.

With what knowledge we do have, there is a capacity to contextualise risk in general scenarios and construct appropriate defences where possible. Popular culture and the *politics of risk* combine, however, to make the contextualisation of risk anything but a rational and responsive process.

The reality is that the determination of risks, their location and their priority from a control perspective is an essentially political question. Despite continual attempts in the languages of policing and of insurance to objectify the classification, representation and management of risk, the calibrations of risk and consequent control investment do not stray far from politics and governance concerns. Never more so is this the case than with considerations of global terror.

Links between crime control and 'law and order' politics are unidirectional. Crime control is crucially dependent on political agendas (Hogg and Brown 1998) and, as the next chapter demonstrates, global politics (and the governance espoused) is dynamic and contested. The contextualisation of risk in the new globalisation is heavily dependent on Western concerns over global terror. Terror relies on context, and there is nothing inevitable about the relationship between terror as risk and global governance.

The initial response to terror attacks on states in the dominant political alliance was a mixture of administrative sanctions, targeted military incursions and exclusion strategies sponsored by international organisations. As these proved problematic and the challenge to their legitimacy intensified, the involvement of ICJ in reacting to terror became more significant. This involvement took the form of international criminal prosecutions, mutual assistance policing, secretive investigation processes and the development of exceptional detention and punishment facilities. The context of the risk was dynamic and contested, and the resultant context of response and control shifted and morphed depending on a variety of political and situational variants (see Chapter 6).

The risk of terror

Moving naturally from modernisation as the crucial motivation for globalisation, it would be fair to assume that issues such as global financial recession, global environmental destruction and the dangers of nuclear contamination present as central risk/security concerns for global governance. While these have their place, and global warming in particular is gaining purchase as an influential risk issue for Western political agendas, it is the risk of terror which is now declared in governance terms as the contemporary risk to world order.

O'Malley suggests (2007) that non-recurring risks like terror, while potentially catastrophic for the risk society, are not statistically predictable:

> Put simply, because these are non-recurring events, or events that unfold so quickly or invisibly that we cannot gather data on them beforehand, they cannot be predicted using statistical risk

techniques. Because of the global scale of risks, institutions such as the family, trade unions and national governments – including the welfare state that itself is based on risk management – begin to lose their functions. (2007: 2)

The challenge to the nation-state, political alliances and a dominant economic culture posed by terrorism has come to the fore in global governance terms despite the little we know of its recurrent risk potential or its predictability. In later chapters I will propose some reasons for this prioritisation which cannot be explained in comparative harm terms. For the present the analysis of crime and risk in globalisation will accept global terror as the risk around which crime control responses worldwide are being constructed.

So far I have been referring to terror and terrorism interchangeably, and to forms of terrorism in a rather generic fashion. A discussion of current global crime risk and its relation to globalisation is an appropriate opportunity to be more specific about the terror and terrorism in question (Walker 1992).

Baxi (2007) has advanced the broadest observation in arguing (as does Pierre Bordieu) that:

... the 'terror' of globalization lies precisely in the fact that it marks an endless warfare against (cultural) pluralism. In this sense, perhaps the remark of Ulrich Beck that 9/11 constitutes the 'Chernobyl of globilisation' deserves a fuller dignity of discourse. (2007: 14)

Baxi's discussion of *wars on terror* and *wars of terror* is also insightful in the way it commences the interrogation of terror with states and styles of governance. He returns to Marx in *Das Kapital*:

... where Marx reads the early phase of industrial revolution as offering histories of so many reigns of terror, to the point of suggesting an integral connection between the rule of law and the reign of terror.

In the context of the 'halcyon days of contemporary economic globalisation' Baxi reflects on the terror caused by Union Carbide in Bhopal, Agent Orange in Cambodia and Ogoniland. These terror enterprises are the intended or unwitting product of alliances between compromised state economic priorities, tragic multinational commercial expediencies and the vulnerable community.

Employing Baxi's retrospective on state or economically directed terror, these may have inflicted far greater harm on humanity and the environment than 9/11. Unbalanced appreciations of risk by globalisation confirm that terror has 'no neutral readability'. The global reality of terrorism is inextricable from the political and commercial contexts Baxi identifies, within which the risk of terror is valued and responded to. For instance, feminist critics have for decades reminded the developed Western states in particular that women are subjected to manifold orders of terrorism. Indigenous people have their own tragic histories about past and present predatory terror. But their stories are marginalised in the priorities of global governance when put against the energies directed at countering politically and culturally motivated emancipist terror enterprises.

> As a potential victim of cross-border terrorism, each and every human has now a stake in a 'terror' free world; this narrative power stands appropriated by the emergent global politics of collective human security which remains utterly confounded by the bio-politics of insurgent 'terror', namely the use of the human body as a weapon of mass destruction. (Baxi 2007: 15)

Despite Baxi's conviction regarding more significant terror risks in past phases of globalisation, in order currently to interrogate the *terror* focus of global governance as it connects to international criminal justice, the prioritisation of insurgent, and to a lesser extent state-sponsored, terror is the crucial model for the risk/security nexus. The complex reality, equity and humanity, despite this recognition, remain to be drawn into the transformed ICJ (see Chapter 9). For the present – and confirming its partiality – international criminal justice has been conscripted into governing (rather than controlling or punishing) the risk of terror.

Risk management through criminal justice

The emergence of the welfare state following the Second World War could be seen as a consequence of risk appreciation. The realisation in state agencies at the time was that by taking on greater responsibility for education, health, housing and family services not only might risks be better managed, but also the authority and coverage of the state would be greatly enhanced. The state came to intrude more personally and perennially into the lives of the citizens to provide greater social security.

Criminal justice administration is a key determinant of state authority. Even though all aspects of criminal justice are now subject to private sector provision, they are in this form usually dependent on state licensing or sponsorship. The state in neo-liberal decline has divested more and more of its service delivery to the private sector and countenanced commercial arrangements to satisfy burgeoning businesses in personal safety and property protection (Shearing and Stenning 1981). In so doing, the state has retained its position of auctioneer as well as monopolist over criminal justice provision.

Since the Industrial Revolution in the UK, Europe and America, the state has adopted responsibilities in policing to ensure a compliant workforce and the perpetuation of public order which complemented capitalist enterprise (Reiner 2000). Not long prior to this the state took over imprisonment which up until the Enlightenment had been the concern of private organisations or local government (Ignatieff 2003). The courts had for some time been a growing province of the state.

Within this framework the state has enjoyed capacities to define and meet the essential risks which justify criminal justice intervention. As criminal justice accompanied governance into a global context, it was natural that risk management internationally should fall to criminal justice, where risks were determined against the sanctity of private property, or to the personal safety of citizens and communities.

Crime control, as a primary state influence over community safety, is currently shaped by risk reduction techniques. Criminal justice priorities from a state perspective have fallen into line with neo-liberal retributive justice paradigms wherein the autonomy and responsibility of the citizen is confirmed (as offender and victim) and state or private justice intervention is designed to prevent and contain the harm which crime presents.

Until recently institutional criminal justice has played a less significant role in the authority frameworks of international representative bodies which formally manage global governance. Also criminal justice has not been so important (until recently) in grounding the dominance of international political alliances. Prior to the activation of the ICC, international criminal justice had simply confirmed global governance as an itinerant institutional device giving effect to the victor's justice.

It has been the developing role of international organisations in peacekeeping and post-conflict restoration which has promoted a growth in formal ICJ going beyond state-centred criminal justice commitments. At the informal level, truth commissions and other *grassroots* resolution mechanisms have emerged as crucial influences in conflict resolution and state formation (Braithwaite 2002). The shift from being a minor to a major player in global governance has for ICJ, not surprisingly from both political and cultural perspectives, heightened its relevance and utility as a control agent. The growth of ICJ accompanied alliance expansionism and economic modernisation received an unimagined boost from risk/security necessities post-9/11. Crimes against humanity, genocide and terrorism tragically have featured as transnational crimes well before this ICJ growth industry and its risk/security flashpoint. Even so, with the identification of these crime risks as pressing global threats to world order (and particularly as challenges to the progress of economic modernisation) the nexus between global crime and risk/security globalisation is a fertile political context for the advancement of ICJ in risk terms. Global terror has been the rocket under that advance.

The crime / globalisation nexus[1]

The crime/globalisation nexus is important to:

- challenge contemporary representations of crime;
- engage popular wisdom about the causes of crime;
- expose the influence of crime over social and cultural transitions;
- demystify both crime and globalisation; and thereby
- offer the potential to rationalise control, diminish crime and reconstruct crime relationships and crime choice.

Crime has been a silent partner in modernisation.[2] Within a contracting world, crime and its traditional boundaries are transforming into predictable and active features of globalisation. For instance, international trading in illicit drugs is recognised as a globalised phenomenon. The crime organisations which manage the trade are multinational, and the capital they produce and proliferate globalises other crime markets.

The marketing of crime opportunity can complement *deep state* agendas. For instance, the recent opening up of drug trafficking routes from Afghanistan through Tajikistan and into Russia has been fostered through alliances between a fragile producer state, a compromised international presence, an unstable and economically non-viable transit state and a well developed organised crime market in the reception state.[3] Each referent community along the way –

and their governments – manipulate a backdrop of global political marginalisation and economic/cultural imperialism to justify and neutralise what might otherwise be more objectively condemned.

Globalisation creates new and favourable opportunities for crime. This cause and effect is the consequence of what Harvey refers to as the 'compression of time and the annihilation of space' (1989: 294–5). Commercial crime relationships in particular are set free through market deregulation to benefit from opportunities not dissimilar to those enjoyed by multinational enterprise operating beyond the jurisdiction of the individual state and the limitations of legitimate market regulation. The deregulation of international commerce and the internationalisation of communication have enabled violent resistance to flourish along with the spread of cultural fundamentalism.

The globalisation of crime represents the potential to view many crime relationships unburdened of conventional legal and moral determination. Globalisation working towards a common culture is intolerant of difference by arguing for a preferred politic (democracy), a preferred economy (modernisation) and a preferred value structure (materialism) by emphasising the integrity of new domains of legitimate and restrictive citizenship such as the *global community*. Terrorism in such discourse is determined by global governance as an attack on global citizenship, and efforts at its control have recently justified extraordinary military and law enforcement interventions on behalf of this amorphous *global community*.

The process of time-space compression which is globalisation has enhanced material crime relationships so that they require analysis in a similar fashion to any other crucial market force. The claim of globalisation is that:

> Spatial barriers have collapsed so that the world is now a single field within which capitalism can operate, and capital flows become more and more sensitive to the relative advantages of particular spatial locations. (Waters 1995: 57–8)[4]

The context of terrorism is such a (dis)location.

The nexus between globalisation and global crime is keenly identified in risk terminology. In a contracting globe, where pluralist cultural, economic and religious values are tolerated only insofar as they do not significantly challenge the norms of a prevailing political alliance, world order has come to rely on a risky mix of domination and violent resistance. Criminalising that resistance is risky. Violent security responses are risky. Predicating globalisation on risk and security where criminal behaviours comprise a major risk and outstrip the risks which victim communities prioritise, is riskier still.

Conclusion

Recognising its limitations, the *risk society* is an important analytical location for examining the risk/security nexus in new globalisation. The *global community* as a risk society is preconditioned by terror and its control. While the neo-liberalist project can be seen as setting the divide between terrorist and victim cultures, it would be unfair and overly simplistic to see global crime risk as entirely or even primarily a consequence of neo-liberal politics. To do this, bearing in mind the enormous influence of neo-liberalism in the later modern period, might lead to massive over-prediction of catastrophes for world governance and order resulting from risk and security overreaction.

> ... criminologists have to beware of falling into line with catastrophic forecasts of complete transformation in justice being effected by such developments as the risk society. Among other things, neo-liberalism itself has been the ascendant political rationality through which changes in the direction of risk have been mediated, then it is to this politics, rather than to complete transformations of modernity that criminologists might rightly wish to turn. (O'Malley 2007: 12)

Pat O'Malley refers to the 'uncertain promise of risk' (2004). How much sharper is this reservation when transferred to global crime risks and globalised security responses.

The following analytical themes can be extracted from the recently developed connection between global crime risk and global governance:

- Like many forms of crime risk, global crime risk is difficult to evaluate and predict.
- As a result, convincing empirical evidence concerning global crime risk is rare and underdeveloped.
- Crime risk, particularly that posed by global terror, is not dependent in its prioritisation on comparative and conditional measures of harm to the global community.
- Recognising this, the context in which global crime is identified and represented will be the significant factor in its prioritisation.

- The anticipated challenge to governance from particular global crime types will also depend on the contexts of its identification and representation.
- Security responses to risks posed by global crime may have as much to do with the context of their identification and representation as they do to any future challenge to global governance which they may pose.

Notes

1 This nexus was proposed and discussed in detail in Findlay (1999b). In the present context the nexus should now be taken as covering globalised crime and the 'new' globalisation.
2 For the purposes of the analysis to follow, modernisation is taken to involve a capitalist system of commodity production, industrialism, developed state surveillance techniques and militarised order (see Giddens 1991: 15).
3 This is well documented in Paoli, Rabkov and Reuter (2006).
4 This is another paradox of globalisation in that spatial locations exist and also vanish. If locations are distinguished by borders or entry and exit points, and if these collapse, then how can a location be defined? For the relationship between the local and the global in international criminal justice this dislocation is of particular significance.

Chapter 3

A review of global crime problems – studies of crime as global risk

Belief in the power of globalisation reinforced ontological insecurity. If one accepted globalisation as a powerful economic and social force that necessitated new rules of politics, then the same power had to be associated with the 'parallel globalisation of terror'. For that reason, the logic by which the process of globalisation was believed to work was used to describe the development of new threats ... The perception of the threat of terrorism fed on the west's construction of its own future in terms of a powerful process of globalisation. As the dark side of globalisation, terrorism had a power to equal the bright side of globalisation. (Rasmussen 2002: 332–3)

Introduction

To appreciate the nexus between crime/risk and security/control there is a need to take any discussion of global crime problems down to risk specifics. The current political moment for global terrorism and organised crime provides a case study focus from which the security of the citizen/victim and the exclusion of resistant communities will later be interrogated.

The interface between the dominant political/security alliance and the organised criminal/terrorist is disentangled in this chapter by recourse to motivations such as profit, market advantage and domestic power struggles, consistent with important drivers of globalisation. In the analytical spirit of investigating enterprise instead of perpetuating ideology, I focus on underlying themes of 'misrepresentation' that resonate across the talk of crime risks, their problematic connections and the distorted justifications provided for control overreaction.

The thesis of this chapter is that a central risk paradigm in the risk/security nexus in globalisation currently is terrorism, and as such provides a unique foundation for security responses. Law enforcement agencies in particular are persuaded by material connections between organised crime and global terrorism. This has the consequence of heightening the risk posed by both crime types and, through association, their challenge to world order. This scenario provides, I suggest, a powerful but deeply problematic platform for radical criminal justice responses in the name of global governance. It has also seen a reordering of global crime and control priorities which gain presence and significance from long-standing misunderstandings of the governance challenges posed by organised crime.

The case studies, crucial to the development of the analysis to follow, chart the connection between corruption and modernisation, organised crime and corrupt opportunities, and terrorist enterprise and organised crime convergence. Globalisation explains the growing interest in corruption even where it is an identifiable consequence of modernisation. Globalisation can also explain the alleged connection between organised crime and terrorism more strongly cemented through political rhetoric than enterprise.

Imagining risk

Since Donald Cressey's work on organised crime as the 'fifth estate' (Cressey 1969), its threat to legitimate government has been identified. Politicians and criminal justice administrations for decades have chosen to represent the organised crime *menace* as an attack on the institutions of the democratic state and as a physical and financial danger to society (Findlay 1986; Findlay 2000). This is consistent with the approaches of governments in the United States and Italy when constructing the *reality* of the *mafia* in their countries for more than a century (Smith 1975), and the representation of organised crime 'colonisation' in the transitional Eastern European states (Findlay 1999b).

More recently, the often unquestioned connection has been drawn between organised crime and international terrorism (White 2006) with similar political interpretations in mind, but now the threat is to global governance. Organised crime is presently cast as a transnational, cross-border problem, with alliances returning to the distinctly political[1]. In global terrorism, the world is said to be confronting a new organised crime opportunity, the local manifestations of which are inextricably linked to international conflict and the threat is directed against global communities (Findlay 2004). That is the risk. The security response is cast for these communities to sever the financial link with organised crime by alienating those in their midst who endorse or profit from the terrorist project.

This chapter commences with a discussion of terrorism as the contemporary organised crime.[2] The common characteristics of terrorism and other forms of organised crime are suggested in a consideration of enterprise theory. In order to effectively indicate the market potential of organised crime and the manner in which control strategies may enhance that skewed market we look at the importance of corruption as a facilitator of illegitimate enterprise. Once this is done, the market realities of organised crime can be more effectively reflected on, in terms of whether terrorism is worth any such investment.

Even were we to reject the link between organised crime and terrorist funding, there is a strong argument to say that the consequences of organised crime are no less destructive of legitimate states and their economies than may be those of terrorist attacks. The importance of globalisation in stimulating organised crime as terrorism is critiqued through a discussion of the risk posed to market integrity, and the development of strong state economies set free from criminal or illegitimate alternatives.

Contemporary globalisation negotiating risk and security (see Chapter 1) has necessarily been predetermined by the prevailing political concern with international terror.[3] Radical responses from the states, regions and internationally have cemented global political alliances and changed the relationship between due process and criminal justice in the name of national security (Rasmussen 2002). The chapter concludes by speculating on how globalisation (and terrorism as one of its contemporary characteristics) is influencing the appreciation of organised crime and associated control strategies. The implications for international governance, if these two contemporary crime types are such virulent challenges to it, require initial consideration.

Governance under challenge

Beneath this apparent contest between organised crime, terrorism and the state are more complex and less apparent mutual interests at a deep *state* level.[4] There is significant evidence that both during the 'Cold War' period and in ongoing instances of transitional state conflict[5] alliances have been forged between organised criminal enterprise and para-political movements in order to destabilise state governance and thereby reap benefit.[6]

Throughout this chapter the analysis of connections between organised crime/terrorism/governance is observed at both state and *deep state* levels. Regarding the *deep state* there are contemporary examples of powerful clandestine relationships between the security and intelligence organisations of established states, international criminal networks and *quasi states* in the form of separatist movements or terrorist organisations (McCoy 2006). These *alternative state* entities challenge sovereignty, economy, monopolies of force and the whole protectionist fabric of the establish state. Organised criminal enterprise may find a home within these movements, in similar ways to its infiltration of state administration through corruption and black economies (Findlay 1994, 2004). In the *deep state* relationship the challenge of organised crime to democratic governance is clearest.

Easier to substantiate is the destructive relationship between organised crime and market formation. There is ample evidence in transitional economies that black markets in goods, services and even security provision maintain communities where the public and private sector, through legitimate commerce, have failed community need. Organised crime has replaced the state or the corporation in satisfying demand and supply where free markets are a fragile aspiration and the divide between illegitimate and legitimate enterprise has disappeared. For those who equate free market economics with democratic state fundamentals, there is much to fear in the replacement of a closed economy with organised criminal oligopolies.

Where organised crime is the substitute for healthy and competitive enterprise, the essentials of a functioning state, such as taxation for public service, do not exist. If the state is as much responsible for social and military security then organised crime in market replacement represents a commensurate threat to governance, as might terrorism to political legitimacy. Examples will later be provided where terrorist destabilisation creates the economic conditions for organised crime to thrive and for states (and regions) to be weakened as a consequence.

A crucial economic bridge between organised crime and state/economic instability is corruption. It would be worthwhile pausing to examine a regional case study where weak states have fallen victim to corruption as a consequence of modernisation. In small Pacific Island states, the transition to cash economies has been characterised by criticisms of corruption. Closer investigation reveals how the ravages of culturally disconnected trade and aid have left these weak states open to exploitation and even international ostracism for failing to resist the corruption-generating consequences of international commerce.

Corruption – weak states or good business?

The small island states of the South Pacific provide a unique context for exploring the relationship between corruption and modernisation (Findlay 1999b: 77–93). These *nations* are recently independent, isolated customary societies where indigenous networks of influence and dependence provide the deep bonds of community life. In their recent and brief postcolonial independence these states have transplanted political and economic institutions within these indigenous networks (Dinnen and Ley 2000).

From an economic development perspective some of these states are only several generations into cash economies. The majority of the population still relies to some extent on subsistence enterprises, and property and the wealth it brings remains in collective village arrangements. Therefore clan or tribal loyalties underpin all commercial enterprise in a similar fashion to the mutuality of subsistence living centuries old.

Whether harsh or paternal, European colonisation has left the vestiges of foreign governance institutions and trading alliances. Over these, through bilateral, regional and international aid regimes, development protocols have required a commitment to commercial practice which exploits and at the same time eschews customary networks of obligation. The influence of aid donor dependency in the Pacific has tended to weaken indigenous enterprise, and has generated a growing level of reliance on traded commodities instead of traditional and otherwise viable self-sufficiency economies.

Regional and international anti-corruption initiatives, associated with campaigns against money-laundering and resource *piracy* seem to have little impact on Pacific island political or commercial culture.[7] This is not surprising when these small states have been pressured into offshore financial dealing and resource exploitation in a climate where domestic market regulation is weak and preferential.

It is also not difficult to appreciate that market regulation against corrupt business practice will be problematic where the reach of state bureaucracy and its regulatory agencies breaks down beyond the principal urban centres. Even if state regulation were more vigorous and equitable, contractual and commercial parity between the small dependent state and large business enterprises (often integrated into the provision of aid assistance) is unlikely. Unfortunately for these vulnerable states, corporate citizenship as evidenced in business dealings only seems to reflect a concern for the parent economy and not for the welfare of the trading partner and its market viability.

The modernisation project in these transitional cultures comes with a price. Not only have cash economies and state institutions threatened the integrity of indigenous cultures, but an orientalist morality has attached to the financial assistance now essential for the existence of these small nations. Anti-corruption commitments feature in the conditions obliged of these states along with the socio-economic development imposed by donor agencies. Such obligations might be perceived as in the interests of the recipient communities. However, it is when the development strategies facilitate relationships of advantage and dependence later decried as corrupt that their further dependent potential seems unjust.

It is not enough, however, to revisit corruption in transitional societies in order for it to be explained against the background of indigenous relationships of obligation. The imbalance of influence between small island communities and dominant international development programmes enables a more critical and globalised appreciation of forces for corruption and control.

Corruption is a product of the giving and receiving of advantage in illegitimate or exploitative contexts.[8] In traditional cultures, relationships of advantage are the foundation of political and customary power. For instance, in Melanesian societies, the cult of the 'big man' has as much pervaded parliamentary authority as it has corrupt business practice. This means that neat distinctions between corrupt and legitimate political or commercial arrangements in small Pacific island states is rarely possible.[9]

Any successful culturally located representation of corruption needs to recognise:

- corruption as a relationship;
- corruption as a market reality;
- the influence of corruption over profit;
- that morality is not an essential consideration for the definition of corruption; and

- as networks of trust are distinctly culturally relative then what comprises a violation of trust for a corrupt purpose is heavily dependent on the cultural location of the relationship in question.

Corruption is a relationship of power and influence existing within and taking its form from specific environments of commercial opportunity. Power and influence as well as opportunity make up the market for corruption and the market is facilitated by corrupt relationships. This can work in a very similar fashion to the way in which legitimate market influence is constructed and negotiated. What separates legitimate from illegitimate market context is not so much the relationship of dominance and obligation but the cultural setting in which such relationships are maintained and the purposes for which they operate. For instance, what may be deemed a political bribe in a modernised context may seem to the local population little more than the exercise of clan fealty in a transitional culture. It is the purpose behind the alleged corrupt behaviour and the cultural context of the relationship on which it rests rather than the behaviour itself (giving and receiving advantage) which distinguishes the bribe.

An example of the interconnection between authorised frameworks of advantage and corrupt transactions is the way in which politicians in Papua New Guinea have applied their parliamentary allowances. On election to the PNG parliament (where single terms of office are very common) a new member is given a financial allowance to be employed in defraying legitimate electoral expenses. PNG is a decentralised and diverse nation with more tribes and languages than could be found anywhere else in the Pacific. In order that a Westminster style of representative government across such a fragmented country should endeavour to function effectively, an electorate allowance system makes good sense. However, these allowances are now a common source of corruption and the reason is apparent. Irrespective of a magnificent leadership code in PNG which legislatively enshrines parliamentary probity and an aggressive Ombudsman, the allowance has degenerated into little more than a means for funding political influence. Many new parliamentarians gain office only through the support of their clan base. Once in office it is now expected that the organisers of that vote base would be paid for their efforts. The source all too often is the electorate allowance. This reveals the institutionalisation of opportunities for corruption, facilitated through customary obligation and funded through seemingly legitimate sources of financial advantage.

Corruption / modernisation nexus

In small Pacific states there seem to be common imperatives behind contexts of development and relationships of crime. Often similar forms of relationships also exist as strong structural features of customary social organisation which easily translate into commercial frameworks and enterprise structures.

Global juxtapositions of corruption as *bad* and modernisation/ development as *good* fail to appreciate or to reconcile the commonality of their motivation and the interests they can serve when commercial enterprise and materialist profit is their context. Both rely on relationships of domination and obligation and in certain cultural settings these can be adapted to both outcomes.

The contexts of cultures in developmental transition produce marginalisation through crime in a similar way that selective access to wealth creation tends to marginalise. Crime control and the regulation of corruption are also selective and add to the process of marginalisation which in turn stimulates crime and corruption.

In small Pacific states, the contextual interaction and interdependence between:

- customary social structures and modes of development;
- development and corruption; and
- corruption and customary social structures. (Findlay 1997c)

are issues which are strangely under-argued in the literature of criminology and development studies. Looking at both economic development and corruption as integral to markets and enterprise where customary structures prevail is a useful predicate to a deeper analysis of corruption and structures of economic influence and development in small states. This analysis is also transferable to any commercial arrangement where the dominant player is happy to use customary or introduced frameworks of influence and dependency to advance an unbalanced and non-competitive commercial 'market'.

It is in this atmosphere of socio-economic development and modernisation which followed the retreat of political colonisation across the Pacific that concerns for corrupt business practice should be viewed. No matter what aid donors and international financial agencies may prefer, colonial protectionism has not been replaced by a resilient free market and an age of competition. Markets are small and frail. Small Pacific economies have little to trade beyond non-renewable resources. Large foreign trading conglomerates raid the

Pacific for natural resources and lucrative if strangled commodity markets. Business enterprise is commonly a one-way commercial street.

Enterprise theory and a market model for corruption regulation

An enterprise theory of crime and control (Burchfield 1978) refers to motivations (for crime and control) as based on economic profit. Crime here is seen as comprising commercial relationships that foster profit in markets which are criminal[10] or partially legitimate.[11] Crime control may form just one but important market regulator which enables particular commercial/profit relationships (legitimate or illegitimate) to adapt and flourish.

Corruption is one of the relationships that enhance the profit outcomes of criminal enterprise. In fact, its nature, organisation and influence over the enterprise may be reliant on the networks of dependence and advantage created and maintained by corruption. Also, certain commercial aspirations (particularly where these are ambiguous or polyglot) and incentives for market advantage may act as opportunities for corruption.

In some market contexts, particularly where legitimate markets for similar goods and services are either weak or over-regulated, corruption may make good business sense. In other situations, such as where the enterprise and the market are made up of tightly knit communities where legitimate market advantage is hard to engineer, corruption becomes part of the commercial or business culture. This is more likely than not where the enterprise comes in contact with market regulators. Prevailing social connections in any of these commercial contexts may in fact view corruption as a normal or at least tolerable feature of doing profitable business (Findlay 1994).

Efforts at identifying, investigating and controlling corruption would do well to recognise the business advantage promoted by certain corruption relationships, and in particular market contexts. With this understanding it is more likely that control strategies will not simply become another form of market relationship which selectively favours certain corrupt market outcomes while limiting others.[12]

Appreciating corruption as a component of business and as an important indicator of criminal enterprise (with public-sector collusion) has the potential also to explain the relationship between corruption and modernisation. For transitional cultures in phases of rapid socio-economic development the pressure is to move from customary commercial constructions to those which promote cash economies. The indigenous networks of dependence and advantage are supposed to support the aspirations of free-market capitalism but to do so in contexts where the market is either unable to facilitate strong competition or where it is regulated in an imbalanced fashion by layers of overarching economic dependence (Dauvergne 1998).

Within customary societies rapidly transforming into cash cultures, other motivations may predominate over economic profit (Dinnen and Ley 2000). Where the profit motive has taken hold, it may in turn be applied to the advancement of other more important social aims. For instance, in the South Pacific, the culture of the *big man* as leader and power broker might explain why newly elected politicians employ their parliamentary allowances directly and openly to curry favour with their clan or village power base (Findlay 1999b). To the outside observer this might appear corrupt but within its cultural context it is an expected behaviour and is good political *business.* To attempt to control the practice by a crude or moralist control strategy which does not understand the indigenous network of dependence and advantage or the manner in which the exposure to cash for office facilitates these would do little to generate an anti-corruption consciousness in the community. In fact, it might present an opportunity to dismiss corruption control initiatives generally as foreign and culturally inappropriate.[13]

Corruption control in the South Pacific is principally sponsored by the external forces for modernisation. They do so by representing corruption as an indication of poor governance, bad leadership, slack financial regulation and even community immorality (Findlay 2003). To remedy this it is one thing to eschew moral arguments about corruption. More effective is the recognition of the position corruption plays within criminal enterprise and from this the perennial relationship between corruption and the current materialist age of modernisation. This realisation needs to come from within the context of modernised communities (social and commercial) before it can be effectively applied to transitional cultures through the process of modernisation.

A case in point is with the recent attempt by international agencies such as the Organisation for Economic Cooperation and Development (OECD) and its Financial Action Task Force (FATF) to isolate Nauru from the global financial community for failing to be strenuous against money-laundering within its offshore banking sector (Findlay 2003).

Nauru is a small nation-state which during its colonial occupation was ravaged to the point of environmental destruction for its phosphate deposits. After independence it was awarded financial compensation but given little responsible assistance in the management of that trust. Now beyond its extreme dependence on international aid, Nauru crucially relies on revenues from its role as an offshore financial centre, and initially it was encouraged by international commercial agencies and feted by multinational business as well as organised criminal enterprise for the provision of financial services.[14] Following the collapse of its offshore financial trading, largely as a consequence of compromised US banks and the FATF, Nauru was exploited by Australia as a dumping ground for unwanted asylum seekers.

The wealth generated by the financial centre operations of Nauru has been the subject of criticism in terms of corruption and cronyism. Beyond this, however, Nauru has become reduced through the pressures for modernisation to a position of extreme dependence on a money market economy once recognised, now decried, for its potential to conceal financial transactions and deny financial regulation. In this position of extreme vulnerability to corrupt exploitation, Nauru is isolated from the legitimate international financial networks for failing to enforce regulations which would have tended to kill off its one lucrative cash economy. Therefore over-regulation will increase opportunities and necessities for corrupt relationships within and beyond Nauru, without recognising and repositioning the profit imperatives for tolerating corrupt enterprise within that dependent nation-state (see Findlay 2003: 116–18).

The charge is more than hypocrisy when the international agencies are confronted by the vulnerability of the small Pacific Island states. For instance the FATF is said to honour a uniform concern for international commercial probity no matter what the context. If this is so then its good governance *push* should be seen to be equally directed towards the major American banks which funnelled suspect funds to Nauru as it has been to the agencies of the Nauru financial industry and the government. This has not been the case. The FATF, as with its dealings in vulnerable Asian economies, is exposed as partial in its own governance functions.

Having analysed several case studies of corruption in the South Pacific (see Findlay 1999b: 77–93) the following conclusions can be drawn regarding the intersection between the forces for modernisation and transitional cultures:

- The identification of certain commercial relationships as corrupt is culturally relative.

- Political power, where it is inextricably dependent on complex networks of filial support and custom obligation will challenge international notions of good governance and financial probity.

- Politics and commerce are inextricably linked in states where modernisation is rapid and sporadic.

- In transitional cultures, crucial relationships within politics and commerce are influenced and shaped by pre-existing custom obligations.

- Custom obligations may create opportunities for corrupt relationships to flourish while in the local context being redefined (and not always in a positive reaction to corruption regulation initiatives).

- The bonds of custom obligation which underpin political and commercial relationships in these transitional cultures may also stand in the way of regulating and controlling corruption.

- Besides (and regardless of) custom obligation, the public, politicians and the commercial community are sensitised to the dangers of corruption through its potential to undermine national credibility which is essential to economic development.

- Even so, where global concerns for good governance and commercial probity intersect with customary obligation and feudal loyalties in transitional cultures, the process of criminalisation and crime control is problematised.

- Economic development within unchallenged contexts of custom obligation can simultaneously stimulate corrupt and commercially viable relationships.

(Findlay 1999b: 89)

Therefore it is not difficult to perceive corruption as a precursor to market subversion through organised crime while at the same time being an inevitable product of particular development and commercial intersections. Even so, organised crime has capitalised on weak states and fragmented and selective market regulation. In the Pacific this has meant environmental terrorism rather than the creation of terrorist havens as a consequence of black market financing. It is worth remembering that some of the greatest violations of sound free-market commerce in the Pacific have been facilitated by major international banks and corporations. The question therefore remains as to who is the organised criminal and what is terrorism in the region.

Despite these empathies between organised crime and corruption, international commerce and weak economies, terrorism and state reformation, commonality may be confined to the profit, power and market advantage which arises through business enterprise (as distinct from any shared ideologies). Any connection between organised crime, market distortion, skewed commercial opportunity and terrorist resourcing needs to be disconnected from obtuse and shared ideologies and rerouted to enterprise theory. Added to this is the recognition that the link between the financing of crime and terror is often no more than circumstantial or for a concealed commercial advantage.

Common characteristics of organised crime

Questioning whether the foundations of terrorist funding are principally or essentially organised crime provokes the question how and why has this assumed connection developed? I will address this contention in a moment. The answer in a general sense may more likely lie in the way organised crime and terrorism have been represented by the state and its control agencies as threats to democratic governance. Challenging this nexus will naturally open up other platforms for contesting political legitimacy through terrorism now simply dismissed as a consequence of criminalisation (Findlay 2007c).

The first analytical step towards these conclusions is to overview representations of organised crime and terrorism and look for a common root. The more convincing investigations of organised crime recognise its enterprise structure (Burchfield 1978; Van Duyne 1993) and the transnational commerce/profit on which it relies (Findlay 1999b: 49–52). This emerges in part from an appreciation of organised crime as the provision of goods and services in illicit markets, the infiltration of state and legitimate markets through corruption, and the creation and financing of quasi-legitimate business enterprises (Volkov 2002). This parallels the role of organised crime in servicing slum settlements in place of the state[15] and the community building of alleged terrorist groups in failing states such as Lebanon (Napoleoni 2005). Here the division between organised crime and the state and their respective location in illegitimate and legitimate economies is far from convincing (Findlay 1999b).

However, utilitarian explanations for organised crime and, for that matter, terrorism have been largely quarantined as less legitimate than law enforcement's official account. Criminal behaviours are represented as dangerous and evil but often purposeless and destructive of the legitimate state. Both organised crime and terrorism are left open to description as insidious products of dysfunctional social alignments. Even if this is so, these alignments are not the apparent concern for the official account. The enterprise of organised crime and terrorism and its subjective benefit are largely ignored.

Organised crime (and drug trafficking in particular) requires comparative analysis from the local to the global if the complex nature of criminal enterprise is to be understood at all the vital phases of its organisation (see Findlay 1999b: 186–8). In recent times the integral relationships between organised illicit drug trade and the domestic and international interests of powerful states has been convincingly chartered (McCoy 1973). In this setting it is the legitimate as opposed to the deep state which marries organised crime for mutual benefit.[16]

Sophisticated comparative levels of analysis (local, regional and global) are notably absent from assertions about organised crime and terrorist funding. If the developing nature of organised criminal enterprise is to be realistically and less dispassionately confronted, the analysis of crime and globalisation is productive (Findlay 1999b: ch. 5). International pressures toward modernisation see regional and international criminal enterprise exploit the instability attendant on economic transition and cultural conflict in order to promote conventional crime business.[17]

Established sources of illegitimate finance and capital are now widely suspected as bankrolling violent struggles for political and cultural change (McCulloch et al. 2004). Even so, there is little evidence-based research beyond operational 'intelligence' to confirm crime as the major source of terrorist funding (certainly beyond its international manifestations).[18] If so, then, why has the organised crime/terrorism connection become part of the language of international policing? Where the link exists, but again where it is not sufficiently recognised in the official account, it is more likely to be evidenced between illegitimate commercial endeavours and state-initiated terror.

Alternately considering organised crime (and international terrorism as its alleged dependant) in terms of enterprise and profit motives also avoids the unfortunate distractions of racism, xenophobia and mysticism pervading the official literature on both phenomena (Van Duyne 1996). This approach may be unattractive to those marketing politics of ethnic division and nationalism. By simply accepting this conventional analysis from law enforcement and intelligence agencies, organised crime is the province of Asian crime gangs, Middle Eastern youth, Italian families or Russian gangsters (Poynting *et al.* 2004: 53–4). In these terms neither organised crime nor terrorism are 'home-grown', always appearing as an external infection, justifying those cultures which tend to protect their border integrity through exclusive migration regimes. Compatible with the nature and origins of legitimate international trading and enterprise, this is not the reality of transnational organised crime, and its distortion makes researching and regulating organised crime and terrorism all the more diverted (Findlay 1994).

Seeing international terrorism as organised crime suffers from similar misrepresentation. Control strategies have been appropriated one to the other in a climate of 'war' rhetoric, wherein criminal justice is engaged and widely compromised (Findlay 2001a). It will be more productive to expose terrorism funding and its organisation to enterprise theories (located within crime or politics) than to base law enforcement on popular culture mythologies. To achieve this for terrorism one would need to adjust the 'profit' motivation for the terrorist enterprise from material wealth (as with drug trafficking) to political power and cultural influence in their broadest senses, which may in turn have their material by-products. Certainly, the critical stages of terrorist enterprises can be qualified as profit driven. In so doing the simplistic distinction between criminal and political formulations is challenged and exposed. This is rarely recognised in attempts to regulate money-laundering and to confiscate criminal assets as an upstream effort to stem the funding of terrorism. But even with initiatives such as the Australian Suppression of the Financing of Terrorism Act 2002 (Cwlth), the unquestioned link between crime capital and terrorism is not critically addressed (McCulloch *et al.* 2004).

I have already argued that one sure way to appreciate the actual motivations of organised crime is in the application of enterprise theory (Findlay 2004). Another consequence of this analysis is the critical edge to test assumed connections between organised crime and terrorism. Through the prism of enterprise theory the best that could be said for any such relationship is that economic profit is a shared platform from which distinctly different objectives are sought. Seen in its limited context, away from political and ideological imperatives, the application of enterprise theory to terrorism as organised crime offers the possibility to:

- disentangle ideology from action;
- understand the stages and locations of a 'trade' in terror;
- identify and appreciate the material motivations for terrorist attacks;
- expose and regulate the financing of terrorism which may be distinct from the religious, cultural and political motivations for terrorism;
- understand why certain phases of a terrorist event and its organisational infrastructure locate in particular jurisdictions; and
- follow the pathways of communication crucial for a terrorist event, and better understand the selection of victims for terrorist attack and their vulnerability.

If possible, a limited, evidenced-based organised crime model for terrorism, emphasises the structural crossover between legitimate and illegitimate commercial enterprise supporting acts of terror rather than their immorality. It further qualifies the extent to which criminal justice should be involved in terrorist regulation rather than military or other political control agendas (Dickie 1994). This rationalised perspective may also reintroduce the importance of state-sponsored terror advancing preferred political and commercial arrangements, being an uncommon analytical outcome in the current globalisation of controlling organised crime and terror.

The intention of the International Convention for the Suppression of the Financing of Terrorism is clearly to encourage similar international criminal justice responses as those now directed to corruption and to money-laundering, and consequentially against the resourcing of terrorism (Tan 2003). The problem with this approach to terrorist financing is its over-adoption. In terms of international politics, an explanation for this lies in the place of criminalisation in efforts to delegitimise contesting ideologies. This conclusion is consistent with a more cultural globalisation project.

If terrorism is crime rather than war or revolution, then accepting the activity of various states in selectively promoting one type of terror against another might enable clearer critique. If terrorism is distinctly integrated within other criminal enterprise (such as arms smuggling, identity fraud and money-laundering) then to a limited extent effective market regulators may be employed in its control, even where violence is the currency for trade (Findlay 1986).

Organised crime as the banker for terrorism

There is much contemporary law enforcement speculation at regional and international levels which declares that organised crime is a crucial fund for terrorism. Occasional evidence of money-laundering associated with terrorism or the transfer of criminal assets to terrorist organisations and enterprises has tended to justify a prevailing law enforcement conviction that by regulating crime cash flows terrorism will be denied. However, there are a number of simple observations concerning organised crime and terrorism that might test this assumption:

- As with organised crime, it is too simplistic and misleading to universalise terrorism and terrorist organisation. A crucial distinction and one which might have a direct influence over whether a terrorist enterprise requires external resourcing is if the organisation behind the terrorist event controls territory or commercial assets.

- Some terrorist events are sporadic, spontaneous and individualised and require little by way of money to promote and achieve their objectives.

- Many terrorist organisations are aligned with recognised or legitimate political movements and gain financial assistance through shared resources.

- Other organisations which are referred to as having terrorist aims or terrorist alliances may gain benefit from donations to overarching religious or resistance movements.

- Some terrorists and their organisations also are active in criminal activity for profit. However, the proceeds of crime which result are as much directed to the maintenance of individual lifestyles as they are to further terrorist activity.

- Organised crime and terrorism may benefit financially and politically through destabilised market structures, without

71

generating identifiable and mutually supportive cash transfer relationships.

- Many terrorists and the organisations they sponsor are independently wealthy through legitimate business or transferred wealth and this legitimate capital base can be redirected to funding terrorism or not, as the case may be.

Having said this, the terrorism usually offered up as being financed by organised crime originates from cells and groups within and outside the state. There is no doubt that in countries such as India, the Philippines, Taiwan, many South American states and even jurisdictions in the US, there are clear incursions by organised crime into politics. This influence can be assured through significant funding. Often in election cycles, crime gangs are the muscle for favoured politicians to extort votes and ensure electoral success through terror and intimidation.

If criminal enterprise is not a crucial financial supplement to the terrorist enterprise which is the focus of globalised risk/security, and if not all significant terrorist activity requires external funding, the effort to defeat terrorism though the organised crime route is at best misdirected. This realisation should have the capacity to require law enforcement to individually justify rather than automatically assume that following the money trail will deny the terrorist the essence of their endeavour.

It is arguable, as has been regularly revealed in organised crime capital and financial arrangements, that examining connections with legitimate banking and financial services might be as productive when it comes to understanding (for the sake of control) terrorist funding. The stories of terrorist groups using drug-trafficking, vice, illegal immigration, identity fraud and poaching to raise resources are unfortunately more populist than the more mundane realities of political and religious sponsorship.

In any case the connections between organised crime profit and terrorist financing may not be causal. Organised crime and terrorist organisations will employ common criminal enterprise for their own quite separate motivations. A good example of this is the illegal arms trade. Organised crime profits from the manufacture, sale and marketing of illicit arms. Terrorists benefit from the trade and may gain ancillary profit from facilitating arms transfer among different terrorist cells. Connected to this is shared training and knowledge transfer which will make possible greater terror capacity. The complexity of this trade and mutual assistance challenges a simple causal interpretation of crime proceeds and terrorist resourcing.

As mentioned earlier, organised crime might not be the great terror bank, but the methods which it employs and the impact on fragile states and fledgling free markets deserves the tag of terrorism in many instances.

Organised crime as terrorism

As with the official representation of the Red Brigades in Italy in the 1970s, the Bader-Meinhoff in Germany and the Shining Path in Peru, ruling states tend to simplify and stereotype the threat of terrorism as organised crime and vice versa. Classifying terrorism as a special form of crime facilitates this and justifies state intervention at a civil level, as constitutional, politically responsible and necessary (Block 1991). This approach, however, ignores the often intricate and diverse organisation behind terrorism and its comparability with other less threatening forms of organised crime. This is particularly so when contemporary global terrorism exhibits and relies on the international enterprise networks essential for other forms of transnational organised crime, such as drug-trafficking, people-smuggling and identity fraud. It also misses spontaneous, disorganised, anarchistic and often as such more dangerous terrorism phenomena such as 'copy-cat' catastrophes.

In the discourse of the dominant Western alliance in particular, the state's response to organised crime and more recently terrorism presents similarities:

- both have been identified as new and vital threats;
- largely from external sources but with local manifestations;
- requiring tough legislation giving new powers to law enforcement agencies, and restricting conventional citizen's rights; and
- justified by the argument that if tough measures are not taken then whole communities and lifestyles will suffer.

This contemporary representation of terrorism features the same *war on crime* discourse that was characteristic of state responses throughout the last century to organised crime, particularly drug-trafficking (Chambliss 1989). In the same vein the obligation to join in an international alliance attacking global terror mirrors the debate behind the UN Convention against Transnational Organised Crime at the turn of this century.

New levels of law enforcement cooperation across borders have been fostered in this climate of acute threat and exaggerated retaliation (Viano 1999). By concentrating on the violent and intimidatory behaviours of organised crime and terrorism rather than on their organisational structures or expressed motivations, the community is more ready to accept strong medicine to prevent terror in its midst. Interestingly, the state has employed the 'terror' of fear concept to facilitate what might otherwise be law enforcement responses that would meet vocal resistance (McCulloch 2003).

Representations of organised crime threat

Smith (1975) argues organised crime is the product of forces that threaten values, not the cause of them. In this regard, if society or the state countenances violence, considers personal gain to be more important than equity and is willing to see the law distorted in the pursuit of wealth and power then such a society or state itself will always be receptive to illicit enterprise whether condoned, ignored or condemned. Such enterprise will become a reality whenever a group of people are willing to take advantage of entrepreneurial opportunities that entail selective law enforcement, violence and corruption to achieve commercial gain (Fiorentini and Pelzman 1995).

When analysing the conventional 'official account' of organised crime it is interesting to note consistency in imagery. Organised crime is:

- the fifth estate (a direct challenge to the authority of government);
- the merchants of terror working towards the theft of a nation;
- the *bankers* for terrorism; or
- the corruptors of democratic government.

Each such representation involves a mixture of the following:

- a subversion of state interests;
- a degree of organised criminal enterprise;
- a potential for violence;
- a deviant counter-culture in terms of morality and collective endeavour;

- commercial power and influence both in the licit and the illicit sense (Passas and Nelken 1993); and
- a threat, whether immediate or long term, to the security of the individual or to the peace and good order of the community.

If organised crime or acts of terrorism are deemed to be challenges to the legitimacy of the state, then governments will move to counter the challenge by neutralising the ideological impetus of the opposition, as much as it will move to neutralise the active threat posed thereby (Findlay 2004). In this process governments *devalue the currency of the ideologies in contest*, therefore giving them less opportunity to exchange, move or trade their ideas.

Continuing the theme of enterprise, states can devalue a currency to reduce inflation (of an idea in this case). In today's international political climate the proliferation of particular ideologies is often attacked in this way, i.e. reducing credence and devaluing the usefulness or building blocks of the ideology (Findlay and Henham 2005). For example, when religious fundamentalists talk about terror attacks as *holy war*, the victim cultures retaliate by reinterpreting these acts as illegitimate violence. A central device in such a process of neutralisation is to define the actions of the opposition as only criminal (Matza 1964), and hence to devalue or delegitimise the claims of proponents who cite provocation by victim cultures as the inevitable reason for violence.

This control strategy becomes more complicated when the state, realising the unique nature of the terrorist threat but not wishing to place it outside the rhetoric of criminality, chooses to compromise or exaggerate the more usual processes of criminal justice rather than give credence to the claims of the terrorist through an ongoing military response.

A recent Australian example has been the enactment of anti-terrorist legislation in the most populous state, New South Wales. The Terrorism (Police Powers) Act 2002 created a new offence on top of kidnapping, bombing, hijacking and the widespread destruction of property which have been offences for ages. The offence of terrorism combines and exacerbates these harms and this is the justification for a radical legislative reaction. The special feature of the Act is to give the police power to intrude without warrants against *targets* which might involve whole classes of people and collections of premises. These powers are largely exempt from challenge by the courts and can extend for days. These expanded search powers are built on the general authority of the police and other more recently empowered investigation agencies (Findlay *et al.* 2005: ch. 3). They are highly discretionary and despite the attempt to exclude legitimate industrial and political protest from the powers of the Act, these behaviours might in fact identify a target group.

The violations of *civil rights*[19] (otherwise protected by the International Covenant on Civil and Political Rights, signed and ratified by Australia) include arbitrary detention and invasion of privacy, even against particular vulnerable communities in Australia. These rights-invasions do not need to be justified by a specific act; they can be pre-emptive, and need to be supported by nothing more than 'reasonable cause' as determined by the police. Particular powers such as the strip-searching of children challenge international covenants such as the UN Convention on the Rights of the Child through such legislative justification. All this is legitimised against a criminal threat posed by international terrorism, as yet of unclear significance within Australia's 'local' jurisdiction.

The utility of the criminal sanction in controlling terrorism, as with organised crime, rests with the acceptance by the community that radical modifications to 'due process' are necessary as part of contemporary legitimate government and an essential utilitarian response to the unique threat posed. The same conditions apply to exceptional laws against organised crime from strong states with a commitment to responsible internationalism (Viano 1999). Any criticism of the radical control response is restricted not to issues of legitimacy, but rather to whether the legislation and new law enforcement framework will succeed in its express control objectives. The wider question follows: as with corruption control strategies, how do these extraordinary measures become normalised so that the original effort to treat the threat as conventional crime becomes unattainable?

Up to this point we have been concentrating on local or jurisdictional responses to what is now defined as an international threat. It is important in order to understand the way in which a state like Australia has responded to global terrorism as crime to consider the impact of globalisation in defining the organised criminal behaviour of terrorism, the threat it poses and the obligation imposed on 'legitimate states' to join the global 'war on terror'. How does terror target the state?

Terrorism and the challenge to the state

Loretta Napoleoni in *Terror Incorporated: Tracing the Dollars behind Terror Networks* (2005) looks at Pierson's *The Modern State* (1995) to distil from his nine characteristics of the state four which are shared by terrorist organisations or 'shell states'. These are:

- a monopoly on the means of violence;
- territoriality;
- taxation; and
- public bureaucracy.

The other indicia (sovereignty, constitutionality, the rule of law, impersonal power and the legitimacy of authority and citizenship) may not only be missing from the terrorist project but they may form the objectives of its violent endeavour.

However, as suggested earlier, what comprises the authorised state, particularly in times of weakness, transition and conflict, may not be distinctive from the *deep state* within and the terrorists it sometimes employs. An important feature of para-political analysis is to treat as state-like entities a whole range of organisations and institutions which at first may not conventionally be classified as states. In doing this, the simplistic dichotomy between states and the organised crime/terrorism threat said to be pitted against them takes on a more politically conditional appearance. These state-like entities (direct challenges to the state or not) include:

1 covert organisations, semi-autonomous intelligence agencies, secret societies and power elites which may be well ingrained into the authorised state institutions;

2 criminal structures and enterprises, which exist in parallel symbiosis with the state and may sponsor it or have its patronage;

3 revolutionary and terrorist movements dedicated to the overthrow of the authorised state, seeking territorial control and sovereignty as well as eventual moral and legal standing.

Recognising the growing power of these groups, particularly in drug-trafficking and terrorism, and their *politicisation*, it is strained to talk of their activities and their consequences as either outside the state or diametrically opposed to legitimate state interests.

It is the complex interconnection between states, weak states, deep states and shell states which challenges the representation of organised crime and terrorism as always and only in contest with authorised state interests. Certainly, if we are to concentrate on the economic dimensions of organised criminal enterprise and its involvement with deep state/terrorist projects then the challenge to state institutions and processes posed by such groups is more even and significant. In 1988 the IMF estimated that illicit funds worldwide amounted to between 800 billion and 2 trillion $US. In some states the black economy exceeds the formal economy in GNP terms as well as capital reserves. In Asia it is not uncommon for much more money in foreign remittances to pass through the informal rather than formal banking sectors.

The tri-partite relationship between deep state institutions within authorised states, criminal networks and quasi-state projects is systematic, broad based and influential. This means that a simple push by law enforcement to crack the link between terrorism and organised crime financing will not have a long-lasting influence on the stability of governance under attack from without and within.

Globalisation and terrorism

Essentially characteristic of globalisation, international crime is moving further away from conventional explanations of criminality, despite political imperatives to the contrary, such as those discussed above. The assumed but problematic and specific connection between organised crime finance and global terror supports this conclusion. The same might be said of the definition and understanding of organised crime and terrorism, particularly within multinational economies (Block 1991; Block and Chambliss 1981).

Integral to both globalisation and globalised crime is the internationalisation of capital, the generalisation of consumerism, resource deregulation and the unification of economies. If crime is to be understood as a market condition then its place within globalisation becomes more vital in analysing contemporary appreciations of crime and control. So too terrorism as a disproportionate organised crime concern on the international agenda cannot be disengaged from international relations which are the product of modernisation (Gilpin 1987).

The transitional economies of Eastern Europe have demonstrated the symbiosis between organised crime, emergent private markets and weak state regulation. With these conditions present criminal enterprise facilitates the market and benefits from capital generation in legitimate and illegitimate market settings.

As with the crime and development nexus in general (Findlay 1999b: ch. 2), in conflict-ridden and post-conflict cultures terrorism can be a force in state formation. As I have conceded earlier, terrorism and organised crime may in certain political contexts come into contact as promoters of both political and economic change. Where states are stronger and legitimate markets more resilient, capital generated through organised crime may support terrorism as it works to undermine state forms which in turn will create unstable market conditions in which organised crime will further flourish. Globalisation also exerts pressure for cultural domination and in this way may either benefit from or contest organised crime and terrorism in a global setting.

Globalisation tends to universalise crime problems and generalise control responses. In this respect it complements and is complemented by the dogmatic organised crime rhetoric of international law enforcement.[20] The simplification and generalisation of organised crime in terms of common threats rather than unique enterprises supports control strategies reliant on more law enforcement powers rather than their diversification.

Cultural unity through globalisation is as yet more convincing at a symbolic level. Crime represents unequivocal symbols around which global ethics are confirmed, such as the war against terror and its partial interpretation and promotion of Western models of liberal democracy (Findlay 2004). Crime control claims an irrefutable mandate for global order and a symbolic terrain across which order rules. Consistently the internationalisation of law enforcement responsibility for organised crime has ranged from the symbolic (requiring from national jurisdictions an unambiguous – and largely uncritical – commitment) to a common language and uniform analysis of the organised crime menace in particular (Block and Chambliss 1981).

The local and the global – terrorism as an organised crime threat: the Australian context

Australia, as a minor player in the dominant global alliance, is now more aware of the terrorist threat beyond its borders and its potential for victimisation. Unlike the US and the UK, Australia has not yet been targeted (beyond the tragedy of the Bali bombings) with a major terrorist assault. Even so, Australian legislatures have enacted some of the most intrusive national security legislation, justified by the ever-present threat of terrorist attack.

With Australia's history of protectionist and exclusionist migration policy, Muslim communities in Australian cities are ghettoised and vulnerable to racist reaction. In Sydney in particular recent episodes of public disorder have exposed simmering racial tensions between Middle Eastern migrants and other young Australian communities and have boiled over into systematic violence. Politicians and law enforcement agencies have fermented this discord by stereotyping the terrorist threat as at home within Muslim neighbourhoods, although there has been little if any convincing evidence of this. As such, the terrorist risk and control *moral panic* has not progressed much from the symbolic, even though the rights of citizens have been significantly compromised in the rush to achieve security in the public psyche.

There is much about the representation of crime as a global problem[21] which implies a more structural set of relationships than do the localised representations of crime as people and actions. This has been a recent trend in Australia and internationally, to move the conceptualisation of organised crime away from 'bosses', through ethnic and family groupings, onto enterprises (cartels, syndicates, networks). The depersonalisation of organised crime has transferred the control focus from the jurisdictional to the global and recognised the structural agility of criminal enterprises. This agility (and durability) explains the perpetuation of organised crime even when local control operations successfully prosecute the individual (see Robb 1996). With terrorism, the control talk is about cells in networks, and while the 'Mr Bigs' of terror evade capture, the organisations which they are said to lead (and their financing) is both an international and local law enforcement endeavour.

Conventional representations of organised crime – lessons for the interpretation of terrorism

A widespread and prevailing interest in crime is a desire at community levels for simple and convincing evaluations of crime problems. So saying, the *local wisdom* about crime is both problematic and indicative. While usually failing to provide a sufficient understanding of crime in context, this *wisdom* goes a long way towards identifying what is troubling people about crime, and where and in what form it is feared. Current media concerns in Australia about Asian organised crime reveal a prevailing racism in the Australian community. For example, these representations, as they implicitly hark back to the *white Australia policy* of the 1950s, are not efficiently countered through decades of political ascription to multiculturalism.

The relationships, dynamics and consequences of crime are derived mainly from popular impressions rather than critical scholarly analysis. Popular impressions determine climates of fear and isolation which impact on the quality of life within communities. This is more so than actual crime victimisation, particularly when the latter, as with September 11, is embraced locally and internationally.

All too often the desire to know more about crime within communities has been satisfied by misleading political and law enforcement discourse or academic equivocation. Partial or unbalanced *understandings* of crime in these arguments themselves become a significant variable in crime situations, thereby influencing the shape it assumes and the effect it renders on its essential relationships.

The interests behind the almost chronic misrepresentations of organised crime (see Findlay 1992) have the power to endorse as well as deny its significant and constant justification for or against social change. However, the analysis of organised crime both in its local and international setting has the potential to unmask these interests and thereby challenge the misconceived stories about such crime.

Social situations of organised crime / terrorism – domestic and beyond

Viewing global representations of organised crime as against actual social relationships which foster criminal enterprise (Robb 1996), any useful analysis will concentrate on the social *situation* of crime rather than elusive and unconvincing speculation about causes, consequences and trends. It is from a culturally specific grounding that explanations are possible as to why:

> ... certain forms of behaviour become prohibited by criminal law and are defined as 'crime'; certain acts and persons are selected by, and become subject to, processes of law enforcement; certain acts and persons are fitted with the label 'criminal' through a process of adjudication; and criminal 'identity' is maintained, developed and transformed through the interpretation and reaction of others. (Hester and Elgin 1992: 11–12)

In Western nation-states today it seems the community's preferred perception of organised crime and terrorism as the product of foreign, violent and subversive cultures serves as the justification for the preferred and largely uncontested style and direction of law enforcement. Crime targeting is more and more directed against certain ethnic communities and youth cultures. Law enforcement authorities have adopted an American approach to the organised crime menace, and American popular culture has influenced community understanding of that menace as a local and global phenomenon.

Mafia-style mystique supports the community's need for a distinction between the 'real criminals' and the rest of society (see Box 1983). Such a distinction was shaped into a series of firm expectations about *mafia-style* organised crime, and *al-Qaeda style* terrorism. By simplifying, generalising and thus mystifying organised crime, the complexity and ubiquitous influence of organised criminal activity and its link with capital at all levels of commercial and economic life is obfuscated (Findlay 1992). Domestic or world *mafias,* commonality in representation, enforcement practice, political discourse and community appreciation of the menace tend to support and confirm an image of organised crime which is at once local and global.

As long as organised crime is understood as an alien conspiracy dominated by ethnic groups it will remain difficult to understand how it actually operates. Effective state control incursion into organised crime, and more particularly regionally sourced terrorism, depends on analysis that rejects or avoids these stereotypes. Insurgent terrorism has carried this *externalised source* representation which means that domestic terrorist events no matter how localised and integrated are employed to justify offshore responses to break *networks* and to halt ideological infection.

Concepts of conventional crime have traditionally relied on some cultural or jurisdictional situation for their relevance and impact. Implicit in this is the expectation that crime stops at national borders, or at least that it has localised interests. Why then is it so different when law enforcement approaches organised crime or insurgent cross-border terrorism?

The jurisdictional boundaries of conventional crime are explained in terms of legal convenience and legislative limits. In a cross-border or transnational sense jurisdictional control responses are problematic. As piracy, smuggling, abduction, gun-running and counterfeiting have been crime problems for centuries, so too the laws of individual nations have been powerless to control them. If organised crime and terrorism are determined as offshore threats, transnational in their coverage, then they too will require unique multilateral or international law enforcement. But what is new about this and why should global governance be so concerned with selective transnational criminal justice?

Transnational crime such as terrorism is new only in its technologies and reach, along with the manner in which law enforcement and international agencies have recently identified it as a priority. Again, the selective political representation of crime is the explanation for such a trend. For instance, as governments realise the potential for criminal enterprise to endanger world market structures, capital transfer, national security and international transport and communication, crime targets are selected for cooperative action while others, like environmental degradation on a scale well beyond the reach or harm ever caused through terror attacks, are largely ignored. Strategies have been developed, for example, to prevent and prosecute commodity futures fraud and abuses, but an international approach to crimes against the environment is yet to be convincingly settled.

The other difference with transnational crime, represented as a recent problem for globalisation, is the manner in which crime control is reshaped in order to address the difficulties with jurisdiction. Crime control is, in this context, at least a bilateral and more likely a multilateral endeavour. However, in many control strategies for transnational crime the bilateral efforts are stimulated by globalised representations of crime and control priorities.

As indicated earlier, criminal justice control potentials are becoming more interconnected within globalised crime control agendas, despite America's preference for bilateralism and autonomy. International criminal law is developing as a new and expansive level of legal regulation. Somewhat surprisingly, however, international criminal law supports an international criminal justice process reliant on discrete operational justifications such as crimes against humanity rather than organised crime. If all crime beyond, say, genocide and terrorism is to develop a transnational potential and a globalised response, then the unique risks accorded terrorism in particular will require a more fundamental interpretation, particularly in terms of the violence they generate and how they can be compared with similar forms of victimisation.

The essential interaction between local and global crime concerns will be the predominant feature of criminal justice into the next century. Organised crime as terrorism cannot but help being a priority for international criminal justice, as well as international relations, if their representation is more closely calibrated with the enterprise which fosters them and the nature of the harm they produce.

Conclusion

The empathies between organised crime, terrorism and state reformation are somewhat limited. A unique insight offered in this chapter is to confine commonality between organised crime and terrorism to the level of enterprise (as distinct from any shared ideologies), while critiquing the link between crime financing and terror as often no more than circumstantial.

The mutuality of corruption, organised crime and terrorism as concerns for global governance is suggested by their common representation as crime risks more than the dangers they pose relative to other international crimes such as environmental degradation, people smuggling and cyber fraud. These case studies bring us back to the realisation that the place of crime/risk for global governance may not be dependent on quantifiable and comparative challenges to global security.

Maybe a better way, from the perspective of global governance, to view the crime/risk determination is to inject challenges to normative integrity, economic dominion and cultural hegemony rather than focus on the harm posed to humanity. If in doing this we need to reinterpret priorities in global security then this should come as no surprise.

The chapter to follow is concerned with visions of global security as they are challenged by selectively nominated crime risk, evoking military and then criminal justice responses. From the above analysis it does not require restatement that the partial representation of crime risk by the state and its control agencies, as for organised crime and terrorism, will determine threats to democratic governance. Challenging the governance rationale behind these representations and consequent prioritising may open up other platforms for contesting the legitimacy of terrorism and its readability. How convincing any of this will be for the legitimacy accorded to violence by communities on either side of terror should be crucially significant in relating risk/security to governance.

Notes

1 This is not new. An examination of the historical literature on the Triads in Nationalist China clearly locates the connection between organised crime structures and financing with contesting political movements.

2 The link between organised crime and terrorism is not necessarily a new phenomenon. On the contrary, the earliest identified manifestations of organised crime in Europe, China and even Japan demonstrated a motivation to undermine and overthrow established rule. In fact, Chinese Triads were, at the turn of the nineteenth century, bound up with the Nationalist struggle in China. The difference today is that the international nature of organised crime as terrorism is clearly directed against global political cultures, influences and domination.

3 Some argue that without the strange conflation between fundamental Islamists and the neo-conservatives in the USA (and the terror which emerges from this) the wider community disengagement from conventional politics would be much more universal. (See the documentary *The Power of Nightmares* (SBS 2007).)

4 For a discussion of the *deep state and para-politics*, see Tunander (2006).

5 Examples are provided in Reno (2006).

6 These benefits can have the common outcome of overturning state authority but may be motivated by distinctly different purposes and with often opposing eventual expectations.

7 For a detailed discussion of this and the impact of aid dependency see Findlay (2003).

8 Note the failure to settle an exclusive definition of corruption in the UN Convention against Corruption (2003).

9 Two case studies (the collapse of the National Bank of Fiji and the negotiation of false bank guarantees in Vanuatu) are detailed in Findlay, (1999b: 81–9). These reveal where legitimate commercial arrangements and institutions so easily are corrupted through exploitative and illegal relationships of obligation.

10 In saying this, these markets may intersect with legitimate business markets often running parallel to the criminal enterprise.

11 Examples are such as where money from other criminal enterprises is processed through the legitimate financial and business sectors.

12 For a brief examination of how this works in the case of drug law enforcement see Findlay (1999b: 101–4).

13 This was the case in the example provided by Findlay (1999b: 85–9).

14 It has become apparent that certain US banks were instrumental in applying money from Russian organised criminal enterprise through the Nauru offshore banking shell to their advantage, despite being exposed by international regulation agencies.

15 See the discussion of the *favelas* in Brazil in Findlay and Zvekic (1992).

16 This also gives weight to Napoleoni's caution that the distinction between state and non-state actors may be false and misleading. In some situations alleged terror organisations such as the Palestine Liberation Organisation (PLO) and Hammas have larger and more community interconnected bureaucracies and finances than do the 'shell states' in which they locate (2005: 67).

17 Volkov's (2002) intriguing examination of the place of protection and extortion rackets in the emerging Russian private marketplace exemplifies this trend.

18 Indeed it seems that organised *philanthropic* contributions from 'offshore' communities play a more significant and constant role in financing organisations and movements suspected of terrorist involvement.

19 In their common law and legislative forms in NSW, or as protected through the administrative guidelines governing police practice.

20 This rhetoric is picked up and promoted by Australian enforcement agencies with a brief to investigate organised crime – see National Crime Authority (1996) *Annual Report*. Melbourne: NCA.

21 In referring to a problem as global, the interpretations of Galtung (1995: 29) are useful:
- global in the sense of worldwide, being shared by a high number of societies;
- global in the sense of world-interconnected, with causal loops spanning the whole world;
- global in the sense of world-system, applying to world society as such.

Chapter 4

Risk and security – studies of global crime control responses in the context of international security

> The paradox and novelty of the globalisation of violence today is that national security has become a multinational affair. For the first time in history, the one thing that did most to give nation-states a focus and a purpose, the thing that has always been at the very heart of what sovereignty is, can now be protected only if nation-states come together and pool resources, technology, intelligence and sovereignty. (Held *et al.* 1999: 490)

Introduction

Security and its maintenance is a global growth industry. For instance, the UN's consideration of employing private security services as an option in discharging its peacekeeping mandate is indicative of a new global phenomenon. That is, non-governmental, privatised and commercialised groups are being increasingly relied upon across both sides of emerging global security challenges. This might be to provide even military or humanitarian services.

Crucial *humanitarian space* in a global sense is no longer the exclusive mandate of representative international organisations, their conventions or their institutions. Peacekeeping as a security strategy is now a matter for multilateral and multinational commercial and constitutional engagement. As dominant political alliances have colonised many of the security functions of the nation-state in the protection of global order, commercial security enterprises have moved into the democratic security void to challenge or to shore up nation-states in transition (DuPont *et al.* 2003).

The recent rise of commercial security providers within global governance considerations suggests an essential blurring between the boundaries of conflict. It is currently unclear, as the security dimension of global governance intensifies and conflict proliferates, what distinguishes between combatants and civilians, between crime and conflict, and between security maintenance and repression. One thing is clear: that a humanitarian security and peacekeeping culture is giving way internationally to deterrence-based security priorities. There is, as a consequence, the gradual shrinking of *humanitarian space* as *humanity* and its protection are politicised in the name of security. Humanity (and its protection) in such a climate becomes 'another weapon in the operation' (Cockayne 2006).

The impact of new security players internationally has significance for the nature of conventional governance arrangements. For instance, the increasing reliance on private or commercial security provision challenges governmental functions and monopolies of force (national and international). The essential accountability of the nation-state or the international organisation reliant on structures of democracy may have little purchase over the commercial arrangements which engage and direct private security provisions. This not only will redefine the nature of *humanitarian space* but, in the name of security protection, perhaps undermine state-building where it is against client interests.

The issue here is who should and does have legitimate access to the legitimate provision of violence for governance sake. The regulation of violence in challenging or ensuring global governance in the name of security is the focus of this chapter.

Studying risk and security

From the particularities of global crime problems and their justification for security responses to *new* risks comes the need to investigate control case studies. Terrorism is the global crime threat which has tended to distinguish the legitimate use of violence in the current phase of globalisation. From this has emerged new and powerful expectations about the capacity of criminal justice to ensure global security as well as punish the terrorist. Paradoxically, while the desire to enhance the protective functions of international criminal justice has lead to expanding institutional and jurisdictional presence, some evidence suggests that along with other forms of violent reaction the world may be less secure as a consequence of the 'war on terror' (Abbott *et al.* 2006).

This chapter takes non-state terrorism as a focus against which to interrogate violent justice responses. *Violent justice* incorporates crime control responses, aspects of which mirror the criminal behaviour against which they may be applied. The actions of criminal justice agencies may be violent, or the institutional procedures may be coercive to such an extent as to constitute violence against the rights of the individual. In this respect, such responses might violate some of the central procedural protections which define a control response as just.[1] The debate surrounding the detention by the US of *non-combatant* prisoners from Afghanistan at Guantanamo Bay recognises the violent and aberrant nature of control responses justified as they are as part of the *war on terror*. At the same time, the US administration has argued before the Supreme Court that this detention response is nothing more than an addition to legitimate military justice options and as such would come within a broad interpretation of the institutions and processes of criminal justice.

The courts and certainly human rights activists have not been convinced by these assertions. Those detainees released from Guantanamo Bay with stories of torture, solitary confinement, religious persecution and denials of due process give evidence of a system of injustice and abuse which has been calculated to prevent the intrusion of natural justice.

What goes uncontested is that these novel control responses are violent. For the purposes of the analysis to follow the claims by the state (and in most cases by the dominant global political alliances) that such responses come within an expanded framework of criminal justice indicate their political rather than moral location. The dislocation between what the state claims as justice and what critics challenge is hardly new. The abuse of power literature surrounding the flawed trials of the Guildford Four and the Birmingham Six (Walker and Starmer 1999) in the UK is resonant of the same critique. The principal difference in miscarriages of justice campaigns from the more recent concerns about enhanced military justice centred on whether it was conventional justice institutions abusing their power rather than unique institutions and processes being created to abuse. In any case, justice is in contest and the state's claims are in question, but violence remains as a common control theme. In Chapter 7 we will explore these justice distortions as representing a distinct *para-justice* model.

Violence is also the motivator for less controversial international criminal justice responses and will continue to stimulate the development of formal and less formal criminal justice contexts into the future. Along with genocide and other crimes against humanity, global terrorism will certainly remain as a concern for governance and the application of international criminal justice within it. This current concentration on terrorism as a primary purpose for global justice responses also merits critical review. It would be wrong to assume that it is the present prevalence and extent of international terrorism which necessitates the radical redirection of global control strategies. Terrorism has a long history as a method of ideological and political resistance and cultural conflict. In the twenty-first century terrorist campaigns and conflagrations have come and gone, posing threats to national, regional and international security equal to the aftermath of 9/11. If so then why did 9/11 prove to be such a turning point in control rhetoric and control strategies? Where did the war on terror come from, and how did criminal justice become so enmeshed in the global control response? This chapter suggests that the negotiation of violence is a key to understanding these considerations.

Criminal justice and terrorism

As in 2003, with Australia's military and policing intervention into the Solomon Islands for the purposes of re-establishing security and order (see Cockayne 2004), dominant states are assuming regional or global responsibility for failing states. The imperative for this may be, as in this case, a concern for national security through the restoration of governance and order in the failing state. What would otherwise be seen as a challenge to the national integrity of the recipient state, political agendas and power dynamics in the dominant state spark forceful offshore incursions claimed to protect domestic and regional security.

Criminal justice processing of terrorist violence is not exceptional, particularly where jurisdiction is uncontested. The former British Prime Minister Margaret Thatcher, when confronted by terrorist violence in the 1970s, declared the Irish paramilitaries as *criminals* and had the control response of internment converted to imprisonment overnight. Timothy McVeigh, judged responsible for the second most deadly terror attack in contemporary US experience, was treated as a criminal despite his religiously grounded right-wing ideology.

Even, as with the trial of the Lockerbie bombers, where issues of jurisdiction and dominion proved complex, a specially constituted criminal justice resolution was a primary control response.

In terms of global terrorism in its current phase as a focus for crime control responses, this chapter is more interested in the post-9/11 predilection for violent reactions to terrorist incursions. Whether such state-sanctioned violence is eventually tempered by a criminal justice context does not diminish the significance of violent retribution as the response of first call.

The connection between terrorism and violent justice responses is well noted (Braithwaite 2005). However, some essential critical dimensions of the justice/terror nexus would benefit from more detailed unravelling in order to sharpen prospects for both the legitimacy and control potential of international criminal justice as a preferred response.[2]

To provide the clearest foundation for the justice/terror nexus within the new model of globalisation necessitates avoiding direct engagement with the rich literature about state crime as terrorism. Much of this is undervalued in a political climate that would rob terrorism of meaning or would even wrongly equate an attempt to critically review the abuse of state power with support for the terrorist project.

In addition, while the history of retributive punishment grows out of contexts where justice was terror and its merciful avoidance added power to judicial authority (see Thompson 1975), the argument to follow accepts the justice/punishment alliance. Punishment is often violent, and justice in its retributive form relies on punishment outcomes.[3] Punishment, be it for deterrence or retribution, is a powerful purpose for justice as it confronts terrorism, in any control strategy.

Empirical substantiations of the relationship between terrorism and violent justice responses are not only challenging but when attempted they are often inextricably tied to problematic normative and political preconditions which may be central to the terrorist conflict under investigation. There has as yet been insufficient research into such connections, particularly from the perspective of intervention strategies employed by states and alliances to counter real or perceived terrorist threats.[4]

The discourse on terrorism today, largely journalistic or political considerations or 'insider stories' (Heffelfinger 2005), is not well supported by hard data on human and organisational behaviours, or by the manner in which these form patterns and reactions. Besides the practical barriers to research in the area, without well-developed theoretical dimensions for analysing this relationship, the discourse remains confined to journalistic assertion and political critique.[5]

More than this, it might be said that the predominating *mythologies* concerning global crime and criminal justice responses (explored in other sections of this book) obviate the necessity in the minds of politicians and governments at least to gain a critical understanding of this relationship. In fact an informed and impartial context for debating global terror will challenge many of the prevailing *realities* which fuel the *war on terror* strategies preferred by the dominant political alliance. It suits political discourse rather to deny the existence of any such relationship in the context of legitimate governance.

Even if a sound theoretical connection is proffered, the researcher may still battle for access to the data which would enable empirical analysis. This data is all too often concealed within military intelligence and hidden in the partial consciousness of contesting agencies and institutions with a real interest in seeing it remain secret or misconstrued.

This does not mean that the empirical enquiry is futile. As the prevailing *war on terror*[6] lurches from disaster to disengagement, more popular knowledge about the utility of violence and its contextualisation is on the rise, despite the efforts to restrict the flow of knowledge. Electorates and referential communities are becoming cynical and disenchanted with the perceived wisdom of their ideological champions and therefore are keener to seek out and receive another story. The other story of Guantanamo Bay, of weapons of mass destruction, secret prisons and rendition, of liberation movements in Lebanon, the Sudan and East Timor, and the actual threats of nuclear proliferation are in the public domain. However, *the facts* remain contested. This being so, the analysts' task is more than finding and formulating data. It also requires a conscious campaign to counter the misrepresentation of the other side. In this way the empiricist cannot resile from the role of advocate for more reasoned, even if still partial, representation.

When seeking a more enlightened understanding of the justice/ terror nexus as it is presently played out in *war on terror* global politics, a preliminary deconstruction of what drives the connection is useful, if rarely attempted. The initial dimension is violence, its purposefulness, the relativity of this and the manner in which both terror and justice interventions employ and justify violent incursion. Implicit in this dimension is the common practice within dominant political alliances of denying purpose to the terrorist, or at least any purpose which can claim rationality and hence that it is legitimate. The segregation of the purposefulness of violence introduces considerations of legitimacy and with them the foundations of international authority. Further, terrorism becomes redefined not only in terms of its violence, but also more against its mindless or malicious irrationality.

Another dimension is where the meaning of violence is contested in the violent event. Considerations of *truth* naturally follow as the prize for the contest and the purpose of violence. Truth here is obviously a relative concept and in order that its legitimating potential is resonant across opposing but supportive referent communities (see Chapter 7), truth is seen to encapsulate common values which bridge the violent divide.

Negotiating violence

In any violent struggle there is the victor and the vanquished. The contemporary political context within which international terrorism and hegemonic justice responses are played out is itself predetermined by victory and subjection in a wider and deeper historical sense. Victor's justice may predetermine the authority foundation through which further justice responses are advanced. Terror on the other hand is a response to victor's justice as much as it is its precipitant. Attendant on 'victory' is the 'morality' of the struggle. This is also conceptually connected to interpretations of truth and the legitimacy/ authority these convey.

One of the spoils of victory is vengeance. Crucial for the direction of violent vengeance (in the guise of retributive justice) is the innocent victim and the monopoly over claims of innocence and the parallel apportioning of guilt. However, as with truth, innocence is both partial and relative. In turn, blame is vehemently contested like any other element of the struggle. The power to apportion blame is evidence of authority, and the resistance against blame in referent communities is a profound challenge to legitimacy.

Legitimacy, a binding theme in the struggle for truth over innocence and to lay blame, is relative to *actual* communities. Crucial communities for the legitimacy of the justice response in particular are those which would otherwise be resistant to this authority. They are the alternative audience both to the message of justice and the irrationality of terror. They are the conscience to be won over or at least alienated from the terrorist mission.

The protection of the individual is essential to the version of justice currently marketed against international terrorism. Victimisation, like citizenship and the right to be protected, is primarily individualised.[7] Terror on the other hand is both discounted and demonised by devaluing the individual and destroying the innocent victim. But this is a more complex dimension of contest. Whose value of whose life are crucial questions, the answers to which further divide justice and terror in contesting the right to life or its destruction.

These dimensions lead back to the image of contest and struggle over legitimacy, authority, versions of truth, rights to innocence and its protection, the power to blame or deny its force, and the price of life.

Purposeful violence?[8] The utility of justice and terror

The utility of terrorism is something that tends to escape consideration in responding to the violence essential for its existence (Rotman 2000–1). At the same time utilitarian considerations drive retributive and deterrent paradigms for justice responses to terror (Braithwaite 2005).

However, it might be seen as too relativist and subjective to confine our conception of terrorism here to claims and counterclaims concerning utility. The same reservations might be directed to measuring terrorism against relative considerations of rationality. Particularly when put against the proportional application of violence in order to achieve stated aims, many terrorist endeavours are excessive and irrational against any measure.

The quest for an encompassing and more universal definition of terrorism is itself misdirected. Even with their faults, the features of rationality and utility will generate contested meanings for terror depending on the nature of the referent community and the violent acts perpetuated. These communities (proponents and victims) are crucial to the determination of the cause and cost of terrorism.

In any dialectical sense there is a need to accept, interrogate and employ the relative meanings and constructions of terrorism. In so doing there is a parallel requirement to discriminate interpretations of terrorism based on purpose and reason. As Tamanaha argues (1997), any such approach will return the analysis to fact/value debates. Avoiding the relativist limitations of value judging terrorism or justice, we can follow Tamanaha's invocation to examine value-based interpretations, grounded firmly in the factual experience of actual social situations.

It is the relationship between terror and violent justice responses that most clearly requires an appreciation of relativities within particular community contexts. Therefore, the social context of processes such as punishment is as significant to the investigation of this relationship as might be the supervening definitional framework.

Retributive international criminal justice focuses on the punishment of prominent perpetrators and if this produces positive consequences for victim communities then it is through the legitimate rendition of vengeance on their behalf as well as the symbolic significance for future deterrence, indeterminate as this may be. So saying, victims or their communities are not the central focus for international criminal trials.[9] In matters before the International Criminal Tribunal for the Former Yugoslavia (ICTY), for instance, there are statutory protections of victim interests but these do not go so far as providing independent victim representation or formal consideration of victim impact (Henham and Mannozzi 2003).

In the show trials of Saddam Hussein and Slobodan Milosovic the prosecutions were presumed to profoundly benefit identified victim communities as well as potential future victims. There is little empirical evidence that from the victim perspective, beyond collective vengeance, the impact of these trials would be deeply felt or long-lasting. What there is[10] deeply disputes the value of retributive justice either for restoring individual victims, or imbuing in their communities a sense that justice has beaten the violence and that benefits will flow because of this. Therefore the question remains regarding the foundations of authority for the application of retributive (and eventually violent) justice responses to terrorist acts and actors. It is one thing to say retribution confirms state authority, but it is much more problematic if authority is claimed on behalf of confused and dissatisfied victim communities.

It has been recognised that both terrorist acts and their punishment may be interpreted as purposeful violence (Butler 2003). Even so, as the violence associated with punishment increases in its scope and intensity, sometimes approaching the nature of the terrorist act, then its legitimacy[11] comes under challenge, if not its utility (Gross 2002).

To justify an extreme punishment response, the violence and violent potential of terrorism is highlighted. However, a moral assessment of terrorism in terms of *mindless* violence is compromised by any corresponding excessive violence of punishment, particularly where this has consequences for innocent communities, in a *law of war* scenario. In addition, its 'mindlessness' challenges the deterrent impact of violent punishment. It also denies the facts that a significant number of suicide bombers today are educated, middle-class young professionals, influenced by much more than religious fanaticism. The decision to kill non-combatant civilians is often based around a conscious neutralisation by the bomber that the outlying victims are as much responsible for the violence as may be any other individual. There is no such thing as the innocent victim in that mental process, beyond those who suffer in the communities which the bomber, in similar displacement, is convinced he represents.

Bentham's 'less eligibility' doctrine as a balance between the utility and humanity of punishment risks compromise through the suffering of innocent communities as a consequence of the harm caused by the punishment directed against the terrorist. In this situation the retributive rationale for meeting with violent punishment the violence of the terrorist against the innocent is also challenged through the commonality of violent reaction.

Claims for utility are dependent on the context of the terrorist and the justice response. So that they are not lost in some confusion of subjectivity, these claims need to be reflected against representations of *truth* and *fairness* said to be essential for the legitimacy of justice responses. The morality of truth and fairness here, I would argue, depends on the innocence of victim communities which a justice response is supposed to champion. Innocence in turn is the foundation on which blame, responsibility and resultant punishment may be more objectively constructed. The problem with this is that convincing representations of innocence are also contextually relative (Gaita 2001).

Contested meanings? The battle for *truth* or the battle over *blame*

When it comes to considerations of 'truth' in the context of terrorist struggle, the contested nature of truth is obvious if also regularly glossed over. Truth is what the suicide bomber is said to die for and what the military and criminal justice responses are set to protect. Can it be the same truth? Obviously not. Then its relativity becomes a contested objective of the relationship between terror and *justice* responses. This contested reality is an important theme for empirical enquiry. How is the subjectivity of truth here to be managed beyond the force-based authority and supremacy of victor's justice?[12]

The paramilitary struggle in Northern Ireland has, since the partition and the imposition of British rule, been a struggle over more than political legitimacy. Its violent ferocity on both sides of the sectarian divide and from the forces of the British state is selectively rationalised as the struggle for the truth of Irish nationhood. True, the triggers for violent events may be religious or cultural bigotry, and the assertion of state authority, but the daily contextual reality of the struggle is contested *truths*.

In the terrorism/response context (both local and global) it is not so much the nature of truth but its contest which is the connection. The protection of truth is the common justification for the exercise of violence on both sides. Even violent retaliation against, say, *genocide* through terrorism claims its legitimacy against *guilty* or *blameworthy* violence where truth is at risk. Yet again the relativity of guilt and blame challenge the advance and democratic dominance of a single *truth* on which the justice response relies.

The recent conflict in Lebanon where the Israeli military allegedly attacked Hezbollah locations in response to the kidnapping of several Israeli soldiers was a stark interpretation by Israel and the UK and USA at least that truth remains on one side of the battle. This alliance initially resisted the declaration of a ceasefire even in the face of significant and disproportionate casualties because the *terrorist violence* of Hezbollah needed first to desist. Despite the tragic consequences for referent victim communities in Lebanon resulting from the violence of the Israeli *justice response* the alliance conceded no terror there. The same was not the view of international aid agencies and other national, regional and international institutions condemning the violence on both sides in terms of its impact on victim communities.

In contest, where responses to terrorism claim the legitimate use of violence, is *moral standing*. Those on the other hand who promote reintegrative techniques as against retribution to more effectively manage original violence recognise that restorative justice relies on the context of a supportive community if shaming is to be positively applied to offenders (Braithwaite 1989).[13] Without a supportive context dependent on a common acceptance of the moral standing of the preferred response, attempts at shaming break down as stigmatic rather than reintegrative. Violence is soon reiterated.

However, in the context of terrorism/response relationships moral standing is at the centre of the contest for legitimacy. Reflective communities, in which both the terrorist and the justice responses are marketed, may oppose the moral legitimacy of each other. These are communities in part galvanised through resistance to the external and oppositional claims for moral standing.[14]

Particularly damaging to the justice response is the resistance of terrorist *communities* over the basis of moral standing. Dworkin's components of the moral standing of law (determinacy, integrity, coherence and wholeness (West 1999)) are difficult for the violent justice response to export when new institutions and processes of incarceration, interrogation, trial and punishment are directed at the terrorist opponent. These novel entities generally contradict or at least strain some of the central protections which make criminal justice in general fair and *just*.[15]

Victor's justice? Victim valorisation

In opening the war crimes tribunal in Nuremburg the US Chief Prosecutor observed:

> That the five great nations flush with victory and stung with injury stay the hand of vengeance and voluntarily submit their captive enemies to the judgement of the law is one of the most significant tributes that Power has paid to Reason.
>
> (Ferencz 2003)

The Nuremburg and Tokyo trials established the courts (military tribunals) and the criminal trial as the legitimate arena for holding accountable those who the victorious in war determine as responsible for *crimes against humanity*. The eventual limitations of the *tribunal* approach, and the emergence of a *second order* justice paradigm which investigates truth and responsibility as opposed to fact and liability, is a feature of the development of international criminal justice.[16]

Narveson (2001) has identified three characteristics of 'immorality' in terrorism:

- the sense of risk it causes the public at large;
- the powerlessness people have from being put at risk; and
- the 'apparent absurdity' of attacking an innocent (and disengaged) victim for a political goal.

Again, the attribution of morality and immorality relies in part on the ascription of innocence and the status of victimisation. Concepts of *risk, powerlessness, guilt, injury* and *blame*, are empowered where awarded on behalf of the innocent victim against the unjustified perpetrator. Terrorist communities become the victims in very similar contexts but from the perspective of victor's justice little regard is paid to their *victimisation* evolving as a necessary consequence of that justice doing its job.

Therefore the subjective distinction of *worthy* victimisation depends, as is essential in all forms of labelling theory, on the authority of those imposing the label and the 'significant others' to whom the label may be addressed. The dominant political alliance claims the authority to determine what is terror and what is not. Victims, such as those of the 9/11 attacks, are valorised by the representatives of that authority, who at the same time demonise the attackers and denigrate the causes they espouse and the communities which give them comfort. But again as with labelling theory, the process of *meaning attribution* is not all one-way traffic. For any meaning to stick it must resonate for the wider audience to which it is directed. The valorised victim may retain the status accorded by a politicised process of meaning among those *significant others* (family, friends, civic leaders, etc.) who accept the authority of the labelling agency and its *take* on the terror enterprise. Crucial in this process are the victims themselves. Those who might challenge or even modify the nature of this meaning and its authority are quickly sidelined and their valorisation denied.

The other feature of labelling theory which is important when reflecting on a relativist valorisation of victims is the dependency on the composition and positioning of the referent community. One group of *significant others* in the USA, after 9/11, may have been in accord with the government's blame laying and victim valorisation. In ravaged communities of Palestinians on the West Bank and Gaza, the *significance* of this labelling process and its interpretation of victim valorisation might have proved to be very different indeed. And with acceptance of or resistance to such fundamental meaning ascription as victim status will follow attitudes to violence and its authority.

As mentioned above, the morality of the justice response (or the terrorist act for that matter) requires *either* community respect *or* superimposed violence (force) to condition its *standing* and ensure compliance. If the claim for standing relies on force rather than respect then the resistance of recipient communities is an important consideration in fashioning the response and expectations for its effectiveness.

Standing even in the legal, non-metaphysical sense has largely eluded analysis of the terrorism/response relationship. A reason for this is that if standing is to have an essential influence over the prosecution of a particular version of truth or justice then the arena within which it is claimed must be mutually respected. Particularly at this level, the *morality* of victor's justice is contested by terrorist violence.

Credibility does not inextricably attend victory in armed struggle. This realisation, as much as any desire for justice and the rule of law, lies behind the transfer of the *enemy* from the battlefield to the tribunal. Paradoxically, the terrorist would hold victory against hegemonic domination in recent military conflict. At the same time the terrorist employs armed struggle in an effort at least to advance a cause to the point where its status in the contest is recognised as meriting a significant (if aberrant) justice response.

The ambiguity of violence as both a challenge to and a confirmation of hegemonic domination is widely apparent in the process of redefining statehood on *the global periphery*. Here in transitional and separatist states where 'global norms regarding the claims of armed groups to self-determination and sovereign statehood are changing'[17] violence is transacted from the status of terrorist coercion to legitimate armed struggle along with the transformation to political legitimacy and global recognition.

A difficulty with any simplified dialectic between the meanings conferred by the terrorist and the legitimate state is the problematic composition of both entities and not just their contested claims to authority. Structuralist political theory, with its focus on the state as an arena and a mechanism of governance and on its agents in domestic politics fails to consider the place of *para-politics* and the *deep state* within the transaction of terrorism.[18] Conventional international relations theory with its emphasis on sovereign states as the core of international affairs largely ignores *states-within-states* which are a feature of terrorist engagement in many transitional political and cultural locations.

Para-politics by contrast is the consideration of *divided sovereignty* with features such as illegal trade, substitute taxation, alternative *armies* and mechanisms of violence. These operate beyond the reach of conventional state authority and, as in Lebanon, may benefit from significant if clandestine sponsorship within the official organs of the state. These *deep states* make the discourse of *victor's justice* and *us-and-them* retaliatory control strategies anything but clear.

Aligned to a more sophisticated deconstruction of the state and its internal dysfunctions, is the relatively marginalised terrorist form where the state and its agents commit terrorist attacks on its own citizens. In such situations, the authority of the state to classify and counteract terrorism will be compromised, at least in those communities against which it strikes. It may even mean, as has been the case in the Republic of Congo, that the reluctance of other states and international organisations to accept and accede to the *terrorist* state's version of the conflict challenges a uniform appreciation of state functioning in the labelling exercise.

Victims' vengeance? The partiality of innocence

It is the image of the victim that drives both the terrorist act and the justice response. What victim has the most legitimate claim to innocence is in contest through terrorism and violent justice. Any resolution of contested meaning will not come from compromise or from violent subjugation. Rather, the latter it seems will exacerbate the risk of violence and its escalation. Where violence is relied upon to answer contested meaning, the altercation naturally progresses on to who is revenging whom. The violent relationship in this progression, therefore, is not only between the terrorist and the justice response but also between each and their respective *victim communities* (see Chapter 7).

With no shared (if not common) morality and a resultant relativity in justice as a justification for violent response,[19] the violent struggle regresses to issues of guilt and innocence. However, where criminal justice institutions within the dominant political alliance are included in the regulatory model, guilt is a consequence of the most convincing prosecution and innocence is more a failure of proof than an absolute state. The shift from military might to criminal justice prosecution (and circumscribed violent punishment) is favoured at one level because of the opportunity to claim some objective legitimacy for guilt and vengeance.

It should be remembered that because of the fundamental dislocation of ICJ from victim communities, where the innocent victim is claimed as the vindication for violent vengeance, it is the guilt of the combatant more than any deep empathy for the victim's situation which will motivate a violent penal response. Violent retribution and deterrence feature more apparently in prosecuting the global 'war against terror' than sophisticated assessments of human security.[20] Those with a responsibility for security recognise that violent justice responses[21] run the risk of generating further violence in communities against which they are launched. Violent punishment as a feature of the justice response will comfort one victim community while at the same time alienating and enraging others. The divergent reception of such violent punishment either as justice or state terror is determined by support or at least tolerance from one community and the resistance of others.

In some respects this mirrors the localised reinterpretation of political corruption against a wider contest for democratic legitimacy. For example, the recent history of *democratic* presidential electioneering in the Philippines has been a history of moral paradox. The wider community and their political representatives are declared opposed to illegal lottery gambling (*jueteng*) and yet it was the slush funds behind the lottery that bank rolls presidential campaigning.[22] The electorate understands this corruption as much as it tolerates the lottery. The intersection is blatant and recurrent. It is only when this corruption spills over into violent reprisals or is exposed by political rivals that the power of community neutralisation gives way to calls for reform.

Communities of resistance? The alternative audience

In the terror/justice nexus, communitarian considerations do not feature anywhere to the same extent as does individual responsibility, outside the setting of terrorist victimisation. But one of the most significant dangers in ignoring communitarian interests when analysing terrorism and justice is to confound and confuse the importance of resistance. Terrorism defined as political struggle rather than mindless evil gains its credibility from support communities.[23] These communities galvanise around the terrorist cause (if not the terrorist act):

- first in recognising the terrorist as the representative of their claims for vengeance and justice;
- next as supporting the terrorist cause in resisting *unjust* justice responses; and
- finally, legitimating the ongoing terrorist struggle through resisting the imposition of competing and contested meanings about justice and terror.

This process of neutralisation/legitimation may even involve flirtation with organised criminal enterprise enforced through violence as a means to maintain economic viability and to attack the social cohesion of rival states. Therefore, for instance, the recent opening up of drug-trafficking routes from Afghanistan through Tajikistan and into Russia has been fostered through unwholesome alliances between a fragile producer state, a compromised international presence, an unstable and economically non-viable transit state and a well developed organised crime market in the reception state (Paoli *et al.* 2006). Each referent community along the way, and their governments, employ the negative backdrop of global political domination and economic/cultural imperialism as in part justifying what might otherwise be more objectively condemned.

Ignoring the subjective meaning of resistance in 'terrorist communities' has the potential to reverse the bonds of cohesion as part of the justice response will be overlooked in favour of punitive attacks on legitimacy. The experience of social exclusion can result in genuine and creative attempts to engage with oppositional communitarian meanings. This predisposition from a good governance perspective can counter resistance through positive rather than negative interaction, and thereby diminish or even reverse the competing legitimacies which foment violent reaction and exclusion.

Another important consideration for the nature and legitimacy of the *justice* response is to turn communities of resistance to the conviction of *not in our name*. No community is homogeneous and even those clustered around a defensive or resistant ideology may at least divide around degrees of acceptable violence. If the justice response can expose (rather than emulate) the excessive violence of the terrorist act then these communities should fragment over the justification for violence and its alternative realities. The susceptible segments of these communities may become unwilling to legitimate terrorism in their name if it is clearly portrayed as excessive, disproportionate or ungoverned violence.

Primacy of the individual? The value of life

Understandings of terrorism and its motivations, particularly of suicide bombings, are often muddied by misconceptions over the value of life. The suicide bomber is dehumanised by accusations of having no respect for the lives of innocent victims. More so, the self-centredness of the act is emphasised through mocking the rewards of martyrdom. As with the earlier discussion of contested meanings, restricting the representation of victim communities to the dead and injured from a suicide bomb ignores the more powerful justification for the terrorist act, that being revenge for other communitarian interests. In the words of one of the co-conspirators in the bombing of the World Trade Centre in 1993:

> The American people must know that their civilians who
> got killed are no better than those who are getting killed by
> American weapons and support. (Parachini 2001)

The respect for human life is impugned against the suicide terrorist
who sacrifices himself and takes along the innocent victim as well.

With the protection of human life as an essential motivation
broadcast with the justice response, the terrorist's apparent disregard
for individual and general deterrence denies the instrumentalist
potential of the ultimate punishment. Where the terrorist rejects
the influence of punishment, only the lives and futures of the
communities of resistance remaining become bargaining currency if
deterrence continues crucially connected to individualised notions of
the value of life.

Earlier I referred to Baxi's interest in the *war on terror* being balanced
against the *war of terror*. The terrorist routinely justifies her or his
actions as acts of war, in which civilian casualties assume no greater
status than *collateral damage*. This diminution of the value of innocent
life outweighed by the natural consequences of war is a feature of war
discourse. To some extent it challenges claims to victim valorisation
based on innocence. The 'law of war' which features both in terrorist
ideology and in unique justice responses to global terror recognises
the utilitarian justifications for sacrificing the innocent. Even the lives
of allies are sacrificed largely with impunity if the fire is 'friendly'.
Yet for the sacrifice of the innocent to be convincingly represented
as either 'friendly fire' or terrorist atrocity depends on a subjective
evaluation of the nature of the violence rather than some absolutist
measure of the sanctity of human life.

Maintaining dichotomies? The *us and them* story

Definitions of terrorism as illegal and immoral and representations
of terrorists as irrational and inhumane perpetuate the essential
divide between good and evil, war and terror, legal and illegal, so
essential for the 'righteousness' of a justice response. However, it is
important to contest these dualities if justice control strategies are to
avoid further galvanising the divide which in turn justifies terrorist
communities:

> In the absence of specific evidence to the contrary, it is reasonable
> to impute to terrorism no lesser rationality than that which social

analysts routinely ascribe to other actors and which, in any event, is requisite for the conduct of their operations. Rational agents are not systematically unable to distinguish efficacious from inefficacious activities. (Lomasky 1991: 87)

Dichotomies also lie at the heart of definitions which see terrorism as illegitimate *war*, aberrant politics or misguided morality. Lomasky continues:

> ... any purported definition of terrorism will itself be laden with moral and political baggage. Most individuals who employ violent means in their political activities prefer to speak of themselves as 'urban guerrilla', 'revolutionary' or some such. Thus the bromide 'one person's terrorist is another's freedom fighter'. One need not accede to the implied relativism to acknowledge the absence of firm and generally accepted criteria of application for 'terrorism' and its cognates. (1991: 86–7)

From this too can be drawn a more complex image of the terrorist struggle and the *corrective* response beyond the realm of bilateral military analogy. This is not simply a tension between states or separatists, cultures or counter-cultures, ideologies and hegemonic alliances. It is through terrorist violence and the violent *justice* responses that the democratic state and the *deep state* contest. It is where the *deep state* employs terrorist violence (its infrastructure and foot soldiers) as a precursor to manipulating the justice response to confuse and violently undermine democracy as the functional authority for apparent state governance.[24]

The suggestions that there can be or are meaningful relationships between terrorism and justice responses verges on the heretical in a political climate where truth is no longer marketed as relative, justice is only subject to a single 'democratic' morality, blame travels in only one direction and innocence crosses no violent divide. Yet this simple and singular political reality seems incapable of promoting easy effective or lasting victories in the war on terror. Such may depend on a more realistic recognition of the place of violence in struggles for global governance that recognises and explores symmetries as well as difference.

Conclusion

This chapter has employed instances of terrorism and violent justice responses to explore the relationship between an identified global crime risk and preferred retributive models for restoring security. The violence inherent in the risk and the response is a common theme. What comes from a study of the relationship between crime risk and security responses is the importance of contextual relativity when ascribing meanings to violence and justifying its application in particular settings.

There is nothing new in the observation that risk and security are relative. However, for terrorism in particular, the revelation that this relativity is uniquely dependent on the construction and representation of referent communities is significant. What makes a victim, and thereby one worthy of violent protection or revenge? In the context of global governance, I suggest it is more important to consider victim valorisation and legitimacy in the context of communities rather than focusing the main attention on individual citizens and their rights or otherwise. A reason for this is the crucial role played by *significant others* in authorising or challenging the factors discriminating (as well as connecting) violence and justice.

The chapter has explored this problematic process of meaning attribution of justice, violence and terror as preconditions for governance. The crucial analysis of legitimacy suggested that fundamental meanings like who is the aggressor and who is the victim will both modify *and* exacerbate risk and violent responses, depending on their community context. Clashes over the legitimacy of violence impact on risk and security and should thereby be reflected in global governance resolutions.

Due to the concentration on cultures and directions of violence when determining regulation as opposed to a deep understanding of its contested legitimacies, critical connections between violence and justice are ignored in settling governance strategies. The consequence for global governance is the concern of the following chapter.

Notes

1 For instance, the protections afforded accused persons and suspects as set out in Article 6 of the European Convention on Human Rights.
2 For a more fully developed critique of contested legitimacies, as these exist in both justice and terror contexts, see Findlay (2007c). (Suffice it to

say, for the purposes of this chapter, that misunderstandings about the relativity of justice and the crude delegitimisation of terrorism underlie much of the political discourse around the *war on terror*.)

3 For a critical discussion of this see Braithwaite and Pettit (1990).

4 Some exceptions to this are represented by Silke (2003a, 2003b).

5 I am not suggesting that theorising on either component of the relationship is absent. The work of Crenshaw (1994), McCauley (1991) and Silke (2004) presents supportive arguments for analysis. What they do not fully achieve is a detailed interrogation of the connections between terror and justice responses in the broadest sense.

6 For a charting of the post-9/11 *war on terror,* see International Peace Research Institute Oslo (2006).

7 For a discussion of the problems associated with managing international criminal justice only or primarily within an individualised rights paradigm, consult Chapter 9.

8 For a discussion of the psychologies of terrorist violence see McCauley (2005).

9 This is critically interrogated in Findlay and Henham (2005).

10 For instance, Albrecht *et al.* (2006).

11 For a discussion of the issue of legitimacy in general see Crenshaw (1983).

12 There is a need here for a more detailed consideration of Weber's conditions for the authority of the state.

13 See Braithwaite (1989).

14 Moral standing as a legal/constitutional claim to legitimate voice is discussed in Winter (1988).

15 For a discussion of the detail of these changes in US criminal justice and their impact on due process see Gross (2002).

16 For a deeper discussion of this read Findlay and Henham (2005).

17 For a discussion of separatist states and their application of violence to early state formation see Reno (2006).

18 For a discussion of both concepts see Tunander (1997).

19 Up until now I have been connecting justice and violence in a fairly casual and erratic fashion. It is useful to recall particular forms of punishment as the legitimate inclusion of violence in justice.

20 For a discussion of the potentials in a 'human security' approach to the pressures resultant from social development (often argued as fertile ground for terrorism) see Jones (2004).

21 Again, here I employ the term 'violent justice responses' not to cloak the violence with justice as its legitimator, but more simply to identify from where and how the violence emanates.

22 For a discussion of this history see McCoy (2006).

23 The importance of victim communities as referents for terrorism is discussed in Silke (2003c).

24 Recent histories of 'deep state' subversion are contained in Tunander (2006).

Chapter 5

International criminal justice and governance

Today we are living through another political transformation, which could be as important as the creation of the nation state; the exclusive link between geography and political power has been broken down. Our new era has seen layers of governance spread within and across political boundaries ... The stuff of global politics already goes far beyond traditional political concerns. Drug smugglers, capital flows, acid rain and the activities of paedophiles, terrorists and illegal immigrants do not recognise borders; neither can the policies for their effective resolution ... But it is not clear which factors will determine how far old (governance) institutions can adapt and whether new institutions can be invested with legitimacy. (Held *et al.* 1999: 488–9)

Introduction

International criminal justice is sufficiently well established to merit an overview of its origins and institutional development. This chapter commences by identifying the institutional indicia of international criminal justice and their close connection with individualised international human rights protections. Controversy over motivations underlies these structural and process signposts of justice. Has formal international criminal justice emerged in response to novel and genuine concerns for the safety of humanity, or is it a manifestation of partial global governance priorities in post-conflict scenarios?

Aligned with questions about where from and why international criminal justice is the distinction of an international criminal jurisdiction. Without a victim community jurisdiction in particular I argue that the integrity of international criminal justice as a unique justice paradigm is suspect. In this sense jurisdiction is much more than spatial location or political entity. An open, inclusive and integrated international criminal jurisdiction designates its *justice* and *governance* potential. The *humanity* which is to be protected and the nature of inhumanity that is prosecuted suggest new notions of constitutional legality and standing which can develop beyond the symbolic or politicised global communities.

The chapter then contrasts the pervasive but arguably less politically potent *alternative*[1] incarnations of international criminal justice. Truth and reconciliation commissions, for instance, could be said to have ensured the relevance and inclusivity of international criminal justice to a host of victim communities otherwise excluded from the formal institutions. On the other hand these and other less formal justice manifestations are criticised for not protecting the rights and interests of victim stakeholders. Nor do they, or do the tribunals, satisfy the complex aspirations of victim communities (Albrecht *et al.* 2006; Weitekamp *et al.* 2006). The chapter reiterates our earlier contention that for ICJ to better recognise legitimate victim interests then the international criminal trial will require transformation.[2] Also for the international trial's conflict resolution potential to be realised, it must be legitimated through the interests of victim communities.

In its concluding sections the chapter foreshadows the connections between global governance and ICJ. From this relationship I speculate on the future development of ICJ, more specifically to be developed in the chapter to follow in the context of governing through globalised crime.

International criminal justice?

Whichever specific point in time one posits as its origin, the connection between formalised international criminal justice and individual human rights is inextricable. The majority of commentators assert that the creation of the International Military Tribunal at Nuremberg marked the birth of formalised international criminal justice.[3] These proceedings clearly enunciated that individuals had actionable criminal liability under international law (Clapham 2003: 31) and, according to Teitel, this international response to the atrocities perpetuated by the

Nazis signified the beginning of the modern human rights movement (Teitel 1999: 285).

The Nuremberg Trials were closely followed, and to a large extent overlapped, the Tokyo War Crimes Trials, where Japanese Class A war criminals were brought before the International Military Tribunal for the Far East (IMTFE).[4] The legislative consequences of these tribunals were:

- the incorporation of the Genocide Convention (1948) into international law;[5]

- the formal recognition of international human rights law through the UN adoption of the Universal Declaration of Human Rights (1948)[6] and;

- the formulation of the Geneva Convention (1949).[7]

Despite this initial energetic conflation of international human rights instruments and criminal justice institutions, the intervention of the Cold War saw both the concept and practice of international criminal justice removed from the forefront of global politics and relations.[8] Indeed, it became clear during this period that a more permanent grounding for international criminal justice would rely as much on favourable international political hegemonies as on strong legislative mechanisms endorsing human rights and international criminal law.[9]

The 'revival of the international criminal justice project' (Megret 2002: 7) came in the 1990s, with the creation of international criminal tribunals for the former Yugoslavia (ICTY 1993) and for Rwanda (ICTR 1994). While Beigbeder asserts that the 'essential historical, legal and judiciary basis'[10] of these derived from the Nuremberg proceedings, Clapham argues they have gone beyond the immediate postwar response in clearly establishing 'that crimes against humanity exist as self-standing crimes' (Clapham 2003: 43). That is, contrary to their formulation at IMT and IMTFE, 'these international crimes can [now] be prosecuted even in the absence of an armed conflict' (Clapham 2003: 43).

The ICTY trial and appeal chambers in particular have actively prosecuted an international criminal jurisprudence. Most recently, with the elaboration of joint criminal enterprise theory[11] to enable the indictment of those collectively liable, the judges of the ICTY have identified unique foundations for international criminal law which will benefit its consolidation through the work of the International Criminal Court (ICC).

The Special Court for Sierra Leone (SCSL 2002)[12] is another product of this revived international criminal justice movement, while Indonesia's Ad Hoc Human Rights Tribunal on East Timor and the Cambodian Extraordinary Chambers,[13] although similarly constructed in response to mass human rights violations, differ in that they remain part of national criminal justice systems.[14] The SCSL is also notable in that it runs in parallel with a truth and reconciliation commission. This has led to some interesting crossover between the jurisdictions of the restorative and retributive justice institutions.[15]

Beyond considerations of institutional justice manifestations, significant 'process' events in the recent progression along this international criminal justice continuum,[16] are the *Pinochet* precedent[17] and the entry into force of the Rome Statute creating the International Criminal Court.[18] The *Pinochet* proceedings saw Spain, albeit because of the 'vagaries of British extradition law and practice' (Perez 2000: 189), assert universal jurisdiction in 'a claim to vindicate the rights of humanity as a whole'.[19,20] Furthermore, in terms of precedent, the House of Lords reached an 'arguably revolutionary legal conclusion stripping Pinochet of former Head of State immunity' (Perez 2000: 189–90). For Robertson this suggests 'the age of impunity may be drawing to a close'.[21] Indeed, Article 27 of the Rome Statute also asserts the '[i]rrelevance of official capacity'.[22] Furthermore, in line with the developments of the ICTY and ICTR, the ICC has incorporated within its jurisdiction both violations perpetrated in the course of an internal armed conflict,[23] as well as crimes against humanity committed in the absence of, or unrelated to, any conflict.[24] This has enabled the first indictment issued from the ICC to focus on allegations of crime emerging from armed conflict in the Republic of Congo. For many the creation of the ICC is the institutional culmination of the belief that 'because individuals live under the international legal system, they must necessarily have rights and obligations flowing from it' (Booth 2003: 186).

Motivational origins

While international criminal justice clearly originated as a response to human rights atrocities, the motives underlying its emergence are the subject of much debate. The argument divides around the essential protection of humanity from new crimes and harms which only a global justice response can satisfy, or a wider mandate employing international criminal justice to advance the dominant political hegemony. It could be said that these motivations are not mutually exclusive, and in fact are crucially interdependent if the protection of humanity is to devolve from persistent military intervention. The critics of this alliance suspect that the more independent aspirations for justice will be captured by a dominant political ideology designating the legitimate global community and the citizens worthy of protection (Findlay 2007a).

A genuine humanitarian response?

Proponents of this view hold that the phenomenon of international criminal justice and its practical manifestations are genuinely rooted in a universal desire to protect human rights and to redress those who have been violated.[25] Several of the distinct justifications articulated by the Permanent Members of the Security Council for the creation of the ICTY, when translated into general terms, can be seen to constitute the normative motivations behind international criminal justice viewed as a genuine humanitarian response.[26] Even so, these general pronouncements are pregnant with complex and competing considerations.

To provide justice for the victims

Justice in itself is a moral imperative at the heart of the law and of human rights. Yet there are also practical gains to be made in providing justice for victims, most notably to 'discourage acts of retaliation' (Scharf 2000: 929). In the words of Cassese, the ICTY's first President, the 'only civilised alternative to this desire for revenge is to render justice.'[27]

Colson voices this concern on a larger scale, seeing the potential future outbreak of war as a consequence of rights violations not redressed (Colson 2000: 54). Quoting the ICTY's Deputy Prosecutor, Graham Blewitt, in support of this argument, McGeary observes '[p]eople explain this war as a revenge for atrocities done in the past that were never punished.'[28] In this view, then, international criminal justice derives from a wish to prevent future abuses perpetrated in the name of revenge.

The tension between retribution and revenge is just one dilemma faced in reconciling legitimate victim interests. Once the victims of crimes against humanity or victims of genocide are established and located (no easy task on some occasions), the challenge for international criminal justice is to provide the maximum access for those interests in an atmosphere of rights protection which enables victim integration to the extent that the legitimacy of the justice response is better ensured.

To establish accountability for individual perpetrators

Again, aside from the moral need to address the particular individuals to whom responsibility for human rights abuses can be traced (Colson 2000: 54), there is a practical component to this objective. It stems from the fact that 'the perception of collective guilt only fosters new cycles of retribution'.[29] Support for this view is provided by Scharf, who argues that the assignment of collective guilt which characterised the post-Second World War years 'in part laid the foundation for the commission of atrocities during the Balkan conflict' (Scharf 2000: 930). The logic is that reconciliation is impossible in an atmosphere of blame, one faction by another.

On the other hand, an over-reliance on individual liability in instances where crimes and harms were the consequence of contribution may promote show trials, rather than any real attempt to punish proportionally collective responsibility.

To facilitate restoration of peace

This is inextricably linked to the aforementioned justifications, that is avoidance of acts of revenge and the facilitation of reconciliation are integral to the restoration of peace. Peace here is the natural consequence of victor's justice. Unfortunately, in the context of courts and trials it is not the peace that truth and reconciliation can bring. Rather it is a desire for peace which is enforced through conquest and confirmed through liability. From the view of many victim communities it may not be a long-lasting peace.

To develop an accurate historical record

Cassese identifies this as one of the 'notable merits' of 'bringing culprits to justice', since it means that 'future generations can remember and be made fully cognisant of what happened' (Cassese 1998: 5-6). Why is this important? Again the objective is practical – a definitive account 'can pierce the distortions generated by official propaganda, endure the test of time, and resist the forces of revisionism' (Scharf 2000: 932). The presumed logical conclusion is, consequently, that the perpetrators of human rights abuses will not one day be emulated, nor will ethnic violence emerge in response to a distorted truth.[30]

However, through the determination of trial justice presently constructed, truth is not always or even the path to proving the case. What is sufficient as evidence and what stands as fact upon which a successful prosecution can rest is the story that survives the adversarial contest. This is not negotiated truth. Without truth determined, reconciliation may not accompany retribution as the essential outcomes of international criminal justice.

To deter perpetration of atrocities elsewhere

This aim is also viewed as one of the main reasons 'the international human rights community enthusiastically embraced' the *Pinochet* proceedings (Wippman 1999: 473). The reasoning in this respect is that the UK decision to divest Pinochet of his Head of State immunity, along with the Chilean Supreme Court's reiteration of this decision and their initiation of prosecution proceedings against him, will serve to deter 'other dictators in the making' (Wippman 1999: 474) from perpetrating similar human rights abuses lest they too be subject to such treatment.[31] As Perez has stated, 'the calculations of officials responsible for human rights violations can never be the same' (Perez 2000: 189). In a similar vein, it is often proposed that the frequent recurrence of human rights abuses in the twentieth century is partially attributable to the consistent failure to punish those responsible. For example, Cassese argues that the unforeseen consequence of allowing the perpetrators of the Armenian genocide to proceed with impunity was that 'it gave a nod and a wink to Adolf Hitler and others to pursue the Holocaust some twenty years later' (Cassese 1998: 2). Similarly, Goldstone (the first Prosecutor of the ICTY) has concluded that the failure to prosecute Pol Pot (Cambodia), Idi Amin (Uganda) and (at that time) Saddam Hussein (Iraq) encouraged the Serb policy of ethnic cleansing in the former Yugoslavia and the commission of genocide by the Hutus in Rwanda with the expectation that they too would not be held accountable.[32] Thus, Arbour asserts, with respect to the ICTY:

> for the first time since Nuremberg and Tokyo, a serious attempt is being made at punishing, and therefore possibly preventing, the perpetration of the most horrendously violent, large-scale criminal attacks on human life. (Arbour 1997: 535)

It is commonly acknowledged that for many observers 'deterrence is the most important justification and the most important goal' (Wippman 1999: 474) of international criminal justice. However, this is another justification which cannot, without much deeper empirical foundation, stray far from normative ascription.

A politically motivated response

The contrary position, however, is that the commonly purported justifications above disguise less altruistic motivations. 'Surely, international criminal justice also tells another story, one that is at least more ambiguous, more fraught with power' (Megret 2002: 9). At the heart of this view is the disbelief that these reasons provide an adequate answer to the question: 'why would states ever bother to create institutions that might end up turning against them?' (Megret 2002: 10). Instead, Megret posits the view that it is interest shaped by political culture which dictates whether or not states support the international criminal tribunals (ICTY and ICTR) (Megret 2002: 15).

In the context of the Bosnian crisis, several commentators have identified the 1992 media reports of concentration-type camps as the key turning point in the international response.[33] In reactivating the 'religious imagery of the victim',[34] these reports 'touch[ed] at the very heart of European memory' (Megret 2002: 17) and resulted in a public demand for action (Megret 2002: 17). This outcry was amplified by what Robertson calls the 'CNN factor',[35] whereby CNN became a 'recruiting officer for the human rights movement'.[36] Yet it is the way in which this permeated 'political issues and outcomes' which is, in Megret's opinion, the key to understanding how international criminal justice came to be manifest in the shape of international criminal tribunals (Megret 2002: 18). Ultimately, 'the outcry ... [made] it necessary to give the impression that something was being done about the crisis' (Megret 2002: 18). That is:

> the transformation of the Yugoslav crisis from a principally political problem to an ethical one in the eyes of public opinion set off a bizarre and frantic race for historical legitimacy between France and the United States. Each of these states seemed to calculate that, if an international criminal tribunal were to be created at all, it would be in their interest to be associated with the aura of reviving the idea, while not pushing it so far ahead that it would get out of hand. (Megret 2002: 18)

While Megret concedes that there were 'elements of domestic liberalism' (Megret 2002: 19) at play, his commentary is imbued with the notion that the institutional embodiment of international criminal justice was an unintended consequence of the rhetoric of morality activated to appease public opinion. Hazan also views the tribunals as an 'anxiolytique' for public opinion rather than as long-term commitments to international criminal justice,[37] while according to Scharf:

> America's chief Balkans negotiator at the time, Richard Holbrooke, has acknowledged that the tribunal was widely perceived within the government as little more than a public relations device and as a potentially useful policy tool.[38]

In support of their sceptical stance, Megret and Scharf point to the fact that the ICTY was 'remarkably under-funded' (Scharf 2000: 934) during its first years in operation, 'a toy in the hands of the great powers ... reined in whenever it showed signs of threatening the status quo' (Megret, 2002: 21). Yet despite these 'dismal beginnings' (Megret 2002: 21) the outlook is positive. The judges of the ICTY have 'transform[ed] themselves into crusading diplomats' (Megret 2002: 25); as such 'a thorough mix of liberal legalism and realist interest is what characterise[d] the emergence and consolidation of international criminal justice towards the end of the twentieth century' (Megret 2002: 29–30). It remains to be seen 'how far international criminal justice's "own momentum" will take it' (Megret, 2002: 32).

How 'international' is international criminal justice?
The relationship between international criminal justice and national criminal justice

Having reflected upon the institutional origins of formal criminal justice and the arguments concerning motivation, the question naturally follows, how is the distinction 'international' to be established and maintained? Are we merely masquerading some hybrid procedural tradition, or has a new jurisdiction and standing in justice emerged?[39]

Why is international criminal justice required in lieu of national criminal justice?[40]

From the outset it should be noted that the principle of complementarity, central to the Rome Statute,[41] asserts ICC jurisdiction only where national criminal justice systems are either unable or unwilling to try international crimes in accordance with the requirements of due process. Even so, for the USA in particular, the suspicion that the ICC jurisdiction would compromise domestic autonomy has proved a barrier to some states signing up to the ICC mission.

Thus the most pertinent arguments for international, rather than national, criminal justice are those pertaining to the usual instability of national criminal justice systems in countries ravaged by mass human rights atrocities. Aside from the reality that the societies in question will often be 'too fragile to survive the destabilising effects of politically charged [domestic] trials' (Cassese, 1998: 4), the central concern is that these national criminal justice systems may be incapable of conducting impartial proceedings.[42] For example, with regard to the former Yugoslavia and Rwanda, Arbour has stated:

> for different reasons, the national criminal justice system was too incapacitated to satisfy the forms of justice in the context of the enormity of the injury inflicted on the social fabric of these countries by the crimes committed. (Arbour 1997: 534)

Indeed, one of the reasons the Rwandese government itself supported an international tribunal was 'its desire to avoid any suspicion of its wanting to organise speedy, vengeful justice' (Arbour 1997: 535). Thus, as Lord Hope stated in the *Pinochet* proceedings, 'justice must not only be done; it must be seen to be done.'[43] It is on these grounds that Delmas-Marty called for an international judicial response to the September 11 2001 attacks, her concern being that the US national criminal justice system would conduct 'procedures that resemble vengeance more than justice' (Delmas-Marty 2002: 293) and which would violate the legality principle of criminal law – that is that 'crimes must be defined precisely and that laws imposing harsher penalties may not be imposed retroactively.'[44]

Yet while international proceedings would likely be tainted with less bias than national trials, a belief in complete impartiality is overly optimistic. For example, Cassese's assertion that 'international judges have no national, ethnic or political axe to grind' (Cassese 1998: 7) demonstrates a surprising naivety concerning the complexity of global relations. It also contradicts his previous statement that 'international judges *may* be in a better position to be impartial and unbiased than judges who have been caught up in the milieu which is the subject of the trials' (Cassese 1998: 7). This is a more realistic view.

A convincing argument for international criminal justice in place of national criminal justice is the fact that transnational investigation is easier for an international court to accomplish, as is the extradition of those 'who have found refuge in foreign countries'.[45] Furthermore, as Kelson noted in 1944: '[i]nternationalisation of the legal procedure against war criminals would have the great advantage of making the punishment, to a certain extent, *uniform'*, where national courts will likely 'result in conflicting decisions and varying penalties'.[46] Finally, there is the logic that just as domestic crimes are tried in national courts, crimes against international law should be tried in international courts – in the words of Roling, 'an international judge should try the international offences. He is the best qualified.'[47] This argument, however, has not been wholeheartedly embraced – indeed the inclusion of the complementarity principle within the Rome Statute will likely mean national prosecutions are far more frequent than international proceedings. It might also betray the reality that we are some distance away from a truly international judicial profession (Wessell 2006).

How have international criminal justice and national criminal justice impacted on each other?

The concepts of 'hybridisation' and 'harmonisation' set out by Delmas-Marty have been influential (if perhaps overstated) in understanding this relationship (Delmas-Marty 2003: 13). Asserting that the intended operations of the ICC are the modern epitome of international criminal justice, the exercise of these concepts in normative form has been realised in the ICC empowering legislation. So saying, it is too simplistic to offer an analysis of international criminal procedure as the comfortable marriage of dominant traditions.[48] The jurisprudence of the ICTY in particular has shown that any convergence of national traditions is a random and peculiar exercise, heavily dependent on the context of the deliberations.[49]

The Rome Statute is the product of extensive deliberation and compromise amongst numerous states. Consequently, it not only embodies an amalgamation of a wide range of national criminal justice principles, but it incorporates elements of both the adversarial and inquisitorial processes: it is a hybrid being. Tochilovsky provides a detailed discussion of these procedural issues and questions how such 'conflicting visions' will be resolved in practice (Tochilovsky 2002: 268). He points out, for example, the fact that while the Rome Statute and the Rules of Procedure and Evidence[50] 'impose a duty on the Prosecution to equally investigate both incriminating and exonerating circumstances', they simultaneously assume that each party will 'prepare and present its own case' (Tochilovsky 2002: 268). Furthermore, while the common law tradition of plea-bargaining is not precluded by the Rules, judges are obligated 'to seek the truth regardless of any agreements reached by the parties' (Tochilovsky

2002: 268). It is the fact that judicial discretion will determine how these discordant approaches play out in practice that is the source of Tochilovsky's apparent dissatisfaction with this state of affairs[51] rather than an opposition to Delmas-Marty's vision of a 'pluralist, universal conception of international criminal law' (Delmas-Marty 2003: 13). Indeed, this vision is one he seems to share – 'jurists from various parts of the world, representing different systems and cultures, will play a crucial role in further development of a unique international criminal law system in the ICC' (Tochilovsky 2002: 275). If the experience of the ICTY is anything to go by, this dream of a judicial 'internationale' can be derailed by the persuasive preferences of an aggressive prosecutor or a resilient judicial chamber.

The interaction of international and national criminal justice systems does not end here. A harmonisation process is evolving for the ICC, whereby the composite set of principles embodied in the Rome Statute have been legislatively incorporated into the national criminal law of many states. A prime example is the entry into force, on 30 June 2002, of the German Code of Crimes Against International Law (CCIL).[52] In providing for 'the universal prosecution of crimes against international law through the German criminal justice system', the CCIL 'transfers the substantive criminal law prescriptions of the ICC Statute into German law' (Werle and Jessberger 2002: 192). The significance of this lies in the fact that the CCIL establishes 'the punishability of war crimes and crimes against humanity *for the first time* in legislation of the Federal Republic of Germany'.[53] That similar legislation has been enacted in no fewer than 11 countries throughout the world is testament to the strength of the influence of international criminal justice on national criminal justice systems.[54]

With one exception, the Rome Statute does not obligate states to transpose the substantive criminal law of the Statute into its domestic legislation.[55] The driving force behind such reform is complementarity. The expected consequence of this principle is that the 'enforcement of international criminal law through national courts will remain the backbone of the international criminal justice system' (Werle and Jessberger 2002: 194). States, then, have the opportunity to retain their autonomy with regard to the prosecution of violations of international criminal law committed within their territory or by one of their nationals. As Werle and Jessberger argue, this is 'a strong incentive to consider domestic law in light of the *Statute*'.[56] In this subtle way, as Clapham suggests, '[t]he complementarity principle at the heart of the Statute has generated a complementary transnational legal order for the prosecution of international crimes' (Clapham 2003: 65).

Yet, although it has had arguably the greatest impact in this respect, it is not just in response to the Rome Statute that principles of international criminal justice have been transposed into national systems. As Arbour points out (1997: 536), the Statute that created the ICTY[57] bound Member States of the Security Council to cooperate with the Tribunal.[58] Consequently, many countries 'enacted specific legislation permitting them to discharge these obligations' (Arbour 1997: 536). The influence was limited, however, since several states neither undertook such reform nor 'formally notified the Tribunal of their ability to comply under their existing national law' (Arbour 1997: 537). Rehman also argues that there exists 'a strong and influential relationship between national criminal justice systems and international human rights law' (Rehman 2002: 510). Given the incontrovertible evidence of the relationship of international criminal justice with international human rights, it is appropriate to draw on this argument here. The principles of customary international law and the immutable rules of *jus cogens* form the basis for Rehman's claim. While states are required to comply with the latter, there is no obligation to incorporate specifically any relevant provisions into domestic legislation. However, as Rehman points out, '[i]n practice almost all states have adopted constitutional practices to conform to the norms of *jus cogens*' (Rehman 2002: 518). In offering additional support for his overall argument, Rehman proposes that treaty bodies, for example the Human Rights Committee[59] and the Committee against Torture,[60] have influenced the practices of many states, including 'pariah states such as Iraq, Libya and Sudan', having led them to reconsider their own domestic criminal justice system in terms of its human rights policies.

How is *international* criminal justice manifest?

It is a commonly shared view that justice is revealed in the application as much as it may be in the normative aspirations for its outcomes.

Formal institutions

As Scharf argues, '[i]t is one thing to create an international institution devoted to enforcing international justice; it is quite another to make international justice work' (Scharf 2000: 927). For some, that the ICC has no constabulary, no *subpoena* power and cannot sanction states directly in the event of non-compliance may make this latter objective impossible to achieve.[61] However, the most frequently made arguments for the impotence of international criminal justice are the low rates of indictments, trials and convictions effected by the ICTY and the ICTR. In its first six years of operation the ICTY issued 91 public indictments but tried and sentenced only six individuals. Wippman points out, 'these numbers are miniscule relative to the numbers of persons actually responsible for criminal violations of international humanitarian law.' (Wippman 1999: 476). Furthermore, '[i]t will rarely be possible to prosecute more than a representative sampling of those responsible for genocide, crimes against humanity, and war crimes' (Wippman 1999: 480). That this is the case does not bode well for the proposed deterrent effect of the international tribunals and the ICC,[62] casting serious doubt on optimistic proclamations such as '[t]he real story of the new Court may actually be the crimes which never take place' (Clapham 2003: 67). This is particularly concerning when one considers that deterrence was a primary justification for the creation of these international institutions. It also leaves unanswered the question 'how is international criminal justice manifest?'

For Colson, '[t]he starting point [in responding to this question] is to conceive of international justice as a process which in itself has significance, no matter what the expected outcomes of the process are' (Colson 2000: 58). He argues that the investigation and denunciation of war crimes by the ICTY, prior to any actual trials, had two important effects:

1 'Victims and their relatives experienced a form of relief – at last their status as victims was being taken seriously by the international community through one of its institutions' (Colson 2000: 58).

2 'To a limited but significant extent, accusations made against Bosnian-Serb leaders Radovan Karadzic and Ratko Mladic weakened their popular support' (Colson 2000: 58–9).

Furthermore, Colson argues, as does Booth, that, in general, international tribunals ensure that collective assignation of guilt is avoided (Colson 2000: 60; Booth 2003: 185). The overall effect then is one of catharsis. That is, the activity of the international tribunals supports 'the hypothesis of international justice as a cathartic process' (Colson 2000: 60).

It is appropriate to note at this point that not all commentators are of the view that the avoidance of collective assignation of guilt is necessarily a beneficial outcome of international tribunals. Rather,

Teitel proposes, in spite of the proposed advantages articulated above, that 'such emphasis on ascribing individual accountability ... is of questionable value because individual proceedings ultimately obscure the profound role of systemic policy in repression' (Teitel 1999: 298). Locating his criticism directly within the trial process, he argues that 'the insistence on proof of individual motive can be misleading, as it obscures the extent to which persecutory policy is a social and above all political construct' (Teitel 1999: 299). Consequently, there is a need for international tribunals, if they are to continue to assign individual responsibility, to ensure that the 'significance of systemic persecution ... [and] the extent to which the architecture of genocide [and other human rights abuses] [are] political' (Teitel 1999: 298–9) is clear to the world audience.

Returning to the manifestation of international criminal justice, while Akhavan does not share Colson's specific conceptualisation, he provides further support for the view of international criminal justice as manifest beyond the trials conducted in its name. He argues that the mere 'stigmatisation of criminal conduct may have far-reaching consequences, promoting post-conflict reconciliation and changing the broader rules of international relations and legitimacy' (Akhavan 2001: 1). Specifically:

> International criminal tribunals can play a significant role in discrediting and containing destabilising political forces. Stigmatising delinquent leaders through indictment, as well as apprehension and prosecution, undermines their influence.[63]

That international criminal justice is manifest in this way is demonstrated by the fact that:

> the international policy of discrediting wartime leaders, and the criminalisation of the former leadership of Republika Srpska by the ICTY, have allowed new leaders such as Dodik to emerge and to make statements that would have constituted political suicide in another context. (Akhavan 2001: 5)

Akhavan also agrees with Colson that the international tribunals play a valuable role for victims in ensuring that the crimes against them 'do not fall into oblivion' (Akhavan 2001: 1). In these ways, international criminal justice manifests itself in a 'significant contribut[ion] to peace building in postwar societies' and through the introduction of 'criminal accountability into the culture of international relations' (Akhavan

2001: 2). Notably, these achievements correspond with several of the justifications put forth for the creation of the international tribunals.

At the same time it has been the frustration and dissatisfaction of victim communities with limited and exclusive tribunal-based justice which has stimulated recourse to local community justice resolutions. This has created its own challenges to international criminal justice in that the alternative exercises, while being concerned with elements of crimes against humanity or genocide, have been coloured by domestic tensions and compromises.

International criminal justice is also declared in national criminal law. As outlined above, anticipation of the eventual entry into force of the Rome Statute resulted in significant and widespread legislative changes to domestic laws. Furthermore, it has been shown that the requirements of the international tribunals and the rules of *jus cogens* had a similar reformulating effect on national justice. Yet discussions of international criminal justice continually either overlook or underestimate the importance of these changes. Booth proposes that the function of an ICC trial will be 'first and foremost a proclamation that certain conduct is unacceptable to the world community' (Booth 2003: 178). Compatible with this intention, domestic legislation is being enacted worldwide to bring the national criminal law of more and more countries into line with the Rome Statute. Each such enactment represents a step closer to Clapham's 'transnational legal order' (Clapham 2003: 65), at least in a legislative and institutional sense.

Alternative paradigms?

Certainly international criminal justice is not purely the domain of international trial institutions and the processes which flow, or are purported to flow, from them. Expansive efforts to create an international criminal justice outside the framework of criminal prosecution are evidenced particularly in post-conflict and transitional states, the South African Truth and Reconciliation Commission (TRC) being a celebrated example. In the South African case, amnesty was offered in return for 'full disclosure of all the relevant facts relating to acts associated with a political objective' (Dyzenhaus 2003: 366) – as Dyzenhaus points out, this led some to believe that justice, seemingly being unlikely to be achieved given the continuing strength of the old regime, had been traded for the truth. The opposing view, in Dyzenhaus's analysis, is that justice was not negotiated, or sacrificed, but rather 'the way the TRC went about finding out the truth achieved a kind of justice different from – even superior to – criminal or retributive justice' (Dyzenhaus 2003: 366), namely restorative justice.

While this latter view is arguably the more convincing of the two, its most critical ingredient is the implied dichotomy of retributive/ guilt-based justice and restorative/truth-based justice. In this analysis, the two seem to be posited as mutually exclusive, incapable of happy coexistence. We have established, in the context of international criminal justice, that this dichotomy is false.[64] A comparative exploration of the objectives underlying both the 'formal' institutional attempts at international criminal justice and the 'informal' *community* approaches shows, not only that the two can, with institutional transformation, coexist in a transitional context, but that there is also significant scope for restorative themes to be incorporated into the procedural framework of international trials.[65] This has been recognised recently by the Chief Prosecutor for the ICC when commenting on the role of the court in conflict resolution.

The motives for international criminal justice through institutions and institutional processes have been articulated, and form a starting point for the comparative project.[66] As noted, one of the justifications for the creation of international tribunals and the ICC was that they would develop an accurate historical record. This goal also underlies the establishment of truth and reconciliation commissions. However, where the proposed merits of such a record are viewed in instrumental terms by proponents of due process, centred on deterrence of future violence, the objectives of supporters of truth and reconciliation commissions are much more expressive in nature and tied to understanding the interests of victim communities. For example, Coakley expands on the purpose of memory and truth telling in the following manner:

> In order to alleviate the suffering associated with memory, the process of truth telling is seen as an essential component of any attempt at healing and reconciliation ... the truth of individual suffering is a vehicle to achieve both individual and collective healing. The stories of the victims are supposed to move people collectively thus diminishing the legacies of violence by sharing its effects ... This process can help heal society's wounds and restore dignity to the victims of the previous regime. (Coakley 2001: 233)

The contrast between these instrumental and expressive objectives raises several issues. Firstly, the disjunction makes it possible that different 'truths' will be created within the adjudication process, a situation which has inevitably led to debate over what the 'best' truth might be, and for what purpose. While Scharf argues vociferously that 'the most authoritative rendering of the truth is only possible through a trial that accords full due process' (Scharf 1999: 513), he is countered by those who argue that a truth commission operating in conjunction with amnesty provisions 'promotes a process of truth finding in which a fuller picture of the truth emerges than would in a series of trials, since amnesty seekers have an interest in making full disclosure' (Dyzenhaus 2003: 366). The proposed incompatibility of retributive and restorative justice in this view hinges then on the perceived necessity of amnesty for truth. Again, I do not see this as inevitable and by deconstructing this proposed conjunction two questions can be addressed.

Which of the two approaches produces the more accurate and more complete record of events, that is the 'better truth'?

Implicit in the question are the assumptions that (a) the complete truth can never be fully recovered, if for no other reason than the fallibility of human memory, and (b) that accuracy is imperative to the production of truth. In raising this second concern I am careful not to equate accuracy with factuality in any legal sense. As a consequence of adversarial argument in particular, what is accepted as fact to satisfy the requirement of criminal evidence may be more a prevailing argument than truth.

Sarkin adds a realist political dimension to valuing the 'better' truth. In the context of South Africa 'a new nation cannot be built on denial of the past' (Sarkin 1997: 529–30). That civil and political distrust can be overcome through what would effectively be the withholding of truth, it is argued, is illogical.

Scharf cites as support for his view comments by Justice Robert Jackson, the Chief Prosecutor at Nuremberg – most significantly: 'According to Jackson, the establishment of an authoritative record of abuses that would endure the test of time and withstand the challenge of revisionism required proof "of incredible events by credible evidence".'[67] Thus, although he does not state it so explicitly, it seems that Scharf's opinion of the superiority of the criminal trial as a truth-producing mechanism stems from a faith in the rules governing such trials, in particular the rules of evidence and the required standard of proof. A problem with this conclusion rests in the problematic but assumed correlation between truth and what will stand as evidence towards criminal liability. The argument goes that the more probative the 'fact' the more it is truth. The contest between the narratives of the criminal tribunals and the stories of the truth commissions is more particularly determined, I would argue, by the completeness of the recount (and its legitimacy for victim communities), beyond its evidentiary status for tribunal chambers.

Viewing the trial as a series of process-generated decision-making sites, Scharf's standpoint is at the core a belief that each of these sites, or turning-points, tests the evidence such that only accurate information is allowed to be woven into the picture of truth – it is a faith in procedure to filter out erroneous claims and dubious evidence, and thus produce 'the truth'. This, I submit, is misguided.

Firstly, it presupposes the infallibility of the trial structure, without acknowledging the inherent weaknesses of both adversarial and inquisitorial systems when it comes to eliciting the whole story, particularly from a victim perspective. Many rules of evidence, in fact, are designed to circumscribe the fullest recount against the rights of the accused or prevailing probative considerations. From this imperative there is a genuine potential for the criminal trial to distort the truth. Let us begin with the rules governing admissibility of evidence. There are no grounds for assuming that evidence deemed inadmissible is inaccurate or vice versa; it may have been illegally obtained, it may be more prejudicial than probative and lack corroboration, but the possibility that it is accurate (or inaccurate) remains. Judicial discretion to admit illegally or improperly obtained evidence or that extracted under duress because its probative value outweighs its potential benefit may do little more than suggest a relative likelihood of truth emerging from a flawed process. Thus the rules of evidence can operate to produce a partial truth.

Furthermore, the fact that opposing counsel can paint vastly differing stories from examination of the same witnesses renders questionable the truth-finding potential of the adversarial trial. This process of story construction has important repercussions in relation to the 'cathartic' function of testifying earlier proposed by Colson. It highlights the inherent distorting potential of the criminal trial in its search for prevailing fact rather than negotiated truth.

Nina argues that selectivity of a different nature was at work in the South African TRC. In his analysis 'the state is privileging the writing of a particular history ... it is the construction of a very limited and controlled history' (Nina 1997: 66–70). Perhaps most condemning: 'One gets the impression as if there was never apartheid or reasons to revolt against it' (Nina 1997: 69). The core of his argument is that in a 'desperate bid to avoid confrontation with the [whites]' (Nina 1997:

65), the TRC recreated an accommodative, edited history – a history of the very nature held above to be unsatisfactory. Even so, the stories emerging from out of the Commission produced admissions which may never have emerged through a formal adversarial process.

Qualifying any such assertions, further criticism of the South African TRC's truth-finding ability in contrast with that of the trial process comes from Dyzenhaus:

> [A]necdotal evidence suggests that perpetrators often stuck to a script, probably co-ordinated by the few lawyers who appeared time and again with this group, which disclosed as little as possible and attempted to confine implicating others to implicating security force actors who had died. (2003: 367)

Without commenting on matters of accuracy, this critique draws attention to the potential for distortion within the framework of a truth commission, as well as through trial decision-making, because of the necessity to negotiate participant interests or navigate rule limitations. Arguably, as the truth commissions have found in particular, this distortion, no matter what the process of extraction and deliberation, may be heightened and the resultant 'truth' further weakened where the process operates without flexible amnesty provisions.

Are amnesty provisions necessary for a truth commission to operate?

The incentive beyond rare and genuine contrition (which should not be dismissed as an ingredient of truth commission hearings) for perpetrators to provide 'full disclosure' if they are faced with prosecution is indemnity if not amnesty. The challenge is to enable amnesty provisions which are open and responsible and do not essentially sacrifice retributive outcomes for restorative truth-seeking. I argue this is both appropriate and achievable within the contexts of transformed deliberative domains.

It is through compromise with retributive justice (recognising the complexity of legitimate victim interests) that restorative justice and truth-seeking will best be achieved. Indeed a combined model would overcome many of the weaknesses of the two separate approaches in terms of truth-finding, arguably representing a more robust international criminal justice than is currently being achieved. In saying this, we do not advance as a hypothetical model on these lines the creation of an international truth commission to operate in conjunction with the ICC. This has not proved successful in Sierra Leone.[68] The transformed trial mechanism (Findlay and Henham, forthcoming) wherein the judge could move from adversarial trial procedures to truth-finding and mediation has the benefit of encouraging disclosure as truth rather than actionable fact, while the evidence given in any adversarial context could be tested by the judge for the purposes of liability if appropriate. Furthermore, the amalgamation of these approaches would better accommodate the administration of juvenile justice, wherein welfare and restorative agendas are more apparent. Linton highlights this in the context of Sierra Leone – while adults will be prosecuted for atrocities in the Special Court, '[t]he Security Council has stressed that other institutions, such as the Truth and Reconciliation Commission, are better suited to deal with juveniles' (Linton 2001: 237).

Thus far, the discussion has focused on perpetrators' contribution to the truth and the potential production of conflicting 'perpetrator truths' as a consequence of the contrast between the instrumental and expressive objectives of criminal trials and truth commissions respectively. Yet this contrast also translates into two different experiences for victims. As noted, Colson argues that international criminal justice, as manifest through the international tribunals, is a cathartic process. Central to his theory is the idea of 'psychoanalytic catharsis included in the act of testifying' (Colson 2000: 60) and the argument that the purpose, the medium and the setting of the ICTY are all conducive to the cathartic process. The purpose is to clarify *thought* by removing *ignorance*. The medium of testimony allows victims to express their trauma and therefore relieve the stress attached to it, and the setting 'provides a safe and controlled locus ... a properly distanced context' (Colson 2000: 60). The analysis, however, neglects the aforementioned potential for distortion inherent in the trial process. This has significant repercussions for victims' cathartic experiences.

At a basic level, what of those victims who are not allowed to testify? In a purely evidentiary context, their testimony can be deemed more prejudicial than probative and would violate the accused's right to a fair trial. While it is imperative that this right be upheld if the court or tribunal is to achieve legitimacy as tribunals of liability, the refusal to admit a wider range of victim testimony denies the potential of the trial as a chamber of truth. As with many formalist commentators, Colson does not explore the emotional consequences for the victim and victim communities. Victims in the context of genocide in particular want the perpetrators punished but equally need their story to be told. Excluded from trials currently constituted because their testimony may not qualify as evidence, victims conclude that their story was less important, a feeling which, when widespread, may adversely affect healing and reconciliation. From a victim perspective, the legitimacy of the trial process from which their story has been removed will also be impugned.

For those victims who do testify, what is the impact of having their stories selectively constructed, destroyed and reconstructed in examination and cross-examination? Not only are their experiences distorted, but they are taken out of their hands completely and retold through the voices of professionals. This loss of ownership, along with the procedurally enforced restraints preventing the accurate telling of their stories, will more likely lead to increased frustration and dissatisfaction for victims than it will to catharsis. They will not feel, as Colson argues they would, that their status as victims is 'being taken seriously by the international community through one of its institutions' (Colson 2000: 58). Indeed, the validity of Colson's analysis depends on victims being able to take the stand, tell their story and step down; however, the trial operates in a very different way. His analysis is constrained within the confines of the international criminal trial currently constructed and as such relegates the victims and the power of their stories to truth commissions, where the purported objectives are expressive rather than instrumental. With the incorporation of this new level of 'truth' within a transformed criminal trial process, the divergence of justice paradigms would be breached and legitimate victim interests merged within an institution which is to some degree accountable in terms of formal rights and responsibilities.

As Dyzenhaus points out, one claim of supporters of truth commissions is that 'in that process the victim has a role that goes well beyond serving as an instrument to achieve conviction' (Dyzenhaus 2003: 366). The argument continues that, in taking this expanded role in telling their stories, 'victims might find not only that they can come to terms with the abuses, but also that they are "restored" to a relationship of equality with the perpetrators, so that they can develop a sense of agency appropriate for participation in a democratic society' (Dyzenhaus 2003: 366). Coakley draws attention to this function of a truth commission to 'provide a forum for people who have not been able to tell their story before' (Coakley 2001: 234). She notes the writing of one commissioner at the United Nations Truth Commission for El Salvador:

> One could not listen to them without recognising that the mere act of telling what had happened was a healing emotional

release, and that they were more interested in recounting their story and being heard than in retribution. It is as if they felt some shame that they had not dared to speak out before, and, now that they had done so, they could go home and focus on the future less encumbered by the past.[69]

The parallels with Colson's proposed cathartic process are clear – it is simply the setting which differs. Furthermore, Coakley argues that this experience goes beyond the individual, having 'a "cathartic" affect [sic] in society, making it possible for a society to "cleanse" itself through this process of breaking the silence and acknowledging a shameful period in its history' (Coakley 2001: 234).

However, this view is not unchallenged. Dyzenhaus warns that the reality of the South African TRC 'should provide a highly cautionary note' (Dyzenhaus 2003: 366). He points to evidence presented by Wilson that many victims did not get to testify at the TRC, and that those who did 'often found themselves in a micro-managed process in which their testimony was reduced to the empirical data the TRC required.'[70] Wilson argues that the TRC instrumentalises victims' testimonies in the same manner as does the criminal prosecution, the only difference being the TRC does so 'to assist the project of nation-building',[71] whereas the criminal prosecution does so 'to achieve the end of conviction'.[72] This is contestable against the governance aspirations of alternative criminal justice paradigms recognised recently by the ICC prosecutor.

Convergence of restorative and retributive themes

The prevailing challenge in the development of justice globally is to synthesise (and assimilate within the rights framework of the trial process) the formal and informal paradigms for the sake of legitimate victim interests. The further challenge is to integrate the paradigms without sacrificing the rights provided through the trial or the inclusive flexibility of the less formal resolution processes.

The existence of informal manifestations of justice to resolve crimes against humanity, being attempts by communities to realise international criminal justice at a local level, highlights that a variety of legitimate victim needs must be satisfied if international criminal justice is to be realised. They show that the ICTY, the ICTR and the ICC cannot in themselves represent international criminal justice. Rather non-formal resolutions are taking on a victim resonance which cannot be ignored. However, as the victim community surveys establish (Albrecht 2006; DeFeyter 2005; Weitekamp *et al.*, 2006) victim aspirations for ICJ are complex and reach beyond the current capacity of either justice paradigm. The satisfaction of the needs the surveys highlight must be more creatively recognised within the fabric of international criminal justice.

While the development of these restorative processes should not be hindered by institutions designed for more retributive purposes, there is a need to open up the trial as a restorative tool so that it is more inclusive of victim interests and more responsive to community expectations. This will necessitate a reshaping of the formal institutions and community responses if international criminal justice is to be fully realised. A new normative framework which values *humanity* as its focus and *truth* as its outcome will be the driver for change.

An important consequence of international criminal justice better meeting the legitimate needs of victim communities will be the resolution of conflict and the advancement of peacemaking as a stronger rights framework and with retribution on offer. This is easier said than done. The two paradigms of ICJ operate within distinctly separate justice cultures. Restorative justice frameworks have evolved to some extent in opposition to formal adversarial justice. Restorative and adversarial justice prioritise and value different outcomes and work from different motivations. Were it not that victim communities are demanding better access to the potentials and outcomes of both paradigms, the necessary motivation for their synthesis may well be missing.

Braithwaite (2002) claims this for restorative justice when applied to state reconstruction. But in terms of victim community interests this does not now seem to be enough. Then again the limitations of trial-based retributive justice mean that in its formal incarnation, international criminal justice is not as influential as it might be in long-lasting global governance challenges (Findlay 2007c). It has been seen to fail victim communities when reparation and restoration are required.

From a victim community perspective the governance potentials of international criminal justice should not be limited to by-products of a re-emphasised restorative dimension. As the ICC in particular will require productive integration across national, regional and international criminal justice systems in order to achieve its prosecutorial mandate, this will provide an opportunity for justice alliances (or at least understandings). International criminal justice, as a force for good global governance, therefore, will depend on its capacity to resolve conflict and to enhance the national and regional mechanisms for sustaining good governance within a legal rights framework. In achieving this, the recognised interests of victim communities can legitimise the exercise of international criminal justice in all its forms, and will commend the capacity of global governance to resolve and avoid conflict. The transformation of international criminal justice to follow (Findlay and Henham, forthcoming) will allow international political alliances to progress the objective of world peace above military dominance. A crucial factor in reaching such accommodations will be an ability to reconcile, in justice decision-making, the competing claims to truth/responsibility and fact/liability. Difficult to achieve as the process will be, it is the challenge for those who manage the process that leads to international criminal justice coming of age.[73]

Conclusion – justice on to governance

In the new globalisation where risk and security predominates it would be fair to assume that the governance focus would be security. In terms of the practice and achievement of international representative organisations (such as the UN) regarding the provision and maintenance of global security there is some gulf between theory and practice (Miller 1999).

The doctrine of *collective security* (significant in placing security concerns within international relations) asserts that the peace of the international community can be maintained through a binding predetermined agreement to take collective action to preserve peace. Central to this concept is the preservation of prevailing world order against forceful change. In this way the doctrine of collective security is both conservative and inclusive.

Against the present threat to security posed by international terrorism, the dominant political alliance has shifted the collective security imperative to one of collective defence on a global war footing. This approach to security is designed to counter external threats, and especially those which materialise domestically. It is an admission that what binds the citizenry in an otherwise peaceful nation-state must be made secure by moving into the global sphere and sometimes aggressively ensuring global order for the good of the global community, as well as providing a buffer for domestic peace and safety.

The League of Nations was not able to save the world from war.

The UN, created in the image of the League, has inherited many of its structural limitations as a mechanism for global governance and peacemaking. Miller (1999) suggests that these revolve around the following issues:

- which sovereign member state's security interests it is meant to prefer and to serve;
- what agents it will use to keep the peace;
- which instruments are available to it in the task of peacekeeping and security maintenance;
- what obligations sovereign states carry in the cause of peacekeeping and global security.

The concept of universality in global governance failed to materialise in the League and is strained and frayed in the administration of the UN. The UN Security Council demonstrates that universality in global governance is wishful thinking. The unilateral military interventions of the US and its allies deny any pre-eminence for the UN as a representative and inclusive global governance arm. The assumption by the US of a global policing role violates its commitment to collective security covenants and challenges their workability in any case. As the *free world* was pitted against communism in the Cold War era we now see global governance divided over the *war on terror* and the *war of terror*. *Bloc* alliances to manage the security concerns of global governance present a fundamental challenge to governance in liberal democratic form. Similarly they essentially threaten to compromise the independence of ICJ.

For the sake of legitimacy, the injection of criminal justice into global governance models is now more crucial than ever. But not as it happens today. The confirmation of global governance is not just about instruments. Compromise documents as they may be, we have enough of those. In any case these legislative instruments are dependent on compliance or enforcement potential worldwide. As we have seen with the US and its approach to international relations, enforcement is not constrained by the regulatory requirements of international conventions. More likely it relies on political largesse.

What about the obligations required of international organisations in global governance? Recent experience shows that the UN has not been bound by collective security obligations. The genocide in Rwanda is dreadful evidence. States have hegemonic power based on military might, and the Security Council demonstrates that the strong have a louder voice than the weak when it comes to global governance. Beyond this, states have ulterior motives running contrary to compliance with collective global governance. The problem with member states trying to realise their international obligations within an organisation like the UN (or the International Criminal Court for that matter) is the continuing salience of the doctrine of sovereignty. Contemporary international relations, as was the case during the Cold War, indicate that regional configurations around mutual self-interest or limited political alliances based on dominant and shared ideologies are the more likely global groupings. These have become the potent frameworks for global governance in contest with international representative organisations.

From the standpoint of dominant political alliances, or from that of representative international organisations, collective security has prevailed as a key motivation for the nature of world ordering. I will detail later there is nothing new in this. The delivery of reconstruction aid by the US to Europe, through the Marshall Plan following the Second World War is confirmation. Aid was directed to strengthen fragile and transitional state structures against the influence of political directions which were seen as contrary to the interests of America and the continued security of the victorious Western alliance. This alliance-based marketing of military muscle in tandem with development aid for modernisation and economic harmony continues to feature as a regional and global governance strategy. What differs in the present phase of globalisation is the clear dominance of the risk/security focus and the extent to which this justifies the application of diverse and often contradictory regulatory strategies. In addition, the recognition of global crime and control as crucial among these strategies has stimulated the proliferation of both itinerant and permanent justice mechanisms inextricably connected to this risk/security framework.

One of the most fundamental problems with this risk/security focus for global governance, as it influences and applies to international criminal justice, is that the purposes of a legal response to risk and security remain fundamentally political. This is certainly the case for the war crimes tribunals and the post-conflict special courts established by the UN Security Council and endorsed by regional and political alliances. Heads of nation-states and of representative international organisations cannot be relied upon to act as independent arbiters of global security, at least from the perspective of dominant political alliances. The discourse of collective security as an impartial governance aspiration will be defeated by political partiality and the relativity of security to domestic and regional priorities. Chapters to follow discuss what partiality is doing to multiculturalism and any genuine experiments in legal pluralism.

Neutrality in international policing, prosecution and tribunal deliberation is the challenge for ICJ as it supports truly global governance. The agents, instruments and obligations of ICJ can grow out from universal standards and a normative framework which are not essentially politicised. As such, they could satisfy the higher goal of protecting *humanity* from victimisation and injustice. Awaiting the day when there emerges a more cohesive worldwide polity, the permanent institutions of ICJ such as the ICC have a heavy responsibility to demonstrate independent and clear-minded justice service delivery.

Notes

1 The description 'alternative' for these paradigms of justice is misleading in that their coverage of victim communities and situations of post-conflict resolution makes them arguably more significant than formal justice institutions such as the international criminal tribunals.
2 Findlay and Henham (2005) show how this might be achieved.
3 See, for example: Clapham (2003), Booth (2003), Rehman (2002), Teitel (1999).
4 http://www.arts.cuhk.edu.hk/NanjingMassacre/NMTT.html
5 Convention on the Prevention and Punishment of the Crime of Genocide (1948).
6 Adopted by the General Assembly of the United Nations on 10 December 1948. For further discussion see Rehman (2002: 515–7). Although the Declaration is not binding on states, Rehman argues that it 'stands out as the most authoritative commentary on international human rights and criminal justice processes' (2002: 516).
7 For the full text of the 1949 Conventions and the 1977 Protocols see http://www.icrc.org/ihl.nsf/WebCONVFULL?OpenView
8 Perez (2000: 183) argues that the need to maintain Cold War alliances was responsible for the toleration of human rights and humanitarian law violations in this period.
9 This is explored in the context of the war against terror in Findlay (2007a) and global governance in Findlay (2007b).
10 Beigbeder (1999: 49), reviewed by Megret (2002: 8).
11 For a critical discussion of these developments and their limitations see Danner and Martinez (2004).
12 Established by the Special Court Agreement (Ratification) Act 2002. For the full text of this Agreement follow the links from www.sc-sl.org/

13 For details see the Agreement between the UN and Cambodia concerning the Prosecution under Cambodian Law of Crimes Committed during the Period of Democratic Kampuchea (6 June 2003). For an outline see http://www.asil.org/ilib/ilib0611.htm#a1

14 It should be noted that widespread dissatisfaction with Indonesia's Ad Hoc Human Rights Tribunal on East Timor has repeatedly led to calls for the creation of an independent international tribunal. For example, see http://www.globalpolicy.org/intljustice/tribunals/timor/2003/0818renew.htm

15 For a discussion of the case in question and its consequences for the court see Cockayne (2005) and Cockayne and Huckerby (2004). In Findlay and Henham (2005) we argue that both justice paradigms should reside in the transformed international criminal trial for the protection of the rights and legitimate interests of victim communities.

16 Booth views international criminal justice as 'a continuum, a process that was catalysed in Nuremberg' (2003: 191).

17 *R v Bartle and the Commissioner of Police for the Metropolis and Others, Ex Parte Pinochet* 37 ILM 1302 (HL 1998) (hereinafter *Ex Parte Pinochet); R v Bow St Metro. Stipendiary Magistrate and Others, Ex Parte Pinochet* (No. 2) 1 All ER 577 (HL 15/01/1999) (hereinafter *Ex Parte Pinochet II); R v Bartle and the Commissioner of Police for the Metropolis and Others, Ex Parte Pinochet* 38 ILM 581 (HL 1999) *(hereinafter Ex Parte Pinochet III).*

18 The Rome Statute of the International Criminal Court (hereinafter Rome Statute) entered into force on 1 July 2002. For the full text see http://www.un.org/law/icc/statute/romefra.htm

19 Perez (2000: 189). This assertion was made in Spain's second request for the extradition of Pinochet from the UK, since their first request, being grounded in passive personality jurisdiction, was denied on the basis that such grounds would not have afforded British authorities the right to prosecute in equivalent circumstances under British law (Perez, 2000: 190).

20 Other examples of countries asserting universal jurisdiction include the 1987 prosecution in France of Klaus Barbie for wartime deportations of civilians (Teitel 1999: 292) and Israel's 1961 prosecution of Adolf Eichmann for war crimes and crimes against humanity including genocide (Rehman 2002: 517).

21 Robertson (1999), quoted in Megret (2002: 9).

22 Article 27 of the Rome Statute.

23 Article 8 of the Rome Statute.

24 Article 7 of the Rome Statute.

25 See, for example: Arbour (1997), Cassese (1998), Wippman (1999), Colson (2000), Scharf (2000), Rehman (2002) and Clapham (2003).

26 These justifications are set out and discussed in Scharf (2000: 928–33).

27 International Tribunal for the Former Yugoslavia, First Annual Report, at para. 15, UN Doc IT/68 (1994). Cited in Scharf (2000: 929).

28 Cited by Colson (2000: 54) and referenced to in McGeary (1996: 22–7).
29 Mendez (1997). Cited in Perez (2000: 175, footnote 2).
30 In deciding to establish the ICTY, the US Representative of the UN Security Council remarked that the Tribunal would develop a historic record of a conflict in which distortion of the truth has been an essential ingredient of the ethnic violence. Reported in Scharf (2000: 931).
31 This view persists despite the fact that proceedings against Pinochet were subsequently suspended and eventually terminated on the grounds that he was too ill to undergo such a trial. Coincidentally, these proceedings were terminated on 1 July 2002, the same day the Rome Statute entered into force.
32 Reported in Scharf (2000: 926–7).
33 For example: Ball (1999), Bass (2000), Beigbeder (1999), Hazan (2000), Robertson (1999) and Scharf (1997). Reviewed by Megret (2002: 17). Notably, however, these reports were later to be unfounded – see for example: http://www.terravista.pt/guincho/2104/199810/deichmann_9701.html and http://www.balkan-archive.org.yu/politics/conc_camps/html/Kenney.html
34 Hazan (2000: 76), quoted in Megret (2002: 17).
35 Robertson (1999), quoted in Megret, (2002: 17).
36 Robertson (1999: xix), quoted in Megret, 2002: 17).
37 Hazan (2000), quoted in Megret (2002: 19).
38 *Washington Post* (3 October 1999). Quoted at http://www.fair.org/reports/post-war-crimes.html
39 This is critiqued in Cockayne (2005).
40 Cassese poses this question (1998: 6).
41 Article 1 of the Rome Statute.
42 A failure to do so would run counter to the principle of procedure, set out in both the International Covenant on Civil and Political Rights (ICCPR) and the European Convention for the Protection of Human Rights and Fundamental Freedoms (ECHR), which asserts the right of an individual to be judged by an impartial and independent tribunal. For full texts see http://www.unhchr.ch/html/menu3/b/a_ccpr.htm and http://www.echr.coe.int/Eng/BasicTexts.htm
43 Quoted in Delmas-Marty (2002: 290).
44 Delmas-Marty (2002: 289). This principle, from which international human rights instruments do not permit a state to derogate (even in 'exceptional circumstances') is set out in both ICCPR and the ECHR.
45 Arbour (1997: 535). Again this was one of the arguments put forth by the Rwandese government in support of an international tribunal.
46 Kelsen (1944: 112), quoted in Cassese (1998: 8).
47 Roling (1961: 354), quoted in Cassese (1998: 7).
48 The synthesis of procedural traditions in the face of pragmatic compromise and the alienation of other important traditions beyond civil and common law is presented in Findlay (2001).

49 Even down to the influence of research sources is speculated upon by Findlay and Bohlander (2003).

50 Hereinafter 'the Rules'. For full text see: http://www1.umn.edu/humanrts/instree/iccrulesofprocedure.html

51 Henham takes issue with this and in turn proposes an enhancement of judicial discretion it the international court context (see Henham 2004).

52 An English translation of the CCIL is annexed to Werle and Jessberger (2002).

53 Werle and Jessberger (2002: 192, emphasis added).

54 For the full text of the Draft Legislation, Enacted Legislation and Debates relating to the implementation of the Rome Statute into national law see: http://www.iccnow.org/resourcestools/ratimptoolkit/nationalregionaltools/legislationdebates.html

55 The exception is Article 70(4)(a) which provides that 'Each State Party shall extend its criminal laws penalizing offences against the integrity of its own investigative or judicial process to offences against the administration of justice referred to in this article, committed on its territory, or by one of its nationals'.

56 Werle and Jessberger (2002: 195).

57 Statute of the International Tribunal (adopted 25 May 1993). For full text see: http://www.un.org/icty/basic/statut/statute.htm

58 Article 29 of the Statute of the International Tribunal.

59 See http://www.unhchr.ch/html/menu2/6/hrc.htm for details.

60 See http://www.unhchr.ch/html/menu2/6/cat.htm for details.

61 For example Scharf (2000), Roznovschi (2003).

62 Goddard (2000: 464) argues otherwise: 'And even if only a few of the perpetrators of genocide, crimes against humanity, or war crimes are held to account, their examples may serve to deter others similarly minded, and that in itself will be a resounding victory for all humanity.' This view should be compared with the in-depth evaluation put forward by Wippman (1999), which concludes with the uncertainty of the deterrent effect.

63 Akhavan (2001: 1). Notably, the tone of Akhavan's argument indicates his belief that indictment in itself is important in undermining influence, regardless of apprehension and prosecution.

64 Findlay and Henham (2005: chs 7 and 8).

65 An argument for this is posed in the context of the influence which China might have over the development of international criminal justice. See Findlay (2007c).

66 Henham has explored this in relation to international sentencing. See Henham (2003; 2004).

67 Scharf (1999: 513). Quoting a Report to the President from Justice Robert H. Jackson, Chief of Counsel for the United States in the Prosecution of Axis War Criminals, 7 June, 1945, reprinted in 39 *American Journal of International Law* 178 (Supp. 1945).

68 For a critique of this binary approach see Cockayne (2004).
69 Burgenthal (1994), quoted in Coakley (2001: 234).
70 Dyzenhaus (2003: 366), drawing on Wilson (2001).
71 Wilson (2001), cited in Dyzenhaus (2003: 367).
72 Wilson (2001), cited in Dyzenhaus (2003: 366).
73 In our forthcoming book we argue that a transformed trial process, where both mediation and adversarial resolutions are on offer, will have the flexible capacity to better meet complex and competing victim aspirations. Essential for this transformation will be the creative enhancement of juridical discretion (and its accountability to stakeholders). Crucial in the exercise of this discretion will be a capacity to reconcile and determine truth and fact in compatible decision environments.

Chapter 6

Governing through globalised crime

Crucially there are whole new types of crime, some of them taking place in electronic space, where, with instantaneous transaction speeds, state institutions within territorial scope ... are unable to exercise extraterritorial control ... Sanctioned agencies supposed to hold a legitimate monopoly to enforce compliance within their own domain are proceeding helter-skelter to devise novel forms of cooperation with their counterparts elsewhere, but they appear to be stymied by increasing deterritorialisation in matters of economic governance ... In this hiatus the quickening of globalisation obscures the boundaries of permissibility and impermissibility, and problems pertaining to the basic legal and ethical dimensions of the global political economy.

(Mittleman and Johnston 1999: 104)

Introduction

Jonathan Simon in his recent book *Governing through Crime: How the War on Crime Transformed American Democracy and Created a Culture of Fear* (2007) positions the well developed nexus between crime and governance squarely within the risk/security politics of George W. Bush's post-9/11 America. In the context of US home security policy, Simon argues:

- Representations of crime create a domestic control agenda.

- The state's monopoly over criminalisation and control through criminal justice determine them as important fields for governance.

- Criminal justice can be aligned with the family, the school and the workplace as fertile governance arenas.

- Contemporary governance concerns are focused on risk and security.

- Risk is to the *valorised* citizen victim as well as to the state.

- The state defines risk and the selective policing of security against the fear which risk generates.

This chapter takes the relationship between crime and governance to the level of international relations and globalisation. It argues that as important as crime and control may now be to domestic governance, in a global age of crime/risk and control/security the interconnection between crime and governance offers an insight into the future of international criminal justice. In particular, I propose the following:

- Crime (and recent interpretations of global terrorism in particular) are instrumental in the conceptualisation and the promotion of the new globalisation (risk/security hegemony).

- The crime/control/governance nexus has become a prominent feature of international criminal law and criminal justice developments.

- The *global community* (as determined through the conditions of 'citizenship') is the habitas for crime; humanity is the global crime victim; political hegemony is responsible for policing global security (against the risk of terror).

- The governance imperatives of a dominant world order have tended to compromise the delivery and legitimacy of international criminal justice.

Simon (2001–2) identified two metaphorical directions crucial to a particular legislative reliance on crime as governance:[1]

- the rise of the 'street' as the nexus for a war on crime-style governance; and as a consequence
- the extraordinary emphasis this placed on policing in managing virtually all organisations, public and private. (Simon 2001–2: 1053)

From an international/global as opposed to a local/jurisdictional/ state-based perspective this chapter augments these directions towards:

- the rise of the *global community* as the habitas for crime (and eventually control);
- the indication of *humanity* as the global crime victim; and
- the particularisation of a dominant global political hegemony as *policing* international security against crime, especially terrorism.

International crime control has become the discourse of the *liberal democratic* interlocutor. The idealised political subject (the *global community* or *humanity*) is realised through the definition of *actual* threats and legitimate responses (Findlay 2007c). Presidents and prime ministers speak on behalf of victim communities and determine what qualifies as crimes of aggression and crimes against humanity. These political discriminations accord legitimacy to idealised victims and alienate and delegitimise the motivations and actions of those who challenge the dominant political hegemony.

Crime is more than a problem for global governance. Global terrorism in particular has become instrumental in the promotion of the *new* globalisation and *para-justice* control regimes. Along with the argued utility of crime in global governance, the fear of crime and the valorisation of crime victims are identified as vital forces over the crime/governance nexus. With international terrorism justifying a risk/security nexus for global governance, criminal justice is both relied upon and contorted for the achievement of violent control agendas.

While it is accepted that crime may frame the broader role of regulatory power (Garland 2001) it is now apparent in the global context that crime and control have become central planks of international governance in a divided world. Essential for this is:

- the magnification of crime (through terror) as a threat to legitimate world order;

- the construction of the crime victim as *humanity*;
- the representation of the victim as the idealised citizen subject of the global community;
- the responsibility of the representatives of the *global community* to fight crime as part of the process to restore post-conflict societies; and
- that the political subjects of the global community are taken beyond idealised fictions into a realm of security, away from terrorist threat as defined by the dominant political hegemony.[2]

The vast and imagined possibility of victimisation (through crimes against humanity and genocide in particular) has suggested motivations for military intervention and consequential penal regulation. If the fear of crime and terror as a prevailing threat predetermines global political control agendas, then any dominant hegemony claiming the right to identify the terrorist, and the capacity to protect the citizen will retrieve their political currency even if this does not progress beyond narrative representation (Findlay 2007c). Further, as the recent relationship between global governance and international criminal justice suggests, the fragile legitimacy of dominant political alliances has inspired concurrent resort to *para-justice*[3] strategies wherein violence and oppression run contrary to the protective limitations which demarcate conventional justice responses.

The dependencies of global governance on international criminal justice, and in turn on a risk/security environment for globalisation have developed reactively. They are repressive, recursive and regressive. International terrorism has necessitated for the dominant political hegemony a shift away from late-modern economic culturation and towards a containment model which relies on criminalisation and justice/control supports (often following military or violent intervention) to counter the challenge of alternative cultural and political alignments.

This evolution has not been without its radical coincidences, or its long-standing antipathies. The destruction on September 11, grounded in part in the struggle between fundamentalism and the 'liberal' ideologies and perceived economic imperialism of the West, has become the backdrop for the new globalisation. Crime and control within this transition appear as:

- a process to consolidate political victory for a coalition of dependent states through an emergent and formal international criminal justice (Findlay and Henham 2005);

- a consequence of opposed political alignment, wherein religion, economy and morality are determined as the enemy for war discourse at many levels;

- a recognition of the need by the dominant hegemony for legitimacy through 'justice' as well as force in the face of violent challenge;

- a critical growth in specialised technologies and exclusive knowledge that in turn fuel governing through crime/control; and

- the defining of a new set of privileged subjects for government and an old set of enemies for exclusion.

Valorisation counterbalances demonisation. The *streets* to be *policed* are now populated by the global community and are beyond state jurisdiction, legislation and dominion (Roberts 2005). The security of the idealised citizen/victim is the justification for meeting the terrorist risk. Thereby the locally/culturally relative motivations for terrorist violence are subsumed in a more simplistic anti-crime discourse. The indicia of good global governance are successes in the *war on terror* fought in the tribunals and not the trenches.

Yet legitimacy is fragile. This hegemony is a loose and negotiated order. It lacks true legislative, juridical or executive authority beyond metaphor or concession. The citizenship it serves is ceded to it rather than democratically included. Its normative foundation has few deep or common cultural roots. It is searching for a framework of governance. The risk/security nexus particularly mirrored in international terrorism has to some extent recently provided this.

However, the legitimating potential of international criminal justice has, in certain control contexts, been supplemented by the dominant global political alliance, with a *para-justice* paradigm. The violent and oppressive nature of this second level of *justice* has challenged the legitimacy of control interventions as a consequence of denying some central justice *balances* which international criminal justice propounds. The assumed necessity and expediency of *para-justice* has made the legitimating capacity of international criminal justice more potent and less negotiable.

In the context of *para-politics* (wherein both organised crime and terrorism are said to have their place) the characteristics of *para-justice* are predominant in control strategies. The adoption of *para-justice* by the dominant political alliance in this new phase of globalisation reveals an intriguing intersection between the aims and activations of both political forms.

The conflict language of this dominant political hegemony, and the emergence of its strong military imagery in its control discourse (*para* and conventional), are paradoxical at a global level. Wars against crime are designed to replace military intervention with criminal justice. While war imagery invokes a simplistic and dominant process of demonisation as a consequence of 'victor's justice', systematic measures against the criminalised enemy see international criminal justice as well as military intervention engaging both the moral and political threats which they represent.

As with the distortion or dissolution of crucial justice identifiers justified through risk and security, the intersection between international criminal justice and the motivations of global political alliances further impugn the legitimacy of justice and the governance it fosters. The challenge for international criminal justice is to reclaim the separation of powers and thereby the capacity to keep governance just. This will not be achieved simply as a consequence of conflict resolution and peacemaking. International criminal justice must provide a critical and accountable capacity against which to measure the risk/security confluence in contemporary globalisation.

For criminologists, criminal lawyers, international relations scholars and rights analysts, globalisation offers a critical context in which to explore the congruence of crime, justice and governance. The analytical endeavour, therefore, is to reveal how world political domination and cultural segregation is presently negotiated and neutralised in a problematic and partial justice paradigm. What remains for international criminal justice is crucial for projecting future developments in global governance and its legitimacy.

Can globalised crime construct governance?

About governance Foucault suggests that the task of acting on the actions of others (government) is bound up with ways of *reasoning* about governing (Foucault 1997). In the sense of globalised governance within the *new* globalisation, the dominant political hegemony has tended to define what is *knowable* and 'more importantly to produce truth selectively' (Simon 2001–2: 1063). This *truth* has emerged as a by-product of its own strategies of intervention and their legitimacy through the earlier argued crime/security nexus. A particular notion of governance has been rationalised both through challenges to international security and *exclusive* approaches to its restoration.

Therefore, the *ways of reasoning about governing* in the recent global context have in significant measure focused around:

- new emergent crime risks;
- consequent challenges to international security;
- actual harm of the global citizen and global communities;
- requiring a force-based response from the 'democratic' international hegemony;
- legitimating a particular form of international justice intervention;
- repositioning ongoing concepts of sovereignty, citizenship, legal standing and alien attack. (Findlay 2007c)

The translation of this reasoning through epithets and campaigns such as the *war on terror* has moved the nexus between crime and governance from the politics of the ideal into processes whereby criminal justice and the control potentials it offers significantly reconstruct and determine the legitimate interlocutors of global conflict (Findlay and Henham 2005). In fact, global conflict and the reinstitution of post-conflict states are in part now dependent on the arena of international criminal justice for legitimate resolution. Resistance through violence no matter how destructive is marginalised and relegated by the determination of the criminal liability of its principal perpetrators. The tribunal has become essential to the restoration of governability post military intervention.

Global governance around a political discourse of the *war on terror* now relies on risk/security balances. The structures which are said to achieve and maintain these balances (morphology) align with and support the central processes and institutions of global governance where globalisation addresses risk (crime) concerns for security (control).

The features of the relationship between risk and security mirrored in contemporary global governance include:

- jurisdiction – international alliances beyond *super* states and regions;
- location – the *global community;*
- citizenship – idealised members of that community;

- standing – power to determine the legitimate victim, to empower the interlocutor, to authorise the judiciary and to disenfranchise the perpetrator;
- dominion – the dominant political hegemony;
- authority – control over the institutions of international justice first through *victor's* status and then through control of international organisations;
- enforceability – initially through violent military intervention followed by monopoly over investigation, policing, trial and punishment;
- amnesty – monopolisation over rewarding complicity and awarding mercy;
- reconciliation – monitoring the availability of retributive and restorative outcomes.

Employing the example of terrorism and its containment (from the perspective of the dominant hegemony):

- Jurisdiction is the attack against democracy and *liberal* values.
- Location of the attack is within those communities which enjoy democratic government.
- Citizenship is accorded the idealised victim and denied the perpetrator of the attack.
- Standing is only as a consequence of victimisation within the context of citizenship.
- Dominion comes as a consequence of *liberal* democracy under attack.
- Authority is initially force-based but eventually legitimated through the monopoly over justice paradigms pitted against the attack.
- Enforceability comes from superior force, from the widest communication and control over *knowledge* and through the support of alliances and coalitions with mutual risk/security agendas to confront such attacks.
- Amnesty is denied as a consequence of terror, except where it is perpetrated within the hegemony.
- Reconciliation is marginalised in favour of retribution and deterrence to prevent further attacks.

This summarises a passage of crime control and governance within the contemporary international risk/security agenda. To move on and detail the institutions and processes responsible for international criminal justice resolutions of risk would identify further the

147

synergy between justice in this context and identifiers of global governance (Findlay and Henham 2005). These would include (but not exhaustively):

- prevailing constitutional legality as a governance context;
- *supra-national* legislative power to construct governance frameworks;
- a set of rules and regulations for administering criminal liability and punishment which substantiate governance;
- a fabric of public and private policing for governance on the street;
- state monopoly over prosecution;
- power to appoint and authorise judges;
- executive responsibility for the nature and duration of penalty, all formal institutions of criminal justice governance;

It is not difficult to determine the separation of powers implicit in this structure which is said to confirm democratic government.

This too holds for the consideration of *para-justice* responses to crimes such as terrorism:

- prevailing authority to create and maintain alternative *legalities;*

- *supra-national* exclusion of both the perpetrators and the mechanisms for their containment beyond the conventional jurisdiction of the state;

- extraordinary rules and regulations for administering criminal liability and punishment, which in turn rely on complex discretionary delegations and largely anonymous activation;

- a process of investigation and policing which is covert, co-optive, compulsory and confrontational;[4]

- state monopoly over prosecution, and more importantly when to detain and punish without prosecution;

- power to sanction and penalise without the confirmation of judicial authority;

- enforceability through superior force and through the construction of control *technologies*, plus the clandestine application of terror against terror, torture against aggression;

- collapsing of military and quasi-judicial powers and the translation of perpetrators into combatants;

- executive responsibility for the nature and duration of penalty.

These features of competing governance draw closer to the *governance by violence* central to the terrorist enterprise.

Can crime control determine considerations of risk and security?

Garland (2001), as did Cohen (1985) before him, argues that community protection is now the dominant theme of penal policy. The risk here is unidirectional. Crime poses a threat to the security of the individual and the community, therefore the state is obliged to minimise that risk through control. The public supports this. On the other hand:

> In these matters (harsh state control interventions) the public appears to be (or is represented as) decidedly risk-averse, and intensely focused on the risk of depredation by unrestrained criminals. The risk of unrestrained state authorities, of arbitrary power and the violation of civil liberties seems no longer to figure prominently in public concern. (Garland 2001: 12)

Garland says more than that, new crime control developments have *adapted* and *responded* to the late modern world and to its political and cultural values. He advances these developments as 'creating that world, helping to constitute the meaning of late modernity' (p. 194). Along with managing problems of crime and insecurity, he argues, crime control 'institutionalises a set of responses to these problems that are themselves consequential in their social impact'.

Transposed to a global context and with the risk being terrorism and the control response being both violence and *justice* (Findlay: 2007c), strong messages for the managing of risk and the *taming of chance* travel through the new institutions of international criminal justice. These in turn lead on to an environment of international governance in which the citizen accepts restrictions of liberty which would have been intolerable in an era of globalisation outside this risk/security nexus, particularly when democracy was marketed as the ideology of modernisation. Now:

Spatial controls, situational controls, managerial controls, system controls, social controls, self-controls – in one realm after another, we now find the imposition of intensive regimes of regulation, inspection and control and, in the process, our civic culture becomes increasingly less tolerant and inclusive, increasingly less capable of trust. After a long-term process of expanding individual freedom and relaxing cultural and social restraints, control is now being re-emphasised in every area of social life – with the singular and startling exception of the economy, from whose deregulated domain most of today's major risks routinely emerge. (Garland 2001: 194–5)

Prophetically in the global context Garland identifies along with the rise of this partial concern for risk/security control agendas is the characteristic of reaction. A new sense of international disorder pervaded the close of the twentieth century and was accompanied by a renewed interest in global order and world governance. Crucial to governance and order internationally, as seen from the perspective of the dominant political hegemony, was addressing:

- dangerously inadequate controls;
- rapidly and violently emergent challenges to the control of that hegemony.

Initial responses were militaristic. But as is always the case, these were unsustainable. Criminal justice has been conscripted to take management of the control of global risk (Findlay and Henham 2005). Of course this is not an exclusive control responsibility, and more violent repression will always be on call in a climate of risk and security where the threat is erratic and incisive. However, international criminal justice is the attractive medium-term response because of its perceived potential to enhance the legitimacy of the dominant political hegemony.

Another important feature of the control profile internationally is the redefinition of 'community' and along with it notions of jurisdiction, citizenship and standing. Immersed in community is the potential both for legitimacy and resistance.

In a recent Australian context, the Federal government's policy on asylum seekers, the use of criminal justice to 'protect national boarders' and quarantine citizenship is a case in point. This initially was built on a denial of the discourse of political correctness which allowed for the re-emergence of racially based migration constructions.

Boat people became a threat to national integrity and when they were demonised as willing to sacrifice their children in illegal efforts at entry the Australian electorate got behind a party with tough policies which criminalised what later proved to be refugee determinations.

Multiculturalism was an associated victim of government policy which played the race card in the context of national security and international risk. Cultural integrity was degraded and dismissed as ethnic individualism. Particularly focused on Islamic communities and their failure to embrace *Australian values* it was not difficult to equate the threat beyond with the threat within. Whole communities became the target of crime and control identification because of their *otherness*, a difference which was synonymous with the cultural stereotyping of international terror. The crime was as much to be one in a culture or religion claimed by the terrorist rather than evidenced by real risks to security and real threats to sovereignty and citizenship. The application of crime and control to internal rather than international security concerns helped also to endorse exclusive and exclusionist notions of nationhood, citizenship and national identity readily compatible with Australia's place in the dominant political hegemony.

So too the *para-justice* processes employed in Guantanamo Bay have received a remarkably tolerant response from the conventional institutions of justice governance in the US, even if not so among its alliance partners (Meister 2004; Duffy 2005). Arguably this is due to what Garland identifies as a modification of citizenship and the liberties of the democratic state in the face of heightened risk and more problematic global security. Paradoxically we see para-justice compromising freedom for its protection (Clark 2002; Chemerinski 2005).

How do globalised crime priorities inform the political discourse of globalisation?

As mentioned previously, concepts of crime have traditionally relied on some cultural or jurisdictional situation for their relevance and impact. Implicit in this is the expectation that crime stops at national borders, or at least that it has localised interests.

It is the threat posed both by terrorism and organised crime motivating local jurisdictions to adopt international control agendas. Normally this would be resisted on the basis of the autonomy of criminal justice as a state domain even in the face of international crime threats (Findlay 1995). By concentrating on representations of organised crime and terrorism, as well as the state response through criminalisation, the local authorities have translated the international significance of crime threat to justify local interventions which may have little real impact within the jurisdiction concerned. It is an example of the impact of internationalism on localised/criminal justice policy.

The threat of global terrorism as a challenge to *legitimate* political ordering has stimulated the development of extraordinary control responses in a similar fashion to that in which organised crime justified extra-legal state reactions under threat (Findlay 1999b: ch. 5). Organised crime and their economies, enterprises and market manipulations were determined, throughout the last century, as challenging legitimate political and economic governance. Further, the application of violence and intimidation by organised crime in its control aspirations was said to require a response in kind by the state. With global terrorism today, the dominant political alliance emphasises the risk of terrorism to legitimate governance and its capacity to compromise the protections of conventional justice to its own ends. *Para-justice* paradigms are promoted in return and legitimated against the nature of the threat and its own methods of *governance*.

How does international criminal justice relate to global governance?

Predominant and prevailing notions of *truth* are essential in the struggle over the legitimacy of international governance. Dominant *reasoning* presupposes predominance over *truth* as a delineator of the government and the governed. ICJ, in its adversarial guise, may sacrifice the search for truth in preference for crime control, liability determination, law enforcement and punishment priorities.

Justice and governance issues depend on constituencies as well as jurisdiction. As argued earlier, international criminal justice and global governance have recognised the growing mandate and constituency of *victim communities*. This notion engages:

- individual victims;
- the communities of these victims which share their harm;
- where wider communities or groups of victims suffer harm;
- where the crime is directed at community cohesion or cultural integrity, and;

- when violence is motivated by the destruction of what makes communities or cultures (language, art, religion, family structure, etc.).

A justification for international criminal justice is crimes against humanity. In this sense *humanity* has a community or cultural location. Justice should reflect *humanitarian* concerns in its mandate to protect humanity. Such concerns are only partial, sectarian or selective in the way contemporary global governance views *humanity*. Anything outside the legitimate citizenship of the dominant hegemony tends to be removed from the protective ambit of its humanity. The excluded are worthy of destruction rather than protection. The followers receive the patronage so long as they ascribe to the dominant order.

The dominant hegemony in this climate of international terrorism (be it manifested in the genocide of Rwanda, the ethnic cleansing of the Balkans or the anticipated and illusive weapons of mass destruction in Iraq) has significantly transferred militaristic intervention at least in part to the jurisdiction of international criminal justice. This is a transition that carries with it expectations for global governance and the legitimation on which it depends. But in keeping with the agenda and exclusive instrumentation of this political alliance, the morphology of international criminal justice for this purpose is made reliant on common notions of the crimes against humanity, the legitimate victim communities and the appropriate retributive responses. This has in fact meant that the formal institutions of international criminal justice have presented limited pathways of access, exacerbated by professionally removed representation which in turn has not well integrated and connected with these communities. The consequence for global governance has been to limit the influence of international criminal justice in restoring post-conflict societies.

But it is not about victims and harm as it is not about governance outside of context. As international criminal justice transforms to better address the needs of victim communities, then its legitimacy, and its power to legitimate as a crucial component of global governance, will be enhanced.

It would be misleading to suggest, which I do not, that the governance/international criminal justice connection depended on the development of a global interest in the core crimes of genocide and crimes against humanity. For decades now, as EU directives on criminal justice harmonisation and UN conventions on corruption, money laundering and organised crime testify, regional and international penal regulation has been active in governance issues such as migration and market protection. What argues for a more focused interest in the transaction of core crimes as a pathway to governance is:

- the often pre-existing military incursions in the name of valorised victims;
- the consequential reliance on international trial justice in particular to exact victor's justice; and
- the transition to conflict resolution and peacemaking as aspirations for justice intervention.

The connection between international criminal justice and global governance is both symbolic and applied. I will leave symbolism aside for another day. In terms of its designated and located context in an age of global insecurity, the power of international criminal justice in global governance is in recuperating the tattered authority of the dominant hegemony as a consequence of military intervention. And at this level, the justice/governance link is reliant on and determined by the failings of the hegemony as much as the transformational strength and consistency of international criminal justice.

Crime, control and governance – the challenge for understanding international criminal justice

The nexus between international criminal justice and global governance is dependent on crime/risk and control/security considerations for world order. In critically analysing this relationship, its potential for conflict resolution and its problematic influences over legitimacy, it is important to avoid simple causal analysis. Good governance is not the incontrovertible consequence of a justice resolution in preference, say, to military intervention. Particular contextual conditions need examination in order that good governance can be anticipated from any selected governance model. In addition, the partiality of governance motivations which presently infiltrate the exercise of tribunal-based justice in particular requires critical analysis so that the recursive effects on international criminal justice might be countered.

Robert's (2005) *cultural assemblage* well covers the dominant political hegemony which is currently the master of international governance, at least at a formal/economic level. It has come together largely within projects of regional government. Its claims to the indicia of *government* are as yet fragile and primitive beyond military victory.

The international organisations said to house global governance, while representative, are without authority, if minus the support of this hegemony. The legislature, judicial institutions and executive bureaucracies emergent from these international organisations are dependent (particularly in resource terms) on this hegemony. The endorsement and protection of global citizenship currently resides with the hegemony, not in terms of democratic inclusion and representation, but rather through patronage.

Roberts rightly cautions against rewarding these negotiated orders with the established juridical, legal or jurisdictional order required of the nation-state.

> Today, under an onslaught of jural discourse and institutional design, the distinctive rationalities and values of negotiated order, while arguably deserving to be celebrated, are effectively effaced. (Roberts 2005: 1)

Globalisation invites the discussion of governance in terms such as law, justice and bureaucracy, without or above the state. For law at least this requires severance from a narrow notion of legislative jurisdiction. In the *war on terror* discourse there is an invocation to protect *civilisation* and *democracy* against violent assault. It is compatible with this celebration of preferred international political paradigms, to view law as *cosmology*. In this sense law and its institutions are engaged in the enterprise of 'imagining and articulating what we want the social world to be' (Roberts 2005: 6). Law in governance in this sense links the discursive formulation of rules and process to an articulation of preferred world order.

Law as cosmology is also supportive of governance through 'leaders and followers' which goes well beyond the inclusive occupation and responsibilities of democracy. While democracy is celebrated as worthy of protection by the dominant international hegemony, its aspirations to global governance are not democratic but oligarchic. Justice within this oligarchy tends to be institutionalised, formal, non-accountable and professionalised. It is thereby consistent with and supportive of oligarchic governance.

If globalisation even in an age of risk and security retains a commitment towards a single culture (Findlay 1999b), the preferred justice is exclusive and not pluralist in its authority, coverage or outreach. Justice also tends to legitimate oligarchic governance rather than to seek legitimacy from it. This is because the trajectory of international criminal justice (even if not its procedures) is towards a concern for humanity and its communities of victims. This then becomes another ground on which the dominant political hegemony claims the legitimacy of its constituency and their patronage.

This trajectory sees an intersection between the conventional and the *para*-justice paradigms for the advancement of hegemonic interests. Interestingly, common claims for the predominance of security as the framework of governance justify conventional and *para*-justice responses. Where the paradigms depart is around the procedural conditions for justice outcomes, particularly those which are said to give international criminal justice its force in state reconstruction and peacemaking (Findlay and Henham 2005: ch. 8).

Presumptuous as it may seem in fact, the dominant political hegemony has represented its version of global order as legal order, and this is supported by a crude but emergent general jurisprudence.[5] The jurisprudence of international criminal law has a particular place in international governance when compared with other fields of international law. For instance, international commercial law sees courts with national legal orders applying commercial conventions originating at a supranational level. International criminal law has in contrast developed for itself a tribunal/court structure which requires the determination of state authority. The negotiated order which will be the province of the International Criminal Court will act as law at least for subscribing states, and will operate across a ceded international jurisdiction. A globalised legal order managing criminal justice is not simply taken for granted. As with states and their jurisdiction, international criminal justice and its institutions become indicia of governance (local, regional or international).

I argue that Foucault's observation on law's decreasing capacity to code power, to serve as its system of representation, does not hold for international criminal justice and its jurisprudence. The reasons for this I have suggested are uniquely contextual and inextricable within the new globalisation and a very particular enterprise of global governance. This is much more than what Robert's explains as the extended space claimed by jural discourse and institutional forms (Roberts 2005: 24). International criminal justice is now incorporated into the *reasoning* of global governance, I would assert, much more than Simon gives it credit at a state level as metaphor.

In the context of a security/risk nexus the *reasoning* of contemporary governance is created recursively. A formative and fragile institutional hegemony legitimises globalised forms of *truth* through control mechanisms specifically designed to minimise threats to is authority. Hence, although *liberal* arguments trumpet justice as an integral element of the democratic credo (and thereby through their application internationally as indicia of global governance), the reverse seems to represent reality. Bilateral intimidation, regional coercion and military incursion are the preferred international relations.

The reduction of risk (in whosesoever's name) is accompanied by a reduction in civil liberties, a denial of plurality and a marginalisation of civil society. Individual autonomy, so central to the normative politics of the dominant hegemony and its idealised *community,* is subjugated through the sacrifices required to maintain *civilisation* and *humanity.*

Conclusion

At this point the analysis of global governance need not leave concerns over metaphor. However, in a very practical sense, globalised crime problems and control responses (as with international terrorism) are far from metaphoric. In practice, the risk/security regulatory strategies directed against global terror regularly disconnect justice from governance and governance from the diverse global community.

The secularisation of international criminal justice has lead to the emphasis on formal retributive paradigms to resolve conflict and the abandonment of reason to fear on a globalised scale. This may be as much due to fragile and transitional frameworks of global governance, as it is a consequence of the failure to find a universal belief system to underpin globalised forms of justice. Dominant political hegemony provides an ideological substitute for that commonly held morality, so the institutional control of behaviours which threaten the hegemony are justified in amoral terms – terms which do not rely on any notion of a shared reason, shared experience or shared value system. In this sense, international criminal justice as the theatre in which the crime/risk-control/security nexus is tested has been profoundly compromised.

Currently ICJ is a justice largely unconfirmed by universal moralities. As such, it retains limited legitimacy, and its potential to legitimate wider global governance and conflict resolution, while present, will continue to have limited sweep.

Risk and security as threats and needs are procured to essentially justify harsh and intrusive regulatory strategies. The only morally coherent basis for global governance being partial and political is hence a reactive denunciation of those who challenge the hegemony. For instance, in order to justify an extreme punishment response, the violence and violent potential of terrorism is highlighted. However, a moral assessment of terrorism in terms of *mindless* violence is implicated by consequent excessive violence of punishment (Chapter 5). This is particularly so where this victimises otherwise innocent but resistant communities in a *law of war* scenario. In addition, an arguably *mindlessness* in response challenges the deterrent impact of violent punishment, which is offered as the very reason for requiring violent punishment (Braithwaite 2005).

If they are to stand alongside recognised indicia of governance and claim a more long-lasting legitimation, the *new drivers* for globalised justice should represent a renewal of humanistic principles as they find expression in what we have referred to elsewhere as *communities of justice* (Findlay and Henham 2005; ch. 7; also Chapter 7, this volume). To sustain and complement these communities, the foundations for international criminal justice need to rediscover the deeper and more grounded rationality for penality as it is expressed in a more common and perennial justice morality (see Introduction).

In this way the *contexts of regulation* within the globalisation project (see Chapter 9) will be more convincingly identifiable as coherent and resilient value systems essential to (and more tolerant of) relative forms of human existence. Partial and hegemonic justice will be replaced as the influence it now represents in global governance. The metaphor of just governance will have prospects for reality. A natural consequence of this transition will be the diminution of the risk/security imperative, leaving international criminal justice to offer a more accessible, heuristic and normatively convincing role in global governance and conflict resolution.

Notes

1 President Johnson's Safe Streets Act.
2 Due to the constraints on this chapter there is not space here to fully argue the nature of this hegemony or to appropriately problematise its entity and significance. Against the war on terror metaphor (post 9/11) and accepting the place of Western 'liberalism' behind the modernising era of globalisation, this hegemony is equated with the loose (and often unwilling) coalition supporting the US Iraqi intervention.
3 As with *para-politics*, the concept of para-justice has no definitional certainty. Here we are employing the notion to encapsulate those control responses which follow on from proscribed behaviours which in other circumstances might be processed through conventional criminal justice. Violence, intimidation and a denial of due process are characteristic of

para-justice. Rather than being dismissed as institutional injustice *para-justice* makes claims for institutional and process credibility through the determinations of military tribunals in particular, and justifies excessive responses through the necessities of war.

4 For a discussion of these *styles of policing* see Findlay and Zvekic (1993: ch. 2).

5 Claims for the existence and operation of international criminal law are consistent with this.

Chapter 7

Tensions between globalised governance and internationalised justice

And in the Guantanamo Bay case (*Rasul*) the US Government argued that the courts had no jurisdiction because the United States had no sovereignty over Guantanamo Bay (even though a treaty gives it control in perpetuity). Guantanamo Bay might as well have been Afghanistan or, for that matter, the moon. That is why a lot of observers characterised Guantanamo Bay as a 'black hole' ... an area where the force of darkness is so strong that everything collapses – light, gravity and federal court jurisdiction. (Meister 2004: 7)

Introduction

How will international criminal justice emerge as a power in global governance while it remains captured by security imperatives? What is it about alternative justice developments that could challenge the notion of risk societies and reassert the importance of victim communities (both citizens and the exiled)? Can *communities of threat* be transformed into *communities of justice*?

This chapter starts out by discussing some of the contextual realities that challenge both international criminal justice and global governance. The characteristics identified are talked of as tensions, tensions that arise out of the:

- oppressive overemphasis on security;
- predominance of violence on both sides of justice resolutions;

- unbalanced evaluation of risk;
- contradictions inherent in domestic autonomy and internationalism;
- evolution of communitarian constituencies;
- mandate for humanity;
- pressures caused within justice service delivery (formal or less formal) as it is employed for conflict resolution and peacemaking.

However, the analysis does not remain stuck in specific tensions or even strategies for their resolution. Rather it develops into an argument for a communitarian justice model as an affective foundation for global governance. To do this it is necessary to first confront the hard issues: crime, security and violence, and to locate global governance.

Who governs globally?

'The United States and Great Britain share common values and an obligation to work for freedom and justice around the world', President Bush stated (July 2007), in a joint news conference with British Prime Minister Gordon Brown at Camp David. 'After all, we're writing the initial chapters of what I believe is a great ideological struggle between those of us who do believe in freedom and justice and human rights and human dignity and cold-blooded killers who will kill innocent people to achieve their objectives', Bush said. Both men said they will continue to work together closely. Bush thanked Brown for Britain's continued support in Afghanistan and Iraq. 'Success in Afghanistan and Iraq will be an integral part of defeating an enemy and helping people realise the great blessings of liberty as the alternative to an ideology of darkness that spreads its murder to achieve its objectives', he said. 'Terrorism is not a cause, it is a crime, and it is a crime against humanity', said Brown, on his first visit to the United States as prime minister.

'And there should be no safe haven and no hiding place for those who practise terrorist violence or preach terrorist extremism'. Brown said the British have duties and responsibilities in Iraq to support the democratically elected government. ... Brown called Afghanistan the front line against terrorism and said the United Kingdom has added to its commitment in the country ... Bush stressed the commonality of purpose between the two leaders on Iraq.

'There's no doubt in my mind that Gordon Brown understands that failure in Iraq would be a disaster for the security of our own countries, that failure in Iraq would embolden extremist movements throughout the Middle East, that failure in Iraq would basically say to people sitting on the fence around the region that al Qaeda is powerful enough to drive great countries like Great Britain and America out of Iraq before the mission is done', he said. The President said Brown understands that failure in Iraq would spread violence across the Middle East, and that a country like Iran would become emboldened. 'The Western world is in a generation-long battle against al Qaeda-inspired terrorism, and there is no negotiating with terrorists', Brown said. 'The battle must include military, diplomatic, intelligence, security, policing and ideological terms. So we are at one in fighting the battle against terrorism, and that struggle is one that we will fight with determination and with resilience and right across the world', he said.[1]

The *war on terror* has no borders. The fight is between the 'great countries', and the enemies of freedom and liberty. The Western world is at war for the next generation under the command of the leaders of the *light*. Cultural dominion and survival are at stake. Failure in the military mission is anticipated not only to endanger the theatres of war but also to embolden the enemy into new fronts of attack.

This recent exchange between the two leaders of the dominant world political alliance is much more than propaganda. It reveals the foundational belief that they (and perhaps they alone) are responsible for ensuring and protecting global democracy and freedom using much more than military means. It is for them a life and death struggle in which they are engaged, a struggle at a crucial turning point. To lose the war at this point, we are told, would endanger domestic security, invigorate a violent enemy and leave the world on the brink of a new dark age.

Despite the suggestion that the *war on terror* might be progressed through diplomatic, policing and ideological means, the alliance sees its enemy as outside dialogue, beyond reason and without the legitimacy of a rational cause. The evil alter-hero neither knows nor respects any response but violence. A control conclusion so constrained excludes the capacity of representative, conciliatory and even democratic international organisations to achieve peace without first forcing submission. That force, as a first resort of global governance strategies, is the province of the dominant global alliance.

The answer to who governs the globe remains today as fractured and contingent as it was when Batman and Marvel Comics imagined world domination as the battle for superheroes and supervillains. Perhaps little has changed in contemporary international relations since the struggles for Gotham City. The leaders of the dominant political alliance use much the same language as the superheroes of Marvel fame, and seem to share similar views of the ever present threat and their singular responsibility for its aversion.

As in the world of the Marvel Comic, the leaders of the dominant alliance regularly reject the relevance of conventional justice responses and the potential of conventional governance institutions to manage the threat. In fact they deride the incapacity, indecision and incompetence of this regulatory framework and its personalities. For instance, the attitude of the US and its coalition, to the UN and its sanctions prior to the unilateral invasion of Iraq was a real Marvel moment.

The comic analogy does not stop with the celebration of violence as justice for good governance. The nature of the threat posed and the necessity for violent reaction from the forces of good is simplified so as to suggest that 'an eye for an eye' is the appropriate criminal justice governance paradigm. Even so, when the villain is disarmed, and the danger to the world for the present contained, then police, courts and prisons are returned to, so that the conventional justice rituals and routines can legitimate the violent and unilateral superhero. Comparisons with the introduction of international criminal justice following the military intervention of the alliance are more than coincidental.

The Marvel Comic governance structures operating in the world of Gotham City parallel what can be said for prevailing global governance. There is a weak and vulnerable constitutional instrumentality which, either due to administrative incapacity or internal division, is unable to protect a vulnerable population without the supernatural injection of superhero violence. The United Nations is that representative authority in global governance, forced to accept and accede to the unilateralist military intervention of a Western superpower alliance claiming to act for an endangered and otherwise at risk global community.

Economic governance is more universal and inclusive among developed nations of different political but common commercial persuasions. World financial agencies, some structured in a representative or accountable fashion, mainly advance modernisation. These institutions are as aggressive in their intrusions into developing economies (and thereby state integrity) as is the dominant political alliance when confronting contesting governance traditions.

It might be argued that the growing influence of the NGO sector is a break within global governance from compromised representative bodies or aggressive political and economic alliances. However, a close interrogation of those NGOs with greatest influence over global regulatory strategies reveals specialist, single-issue governance engagement or suspect alliances with political and economic ideologies.

Global governance is polyglot. The preferred political ideology is enforced by the dominant Western alliance. The free market economy and modernisation is regulated by the developed economies. Representative international bodies develop international legal, environmental and human rights frameworks which need domestic legal endorsement. Regional economic confederations are emerging as important counterbalances to internationalism. NGOs offer governance checks on an issues-based agenda. Grassroots movements fill the hiatus of failing state governance. Peacemaking and conflict resolution is open to restorative justice. ICJ offers a legitimating function to a range of other regulatory strategies. There is no unequivocal or settled normative framework for global governance. Both the nature and the substance of global governance are strained as a consequence of challenges to and reassertions of cultural dominion.

Tensions between globalised crime and international criminal justice

In a recent speech to the University of Sydney the ICC Prosecutor Luis Moreno Ocampo set out his strategy for selecting crimes and alleged offenders in the court's first set of indictments. The Prosecutor is focusing on a small group of incidents and a limited number of individual offenders who are charged with committing specific crimes against humanity. The strategy targets crimes representative of much larger conflicts and possible genocide, where national courts and authorities are unable or willing to intervene. It is a strategy to protect especially vulnerable victims (such as child soldiers and innocent community 'cleansing'). It is a strategy dedicated to prosecutorial success and to retributive justice. While the Prosecutor seems intensely committed to victim communities, such as the 1.3 million refugees in northern Uganda, he sees the work of the ICC as first being in the interests of justice and not the interests of peace. Perhaps this is a very fine distinction for lawyers to debate.

The most obvious tension between globalised crime and ICJ is the form required for crime to merit international justice intervention. For the justice institutions in particular only a limited and proscribed selection of crimes can be prosecuted through the international criminal tribunals and the ICC.[2] The reasons for this are easily discovered in the diplomatic conferences and resultant statutory instruments which authorised these judicial institutions (see Chapter 5). It was all an intricate process of compromise. Those state parties which had much to risk in exposing their military adventurism to the critical eye of an independent prosecutor or challenge from enemy states argued to protect their citizens (see Chapter 8). The price is a problematic range of global crimes.

An example is the current position with crimes of aggression. During the Rome Conference negotiations, the issue was largely divided between those representatives arguing against its availability and those wanting the ICC jurisdiction to cover this abuse of power (Bikundo, forthcoming).

The opposition against crimes of aggression centred on:

- the argument that it is impossible to adequately define this crime type in order to enable consistent prosecution;
- a strong view that crimes of aggression should only be prosecuted within the domestic jurisdiction where it is alleged the crime occurred; and
- those who felt that the consequences of aggression were effectively picked up through other available crime types.

The compromise was for the conference to hold that crimes of aggression were legitimately within the jurisdiction of the ICC, but to defer the time at which the crime would be defined by the court, and the ICC would take up that jurisdiction (in 2009). It seems a strange argument over the nicety of jurisdiction, autonomy and political compromise. Put it to the man in the street that the ICC would not be concerned with crimes of aggression and they would likely doubt the sincerity of the system to protect humanity.

When paralleled with the *war on terror* the ambivalence of member states over crimes of aggression seems difficult to reconcile. Crimes of aggression are commonly little more than state-initiated or sponsored terror. As terrorism, aggression might be expected to be treated by the dominant alliance with military intervention, aggressive prosecution and calls for universal condemnation. Not so! The reason could be that for crimes of aggression (different to terrorism) the essential interests of the dominant alliance partners and their geopolitical favourites could be challenged by relative interpretations of aggression. By contrast, the terrorist enemy is uncontested in the West. Ascription to the *war on terror* is a precondition for civilised inclusion in Western peacemaking and liberty.

Crimes of aggression are not distinguished in terms of harm alone. Identifying aggressors in conflict is often politically contentious. Victims, on both sides of the conflict as a consequence, are not so easily valorised.

Perhaps the distinguishing feature for regulating crimes of aggression against crimes of terror is the political and ideological gain in criminalising terrorism and the risks in so doing with aggression.

The discussion of tensions in global governance to follow will not remain formalist, tied to questions like what crimes should ICJ be concerned with, why and why not. To more usefully understand how ICJ and governance combine is to move outside the legislative limitations of formal ICJ empowerment and to search for the themes in governance which are compatible (or otherwise) with criminal justice as a regulative framework. Tensions will emerge from normative considerations such as crimes against humanity and their translation into justice processes. Of deeper impact on the thesis that ICJ is now central to global governance, however, are the tensions around the struggle to achieve common aspirations, where justice and governance are grounded in different regulatory traditions.

Tensions over security, development and justice

In their chapter 'Security through international citizenship' Rees and Blanchard (1999) chart the problems associated with an international citizenship model for advocating global security. The assumption is that inclusion through citizenship will advance security by neutralising the risk posed by elitism or civic alienation. The rights protections which accompany citizenship may promote an alliance between the citizen and the state to minimise risk and address security.

However, along with citizen inclusion comes the social exclusion of those without civic standing. Such exclusion provides an oppositional framework for violent contest. Social exclusion over citizenship also has the tendency to focus antipathy on the mechanisms of the state which award or deny citizenship. The citizenship model for ensuring security passes over the vagaries of global citizenship residing within contested and fluid frameworks of global governance and as yet uncertain structures of rights protection.

An additional difficulty when ICJ is invoked to shore up the security of global citizenship is that when terror contests citizenship and standing, then 'justice' responses all too often employ terror to re-establish security (Posner 2002). As a consequence, good governance in a liberal democratic sense is directly undermined.

Security is the motivation for crime control in the locations of global governance. In this sense security has domestic, regional and international implications and these may not always be compatible. In fact, a potent strategy of domestic governance through crime control is where state administrations externalise the threat of terror in order to sensitise citizen communities. The fear of the terror from *the other*, as Simon identifies for the US (2007), has become crucial when regulating citizens in domestic governance. As such it is not surprising that crime/fear/risk and security progression would be exported and resorted to when global order is negotiated by the dominant political authority.

Security is the key to this progression. What then is security? For the purposes of this analysis it includes safety from terror and the fear of terror. Far from a simple aspiration, however, it is the violence that terror demonstrates or threatens which registers locally and globally as the central challenge to security. Yet a central tension posed by security strategies which employ violence and terror against violence and terror is the spiraling consequences of recipient violence and insecurity (Turk 1982).

In this age of globalisation, the threat of global terrorism validates security as a higher priority than liberty (Feldman 2006). Politicians rather than lawyers or judges have claimed the capacity to assess the risk posed to security by terror, and therefore legal regulatory models are considered to serve the political imperative for security (Cassese 1996). While criminal justice responses to outrages such as 9/11 gained prominence as the threat posed sank deeper into the public consciousness, military reaction to protect public health and safety was accepted as appropriate and affective (Posner 2002). The lawful use of force advanced through military and justice intervention raised violence against violence to a level not seen for decades in the experience of criminal justice control.

The coexistence of security and aggressive political intervention has featured in the colonial, mercantile and industrial phases of globalisation. During the Cold War period that followed the carve-up of Europe post 1945, economic and social modernisation were specifically financed with security in mind. The US made it clear that the Marshall Plan for state reconstruction was aimed at the containment of governments and groupings in Europe that might threaten the security interests of the United States. When the OECD replaced the Organisation for European Cooperation in 1961, the US and Canada joined up and transformed the organisation into a vehicle for distributing aid from North America and Europe to promote security and development in the Third World. US postwar development aid to Taiwan, Japan and South Korea was to provide capitalist bulwarks against the USSR and Communist China. In South Korea and Vietnam alliance military intervention followed the failure of modernisation and development initiatives designed to fill security gaps left by the retreat of European colonial powers. Latin America, sub-Saharan Africa and the Asian subcontinent were all recipients of massive Western aid and development injections designed to promote governance and security regimes complementing Western security agendas. As with the current war on terror, much of this *aid-for-security* international relations fortified the resistance groups against which it was directed. Cold War economic and diplomatic patronage (from the USA and the USSR) intensified global divisions that brought the world to the brink of further conflagration before the collapse of the Soviet Union and the consequent world reordering.

There is much value in a recent historical analysis of the nexus between development and security in the context of global modernisation. As I explained in my discussion of modernisation and transitional cultures (Findlay 1999b), in order for the developing world to reap the benefits of modernisation, aid donors and world financial agencies sought cultural as well as economic transformation. Added to this in the current phase of globalisation is the requirement that benefiting states need to cooperate in the *war on terror* and its security imperatives. Failure to sign up not only endangers aid delivery and assistance in modernisation, but exclusion from technological, economic and material interaction with the rich world.

The wider enmeshing of security and development in contemporary international relations has meant that humanitarian prioritisation of aid delivery complements social engineering for security purposes. This resembles the decade-long programme of land and economic reform promoted by the US through the Alliance for Progress. Therein agricultural underproduction, illiteracy, poor housing, substandard health and weak trading were attacked so that the foundations of political revolution might be neutralised. Berger (forthcoming) suggests that the connection between aid development and security priorities led to 'the rise and fall of classic dependency theory'. In its simple form, dependency theory asserts that capitalism produced the underdevelopment racking the Third World, and capitalist aid programmes (focused on modernisation and economic transformation) exacerbate dependencies. In the late 1970s and with the rise of neo-liberalism as a prevailing global political dogma, the authoritarianism and corruption of Third World states were blamed for underdevelopment and regional insecurity. This was accompanied by efforts from the West to politically incorporate the third world states into the dominant liberal capitalist narrative on development and security (Evans 1979). The language of dependency at least was replaced by the aspiration for an economically homogeneous Third World, and there from an incorporated global security project.

Also in the late 1970s, the UN launched a call for a New International Economic Order. This was accompanied by a shift in the West away from Cold War divisions towards the incorporation of North/South relations. The administration of President Carter in the US nominated US relations with Japan and Western Europe as the 'strategic hard core for both global stability and progress' (Brzezinski 1983: 289). This was the introduction, through Carter's Trilateral Commission, of a cohesive and semi-permanent alliance of the world's main capitalist states and economies in order to promote global stability and order for mutual self-interest. It contained the seeds of the Group of Eight which now protects and governs the security of the global economy.

By the end of the 1970s the Brandt Commission and its *North-South Report* (1980), provided a blueprint for the world's major industrial nations to manage the development of the Third World through piecemeal reforms, employing socio-economic development for security purposes. The international financial agencies were drafted into the mission. The World Bank, confronted with an international recession in the 1980s, started work on debt relief to protect the global economy. Consistent with neo-liberalism the Bank declared that underdevelopment and consequent insecurity were caused by excessive state involvement in the economy. The socialist states of Eastern Europe (and along with them the Cold War) were imploding as proof of the argument. The predominant influence of global financial agencies in governing development and security in the late twentieth century had the additional consequence of weakening the UN and its broader development agencies like the UNDP and UNCTAD in which the Third World had obtained an influential representative voice.

In the post-9/11 era the nexus between development and security has taken on particular significance, with a revitalisation of state and alliance security initiatives. Demonstrative of this has been the interaction of:

- military intervention, capacity building and protectionism;
- conflict resolution (through criminal justice and more localised initiatives);
- social reconstruction;
- foreign aid and development policies, bilateral and regional in particular; and
- selective cultural isolation.

A parallel development can be seen in the international NGO sector where governance themes such as anti-corruption and transitional justice have influentially complemented nation-state and alliance initiatives. The UN, through the successful construction of international conventions concerning transnational crime and corruption, has claimed more purchase over governance through crime minimisation and security enhancement. The private sector and commercial security providers in particular have also entered the mix with a greater involvement in national and transnational policing and military services, even including the protection of humanitarian space.

The Clinton presidency advocated an international relations shift from 'containment to enlargement' (Lake 1993).

> Clinton advised that his administration's main goal was not just to 'secure the peace won in the Cold War' but to strengthen the country's 'national security' by 'enlarging the community of market democracies' (OPUS 1996) ... Like the Bush administration, Clinton remained focused on the major powers ... (Berger, forthcoming)

In the George W. Bush administration attention turned to the significance of nation-building. Failing or failed states were propped up and reconfigured in the name of security, provided they conceded to a neo-liberal development and restructuring agenda. Despite the celebrations attendant on the fall of the Soviet Union, and the military commitment to regime change in Iraq, it was the breakdown of viable and compliant nation-states rather than failings in the modernisation project that was held to challenge security. However, crucial issues of history, identity and culture, which have fomented violence and revolution for centuries, have been passed over in this political age of technological and force-based state building (Fukyama 2006).

Crime, justice and state reconstruction

Transitional justice argues that the generation and growth of justice mechanisms in post-conflict states is the way forward for state reconstruction. However, Cockayne (2004) critiques transitional justice through the example of Australia's radical governance interventions in the Solomon Islands. Territorial sovereignty was overridden there, carrying the hope that imported governance mechanisms would generate stronger grassroots governance in that *failing state*. In practice, the political agendas and power dynamics governing these interventions are working against domestic governance empowerment. Even within the transitional justice paradigm Cockayne suggests that attempts to create, build and sustain post-conflict states through the incursion of dominant Western cultures, is inherently ethnocentric and as such unable to deeply ground advocated governance styles.

The problem lies not only with the cultural partiality of this imperial approach to governance capacity building. It also rises out of profound ambiguities regarding the place of law and legal regulation within indigenous and sometimes ungoverned conflict resolution styles. As with colonial regimes and postcolonial nation-building the relationship between introduced and customary law is a tense and dynamic one. Cultures such as those in the Pacific, where custom remains the foundation for social control and introduced governance styles rarely travel beyond the urban centres, demonstrate regulatory frameworks resilient against international influence (Findlay 2002a).

Rather than what Cockayne quips as the 'add the rule of law and stir' approach of transitional justice to bottom-up state reconstruction, he rightly identifies the need to recognise and respond to underlying economic inequalities in any justice-led governance strategy. Grassroots governance in the present age of globalisation needs the opportunities offered through modernisation to complement the resilience of cultural adaptation.

I concur with Cockayne's advocacy of *transformational* rather than *transitional* justice as a way to conflict resolution, respecting the problem that normative governance strategies have the potential to exacerbate (or at least ignore) underlying socio-economic inequities. In rebuilding the institutions for rule enforcement by relying on imported procedural justice (Findlay 1999b), governance strategies are in danger of derailing indigenous conflict-resolution initiatives more generally. Justice institutions and processes will only maximise their good governance capacity in a custom context when they have transformed to include legitimate victim interests in the widest sense (Findlay and Henham 2005). And to avoid the criticism that alternative justice options often compromise victim rights protection, the transformation of governance through justice should focus on victim access, inclusion and integration. The capacity for the ICC chamber to recognise the voice of the victim is a step in the right direction, even though the Prosecutor admits it to be a procedural challenge perhaps that will be managed chamber to chamber.

Justice, and consequently governance in the transformed condition considered here, can rebalance and rejuvenate community relations strained through victimisation. As detailed in the previous section, political power structures, development and economic opportunities which remain compromised in governance strategies more focused on state reconstruction than community regeneration need to be recognised as a crucial challenge to the fairness inherent in transformed justice and governance (Findlay and Henham 2005). This is a vital issue for transitional cultures struggling to make sense of state structures and instrumentalities which fail to support and complement their customary regulatory frameworks.

The growing number of nation-states which have failed to meet the promise of modernisation and development never equitably received that promise or were unable to make the nation-state system work to fairly embrace its benefit. These *failed states* are viewed by the dominant Western alliance as a growing challenge to domestic and international security. Such a myopic approach to international relations reveals the self-interested motivations behind development aid delivery from national, regional, alliance and international agencies. It fails to appreciate the serious strains that the Western state model has imposed on indigenous cultures (Dinnen and Ley 2000). It ignores the destructive and criminogenic consequences of modernisation (Findlay 1999b). It identifies external and culturally insensitive measures of healthy governance as the triggers for intervention and state reordering (see Chapter 3). The *pillars of good governance* approach heavily marketed in developing countries by the super-NGO Transparency International exhibits just this failing. This approach to governance also nominates the security of dominant cultures and economies as negotiating and superseding social and cultural harmony in states in transition (Findlay 1999b).

State failure and the consequent security challenge have given rise to a wide range of development strategies with at the same time a distinctly monolithic response to their security ramifications. In the present phase of globalisation state failure or weakness is not answered for itself through cultural enhancement, capacity building or economic reconstruction, designed to address the local conditions under strain. Following the Cold War, a pluralistic approach to governance gave way to a *one-size-fits-all* exportation of democratic institutions intended to protect and promote the ideal of free market economics. The parallels with European colonisation which first introduced the state to stateless cultures are clear. The expectation is that success in the free market and democracy brings with it security and the rewards of modernisation. Only on those strategically positioned failed states (often resource-rich or geopolitically prized) will military and infrastructure development be lavished despite not meeting the global governance scores. Hypocrisy is rampant in the international treatment of different states for similar human rights abuses. For some states, forgiveness and trust in change abounds. Otherwise it is regime change or intrusions into territorial and cultural sovereignty that rival the colonial phase of globalisation.

The significance of the nation-state and its security can be linked back specifically to considerations of global security. State-centred terrorism, while internationally significant, is more likely to be caught up in the contemporary manifestations of international relations in terms of whether the state itself remains a viable governance mechanism. Resource-rich and geopolitically significant nation-states will be tolerated by the dominant political alliance even when they practise terror over their citizens or their less significant neighbours. It is those states which are determined as rogue that will have even their own democratic determinations labelled as terrorist or illegitimate. The accession to government by Hamas in the Palestinian Authority is a case in point. Once the new governance authority was determined by the West as primarily terrorist, democratically elected or not, the war on terror invective was returned to, enabling overriding regional and hegemonic governance to be reasserted through sanction or violent intervention. War is often the result as seen in Lebanon, the West Bank and the Balkans.

The contemporary technologies of terror have destabilised accepted frameworks for waging war. In response, the dominant political alliance has moved away from a *mutuality of interest* governance model for the *war on terror*. The current preference is to distinguish between *legitimate* and *illegitimate* violence, *justifiable* or *unjustified*, *licit* or *illicit*. International criminal justice is incorporated into violent and non-violent regulatory strategies. Its coalition with political, military and economic governance imperatives tends to challenge the role of justice within domestic models of separated powers (Phelan 2003; Clark 2002). In addition, the incorporation of criminal justice within a deeply politicised regulatory framework shows up its inadequacies for more partial and sectarian governance aspirations (Stenson 2001). The legitimacy of ICJ as an independent regulatory model, particularly in transitional and contested states, suffers as a result.

Inadequacies of justice in global governance – communities of justice

In describing the recent reconstruction of the Balkans, Johnson (2005) critiques ICJ and forms of global governance as insufficient. By not giving detailed consideration to the pre-existent domestic and regional forms of control while endeavouring to replace governance through military intervention with war crimes adjudication, ICJ is likely to leave dormant and resentful those fundamental social and cultural divisions which are the outcomes of genocide and state disintegration. The prevailing governance project of restoring peace and at the same time marketing a distinctly Westernised ideal of order has regularly compromised (for local communities) the institutions and processes of criminal justice complicit in that project.

> The West has offered a template for reconstruction in the Balkans that bestows legitimacy on the post conflict governments of the region in proportion to their ability to comply with the liberal values of regional and European integration, development and good governance institutions and commitment to economic liberalisation. (Johnson 2005: 190)

And it is not only the formal institutions of ICJ in association with global governance that come in for criticism. Reflecting on the example of post-communist Hungary, Kiss (2006) notes that various types of transitional justice were employed in order to reconcile the old and the new regimes. He holds the enterprise ultimately unsuccessful. The reasoning for this conclusion is that in Hungary transitional justice was applied primarily for political manipulation. In particular, retroactive legislation and screening based on secret police files to target and transact past criminality are seen as illegitimate and potentially destabilising methods for community reconciliation. There always is the risk of irrelevance at best when the aspirations of the political elite for justice and governance fail to resonate with the legitimate priorities of victim communities.

The communitarian location of ICJ is crucial to its legitimacy. More than with domestic criminal justice, I would argue, the challenge is for all forms of ICJ to engage both with victim communities and communities of resistance as a central mandate and more equitable and universal jurisdiction. I say this because the crime focus for international criminal justice is genocide, and its protective function is for 'humanity'. The collective and communitarian direction of ICJ is clearly set through the crimes it must prioritise. If, in addition to its restorative role, ICJ is to promote peacekeeping and conflict resolution,[3] then access, inclusion and interaction considerations must rate highly in its service delivery. Victim communities thereby become the first concern. If these victim communities are to reflect *humanity* then those communities which resist criminalisation or give comfort to perpetrators may not be excised from justice on offer. For the prosecution of crimes against humanity it is justice for all.

The main challenge for ICJ as it presently operates (formally or less formally) is to establish and maintain a wide and lasting foundation for legitimacy. The importance of respect and consensus above force and compulsion for any system of criminal justice means that legitimacy which generates consensus is a valuable if fragile prize.

The legitimacy of ICJ is selective and currently contested because of the:

- politicisation of ICJ authority and practice;
- restricted engagement with victim and resistant communities;
- professionalisation of formal justice delivery and the tensions inherent in its varied procedural traditions;
- lack of satisfaction for legitimate victim interests beyond retribution and truth-telling;
- selective availability and application of rights protections to stakeholders depending on the level of ICJ with which they engage; and overall the
- confusion prevailing around who ICJ is meant to serve.

In earlier analysis (Findlay and Henham 2005), we suggest that transforming ICJ into a more communitarian governance arena is crucial to its legitimacy and the legitimacy it offers to global governance at large. The communitarian foundation might better be conceived as *communities of justice.* This conception harks back to the new normative framework for ICJ which I foreshadowed in the introduction to this book, a framework committed to humanity.

Communities of justice as both the essential constituency and the operational domain for ICJ will depend on access, inclusivity and integration at all levels of criminal justice service delivery. This injunction is not limited to victim communities and their rights or to the protection of perpetrators. It should, by the nature of *communities of justice*, be open to the exile, the non-citizen and the community which might otherwise resist determinations of liability. This is the wider challenge for ICJ to engage with victim communities across the divide of individual criminal liability.

It could be argued that this aspiration is impossible to ground in a system where adversarial determinations predominate, at least in the formal institutions and processes of justice. This is so. However, the transformation of ICJ which we have argued for and will detail in the future (Henham and Findlay, forthcoming) moves on from the adversarial model. The importance of truth-telling, mediation (discussed in the next chapter), reconciliation and dispute resolution holds out possibilities wherein oppositional communities can work through a justice dialogue. The adversarial division and the pressure to allocate liability in retributive justice may present a benefit for innocent victim communities, but it tends to further segregate resistant communities that also have legitimate claims in just and fair conflict resolution.

Problematic constituencies – victim communities

The Chief Prosecutor for the ICC recognises the importance of the victim voice in ICJ. In so doing, Dr Moreno Ocampo has declared that victim communities, with which the court has a crucial interest, may deserve justice and compensation. How this is to be achieved within the formalist institutions of the ICC (as presently constituted) and in the environment of retributive justice is a challenge which the Prosecutor recognises.[4]

Therefore *victim's justice* will provoke tensions within the delivery of international criminal justice services and on to global governance. Since the late 1800s in Western justice processes, the state has gradually assumed a monopoly over the prosecution of criminal offences. This monopoly has transferred with little question through victorious military alliances and representative international organisation into ICJ, despite the ambiguity of state authority in global governance. Victim interests, in a community context in particular, face the danger of marginalisation within the wider play of retributive justice. At a symbolic level, the prosecution of global criminals has taken centre stage, with victims assuming minor roles as witnesses or audiences to which the trial decisions are broadcast.

Under neo-liberal versions of justice which concentrate on autonomy and individual liability, the place of the victim in trial and punishment recently has been somewhat rehabilitated. This has led to critical reflections on the purpose of retributive justice and the extent to which harm should drive the determination of sanction (Erez and Johnson 1999). The victim's voice through victim impact statements is given at least normative presence in the sentencing process. How this injection of victim discourse sits with the protected interests of the accused is still unsettled in adversarial trials and is not much clearer resolved in the legislative instruments of ICJ.

Some criminal justice traditions, such as in Italy and Russia, provide the victim the right of separate representation and thereby an active role in eliciting and testing evidence which may be crucial to questions of liability and sentence. Of the international criminal institutions, the ICC in particular has accommodations for victim interest, within and outside the trial. There is a special bureau of the court administration dedicated to victim concerns. Although the victim's voice in ICC trials is specifically limited to very few contexts of advocacy, concerns to communicate the court's deliberations to the victim community are highlighted in ICC procedural provisions.

The UN war crimes tribunals have a varied engagement record with victims. As such the legitimacy accorded to tribunal justice, where it is grounded in community consensus and acceptance, is dislocated and specific. For instance, one of the reasons that the Rwanda Tribunal has held its hearings almost entirely outside Rwanda is concern that the people of that conflict-ridden state would not welcome its presence. The ICTY prides itself on its victim outreach. However, Milanovic (2006) is doubtful whether any move from the tribunal into a transitional justice style outreach has or will be effective in connecting with communities. He is concerned, as was demonstrated by the International Court of Justice action between Bosnia and Serbia to determine who had committed genocide and when, that these central questions of responsibility do not lose touch with victim communities. Milanovic suggests it is time for mediation rather than persisting with *show trials* and resultant superficial outreach endeavours.

> The ICTY's Outreach programme has not produced much success, and the judges and the Prosecutor of the Tribunal must make much more effort to make their work as public as possible, and to pay attention not just to the proceedings of the court-room, but to the appearance of these proceedings out of court … Hopefully the whole process (as well as rights tribunals, and justice courts) will in the long run result in the creation of a set of facts accepted as truth by a large majority of people in the states of the former Yugoslavia, and allow for the resolution of the residual disputes in the Balkan wars.
>
> (Milanovic 2006: 29–30)

Even where there have been genuine attempts at victim engagement by the formal institutions and processes of ICJ, this is made more difficult by limitations in *imagining* the victims of genocide and crimes against humanity. Where the crimes in question are generic and encompassing, their victims will be communities, and the community of victims will be comprised by a variety of victimisation contexts.

Tribunal justice focuses on the individual liability of one or several accused. Collective liability is narrowly interpreted in tribunal jurisprudence (Seiber *et al.* 2007). In turn this has led to a confined construction of victimisation. Victim communities, communities of victims, and individual victims within communities are all vitally connected in the horror of genocide. Criminal law domestic or international has traditionally worried over viable notions of collective victimisation and how they can and should be recognised. This is now a much more significant consideration in the delivery and resolution of ICJ.

The particular difficulties in achieving victim representation resulting out of major terror events, is discussed by Logan (2007). His focus is on the terror events of the Oklahoma bombings and 9/11 in the US and the US embassy bombings in Kenya. In total these atrocities produced over 3,300 deaths and the challenge for the courts in prosecuting and sentencing those responsible was how to recognise the voice of victim families. US President George W. Bush at the time publicly declared his commitment to the victims (Bush 2002).[5] Therefore the courts in the US were on notice that they would need to consider means for validating victim interests. This challenge sits within the wider controversy surrounding second- and third-party victimisation which will always plague victim representation in homicides.

Logan explores the many difficulties that the use of victim statements presents in these circumstances, such as:

- demarking permissible boundaries in terms of victimisation and impact. These are issues for capital (murder) trials in general but may be exacerbated in the context of mass killings and mass victimisation;

- questions of proximity to the actual victimisation for survivors;

- the forms of harm to be recognised by the court;

- guarding against popular emotionalism which may affect the personal experience of victim survivors; and a range of

- tactical problems in giving equal recognition or proportionate weight to different victim voices and how these are to be challenged.

These warrant attention not only for future US mass killing trials which, if the recent past can serve as a guide, are certain to occur. They also should figure in the international arena where mass killings occur with even greater frequency.

As in the US the allure of affording victims a direct personal stake in the prosecution of mass killers is now also making itself felt in domestic jurisdictions. Logan addresses how, and if, victim-centredness can be accommodated in the ongoing effort to maintain *rule of law values* in the prosecution of mass killers. The challenge he sees as transferring logically from domestic to international criminal courts.

The instrumentality of victim impact statements arising from terrorist mass killings is controversial. Should the victim voice, individual or collective, influence sentencing directly, and if so what weight should it be accorded relative to other sentencing principles such as general community protection? Further, in the context of widely feared terrorist events, how can the interests of the accused be fairly separated from victim impact, and community vengeance and mob hysteria?

Then there is the concern for adequately providing legitimate benefits to victims through a trial voice. The UN has detailed this need and associated rights in its *Declaration of Basic Principles of Justice for Victims of Crime and Abuse of Power*. While rarely if ever allowing direct participation of victim voices in the trial process, the international criminal tribunals and the ICC recognise as appropriate this influence in determining punishment.

However, if a more formal trend towards victim-impact statements is to expand internationally, the question of who is a victim needs sharper relief. The ICC is struggling to recognise the *victimisation of third parties*.[6] If ICJ is unable to successfully manage collective liability, what hope does it have in recognising the reality of victim communities?

This being so, is there a peril for ICJ in victim-centredness? The problems of this direction have been rehearsed in detail when considering victim impact statements in homicides. In such cases, no victim voice remains, beyond the voices of secondary parties closely connected to the deceased. This is exacerbated when there is more than one voice to comprise a connected victim community. In the international context, the normative frameworks around harm and victim location may not be as consolidated as they are in the domestic setting:

> While the views of natures and cultures can coalesce on matters of broad importance ... they often diverge on questions relating to more specific normative notions of substantive and procedural fairness ... finally is the basic question whether government should be permitted to deploy victims to meet their didactic ends. (Logan 2007: 47–50)

Then there is the issue of *legitimate interests*. International criminal justice is predetermined, at least in its formal manifestations, by competing rights considerations. Conventionally the rights of accused persons are the first measure of trial fairness. However, in a neo-liberal age *balance* competes with the presumption of innocence to measure the public acceptability of criminal justice. Not every victim interest is legitimate as justice. In many situations, victim interests may compete, and victim communities can divide over what justice interests they prioritise.

Another important theme is the contextual relativity of victimisation. Many violent groups and organisations presently identified as terrorist threats have themselves been victims of harsh repression and counterinsurgency violence. In transitional state conflicts certain sides of the violence hold a privileged identity as both victors and victims, and as such claim considerable domestic legitimacy (Bikundo, forthcoming).

Sovereign decisions on who is friend or enemy are not grounded by force or violence alone, or the authority for their exercise and against whom they might be directed. More importantly this distinction depends specifically on the authority of the sovereign and the legitimacy of the distinction among respondent communities. If either is challenged, the valorisation of victims above others beyond questions of innocence may be challenged, and the determination of legitimate victim interests will be contested as a consequence. How is ICJ to resolve this where military and political discrimination has exacerbated the confusion?

The *valorisation of victims* has essential bearing on which individuals and communities can claim legitimacy in justice resolutions, thereby having a voice and demanding a dominant place for their interests above those of marginalised or *illegitimate* victim communities. As mentioned earlier, and to confound conventional considerations of justice, innocence alone may not be the crucial driver for victim valorisation. The same with risks and responses, it is the nature of authority claiming and exercising the power to distinguish between victims and collateral or resistant communities which confers this legitimacy. At least this is how it pans out within the ICJ dimension of global governance.

To make such distinctions more redolent, the dominant political alliance valorises citizen victims while simultaneously alienating and even criminalising opponents and their resistant communities. Part of this legitimacy project is to neutralise value plurality. There is one model of governance to be fought for, one victim community to be protected and one prevailing justification for violent justice responses.

Violence focus

The relationship between criminal justice and violence is hardly novel. In the US and Australia today there is serious academic debate about legislative justification for the use of torture when interrogating terrorist suspects (Dershowitz 2006; Bargaric 2005). Torture in the process of extracting confessions or encouraging incriminating evidence has featured in legitimate and illegitimate investigation practice throughout the history of criminal justice. Foucalt in *Discipline and Punish* (1989) highlights the importance of violence against the body both as a process for identifying liability and then as essential to punishment as an exemplary social control. Violence against the mind is crucial to the disciplinary regimes on which imprisonment relies as the ultimate penalty in many Western jurisdictions (Christie 1993). In many of the world's economically advanced nations capital punishment is retained as the pinnacle of lawful force which the state exercises against the offender.

If violence prevails as a feature of criminal justice domestically, then why do I make special mention of violent justice responses against global terrorism, authorised through international criminal justice or otherwise? The answer lies in the:

- nature of the violence employed by state agencies in the name of justice;
- compromises of conventional justice processes and institutions in order that violence can be maximised; and the
- manner in which justice and other violent regulatory strategies (such as military forces, or national security and intelligence facilities) combine to facilitate the threat and practice of violent regulation.

Violent regulatory responses are a feature of ICJ in its various forms:

1 *Formal justice institutions and processes* – the more conventional policing and punishment arms of the international criminal tribunals and the violence they demonstrate through compulsory detention, interrogation and the punishment options which can range from restriction on liberty to indeterminate confinement.

2 *Distortions and derivations of the conventional formal justice institutions and processes* – these are less likely to be governed by *due process* style procedural regulation and demonstrate heightened forms of violence such as detention without charge, torture during interrogation and corporal punishments sometimes resulting in death.[7]

3 *Less formal justice institutions and processes* – where violence is less likely to feature within the processes themselves, as compulsion may not be an essential feature of truth and reconciliation or of community justice initiatives. Even so, restorative justice requires the accused to concede guilt before participation and along with such concession may follow a series of compulsory consequences.

Further, informal justice practices have been criticised for leaving participants open to consequential violence and retribution.

President George Bush has argued that 'unusual circumstances' require an 'irregular style' of justice to secure American borders (Clark 2002). With the post-9/11 threat designated as coming largely from *non-citizens*, the denial of convention rights and the generation of institutional and process justice distortions became a predictable consequence of military intervention for this enemy. The *wars* in which the Guantanamo detainees were *non*-combatants were not conventional, and the consequent detention of prisoners from these wars is equally extraordinary. The President was even willing to go beyond what the Supreme Court divided over (Meister 2004), whether he had the power to establish military tribunals to keep the trial of Guantanamo Bay inmates out of the mainstream courts (Clark 2002).

As sinister as were the 9/11 attacks, they did not cause a general recourse to martial law domestically. Rather, the martial law option with all its *justice trappings* was directed offshore. Even the terrorist *threats* were contained in an American territorial outpost, Guantanamo. The detention facility there represents a 'legal black hole' (Duffy 2005) in which the most irregular forms of *justice* are said to be tolerated: isolation, torture, indeterminate detention without trial, constrained legal access and military adjudication. Despite the condemnation from the international legal community (the English Court of Appeal for one) the US administration remains committed to a violent justice distortion as a key response to these 'unusual circumstances'. The justice response in turn, violent as it may be, becomes an 'unusual consequence'.

Some would argue that the danger posed by international terror gave the US administration little choice but to augment traditional justice forms in the management of key terrorist suspects (Eastman 2002). Fine distinctions between lawful and unlawful combatants aside (Fogarty 2005), the due process protections of international law could be seen as vulnerable to the evil purposes of global terror. What challenges any such repudiation is the reality that the threats exhibited in contemporary terrorism may not in fact be so much greater than others which have been effectively countered through the resilient institutions of conventional criminal and military justice. The Nuremburg and Tokyo tribunals after the holocaust of the Second World War are cases in point. However, as I have regularly suggested, risk here is not a matter of comparative harm but rather is redefined in 'the national interest' (Kay 2004).

What provides another inducement to ICJ in contemplating or transacting violent responses, is its convenient inclusion in the *war on terror* discourse. However, even the violence of war is regulated in conventional military engagement. The same is not so in the war on terror. The fundamental distortions in criminal justice designed to easier prosecute this 'war' show that the place of violence in contemporary global governance is far from conventional.

The preference in global governance terms for *law over war* in controlling international crimes such as terrorism may gain a greater relevance as international humanitarian law plays a more important role in ICJ (Chadwick 2003). The *International Humanitarian Laws of Armed Conflict* prohibit the use of terror-violence as a means of warfare in all circumstances of armed conflict. However, *terrorist* enemies do not always share the humanitarian consensus on which these laws and conventions are based. The consequent responses from the dominant political alliance against terrorists in *non-combatant* roles is to turn its back on the protections in the *laws of war* (such as the Geneva Convention). Novel and violent apprehension and detention strategies have been developed in a climate where both sides of the violent aggression deny the necessity of legal regulation. Because of this, for legal regulation to reassert its relevance over novel violent responses, humanitarian law needs to develop to address the violence of global terror as well as the challenge posed to security through more conventional warfare.

Modern laws of war evolved in the nineteenth century from reciprocal pacts designed to ensure minimum restraint among *civilised* people. Any strict contractual approach to mutuality in restraint has been superseded in this phase of globalisation by a more rigid and delineated commitment to global security and order at whatever cost. The cost has emerged as violence to the rights of offenders and victims in the name of risk and security.

The violence focus of governance responses to global terror can be seen as directed against the rights of offenders and communities, as well as against their physical integrity. Michaelson (2003) argues that the criminal law has been 'bastardised' in the name of control and security. The perversion of human rights in the process is evidence that both law and justice have been subverted. The question is whether the terrorist threat can be viewed legally as posing a sufficient *public emergency* that national security legislation is justified in abrogating the obligations imposed by international human rights conventions.

A particular example of violence against the rights of individuals and communities is the recent qualification of migration regimes to prioritise national and regional security (Miller 2005).

> In the years between 1996 and 2001 the immigration system bought into the 'severity revolution' occurring within the criminal justice system. Some describe it as the 'criminalisation' of immigration law whereas others describe it as a convergence between the criminal justice and deportation systems. Under either characterisation, the interaction of the two systems produced outcomes that were unprecedented and even unintended at times in their harshness. (Miller 2005: 95)

This coalition between migration, criminal justice (particularly policing) and security has had an even more devastating impact on those outside citizenship. The stateless, refugees, asylum seekers and *over-stayers* are all the more vulnerable to the violent and intrusive impact of regulatory agencies when their very status is criminalised and the conventional protections afforded a criminal accused do not apply to their condition.

The emphasis on violent justice responses to violent terror incursions has tended to diminish any more sophisticated consideration of the jurisdiction and mandate of ICJ. Formalists will say that both these issues are constrained by the foundation statutes for the tribunals and for the ICC, emerging as they did out of the negotiations in the Security Council or the compromises of state parties to the Rome Statute. Not so if ICJ is appreciated in its broadest sense, incorporating less formal and wide-ranging communitarian justice forms (see Chapter 5).

Tensions over jurisdiction and mandate

The risk of terrorism has also formulated the recent mandate and jurisdiction of ICJ. Mythen and Walklate (2006) refer to the 'changing geography of danger' in their discussion of risk societies and governmentality. To this they attach wider cultures of surveillance and control. By creating atmospheres of fear, as I have previously agreed, the reactions to risk in violent form may themselves be characterised as terror inducing. As much as they are pitted against terror, Mythen and Walklate suggest that neo-liberal states are *governing through terror*. This depends in part on jurisdictions over knowledge and mandates of power over fear creation.

... by delving into the triadic relationship between knowledge, power and risk, we have come across the thorny issues around the uses and abuses of the terrorist problem. Is the construction of a generic discourse of the *non-white terrorist other* causing unwarranted global tensions? Are authoritarian counter-terrorist measures being used to reinforce unequal power relations? To what extent is the hegemonic discourse of terrorism serving to extend the economic, political and cultural pincers of Western nations? (2006: 394)

It may be correct to assume that concerns about the jurisdiction and mandate for ICJ are really around the spread of democracy, modernisation and Western value systems. In order to promote these priorities for global governance, ICJ is now being directed to engage with conflict-prone states. The ICC, through early indications of the Prosecutor, has adopted this as a priority, even if subservient as it is to (but flowing out of) the prosecution of crimes against humanity. The Prosecutor identifies the law of the court as constraining his mandate, and the Security Council and the member states as his constituency. Even so victim communities are recognised by him as an important interest group for the criminal prosecutions of the court. How to recognise victim communities and their need for conflict resolution and peace ongoing within the determination of criminal liability of the ICC is both a procedural and conceptual exercise for its first year of operation.

The constituency of victim communities and a mandate for conflict resolution are more accepted and less controversial within the *alternative* ICJ paradigms. Truth and reconciliation commissions, for instance, were constructed where it was thought (by post-conflict states and peacekeeping agencies) that retributive justice and its institutions could not achieve the legitimate interests of victims within transitional cultures. It is becoming clearer as ICJ develops and gains a more significant purchase in global governance that justice for conflict resolution cannot only be relegated to a second tier of *truth telling*.

Formal and less formal justice paradigms – all about 'alternatives'?

Justice as exercised by the war crimes tribunals is a revealing case study of the inadequacies of formal ICJ, particularly from the perspective of legitimate victim interests (Findlay and Henham, forthcoming). Again with reference to the recent Balkans conflict, the ICTY, which is recognised as the most functional of the tribunals and the special courts, stands criticised for failing to significantly engage with victim communities. Marco Milanovic (2007) accepts that the war crimes tribunal has a role in determining whether genocide occurred and who among the prominent leaders deserves prosecution. But this is far from the end of it. For legalist determinations of individual liability to have any real community clout even as retributive action, they require successful translation to the victim communities which suffered the atrocities in question.

The human rights implications for victim communities of crimes against humanity may not be the central or even peripheral concerns of a war crimes tribunal. But crucially, human rights violations and concerns for rights protection at a community level in particular impact on justice resolutions and their legitimacy in the context of post-conflict peacemaking (Braithwaite 2002). As we have argued in detail (Findlay and Henham 2005; chs 7 and 8), there is a need for the exploration and confirmation of individualised and communitarian rights in a transformed institutional ICJ capacity.[8]

In addition, the Balkan experience highlights the need for a mediation facility in ICJ for establishing wider grassroots responsibilities over genocide, as well as in determining the restitution frameworks that should follow determinations of liability and efforts at reconciliation. Unfortunately the adjudicatory emphasis of the tribunals and their management of sometimes violent justice responses has distracted attention from a more holistic approach to the satisfaction of legitimate victim interests.

Concerning criminal justice in all its contemporary locations, there have emerged recent tensions between institutional processes and communitarian/restorative commitments. These tensions have been papered over or skirted by:

- continuing to demark the separate *territories* for restorative and retributive justice;

- diverting to restorative justice practices those determinations and stakeholder relationships which have been notoriously unsuccessfully managed within the formal processes of justice;

- legislating restorative justice, thereby bringing it within the authority structures of the state;

- capturing some of the communitarian legitimacy accorded restorative justice for more institutional justice processes (particularly those with cross-overs to restorative endeavours);

- positioning justice professionals at the head of restorative processes and practices to assist in this *legitimacy sharing* project;

- allowing the rise of victim interests through the restorative direction, thereby not radically challenging the procedural foundations of formal criminal justice; and even so

- risking the rights of witnesses and victims in the *truth telling process*, and thereby circumscribing their access to the formal justice determination and resolution processes.

Despite these trends, the tensions between the main ICJ paradigms remain. Legitimate victim interests as a recognised motivator for developing ICJ are generating previously incorporated and relegated pressures for a transformation in ICJ. Transitional justice would see this coming about through the growing domination of alternative justice strategies. Critics of this position believe that transformation without integration and adaptation will not achieve sustainable and protective justice contexts in the long term for victim communities.

Conclusion – tension into transformation

International criminal justice has reached a turning point. After decades of experimentation, commentators are asking what is beyond the war crimes tribunals and truth commissions.

One response has been to distort conventional justice for the sake of risk/security. Guantanamo Bay has suggested a new legal order. It confirms the use of criminal justice with the ulterior motive of world-ordering for a preferred political ideology. Domestic and international criminal justice enacted in the name of the *war on terror* demonstrates 'anomie made law' (Paye 2005) thereby distorting normal justice preconditions.

Is anomaly-driven law and process the way forward for a more permanent and prolonged international criminal justice? The administrative, legislative or judicial authorisations of distortions and subversions of more conventional criminal justice processes at a domestic level are challenges for the development of ICJ. Thousands of individuals in the US since 2001 have been arrested and detained without charge and denied conventional criminal justice protections in the name of national security. If anomaly-based justice process reform flows onto the role of ICJ in global governance, then the fragile *separation of powers* model yet to be well-grounded internationally will crumble (Clark 2002). Executive self-proclaimed judicial powers in particular carry the potential to politicise the international criminal courts and tribunals, thereby challenging even the ideology of judicial independence.

The International Criminal Court promises much. It is a necessary move away from the 'shoestring' justice model of the tribunals, both in terms of their sunset duration and their limited jurisdiction. Also, the ICC gives an essential impression of permanence for formal ICJ, not before time. Having said this, as the tribunals and the special courts continue to evidence a failure to engage with victim communities and do little more than speculate on the causal link between retribution and peacemaking, reliance on institutional justice may be as risky in governance terms as is a confidence in the violence of para-justice distortions.

I will argue in the concluding chapter that the outcome of productive connections between ICJ and global governance needs a communitarian commitment in the form of *communities of justice.* The central feature of these communities will be accountability between service providers and vital stakeholder communities, including those that till now have been relegated beyond the reach of ICJ as a consequence of their resistance to the dominant global governance cultures.

Accountability is an essential legitimator for the justice component of governance. Kritz (2002) writes about the crucial need to provide accountability through criminal justice systems for post-conflict states. Accountability increases its legitimating potential the farther it moves from normative considerations to engage with processes and outcomes. Particularly for the administrative sanctions imposed by international organisations (such as economic sanctions) which often precede criminal justice in global governance strategies, accountability about unintended consequences is not a feature of global governance. That is because those who suffer from such adverse even if unintended consequences have up until now largely been communities in opposition to the dominant governance cultures. If not criminalised, these communities are systematically denied a place in ICJ. As globalisation advances dominant governance cultures this marginalisation, unless strategically arrested, will be advanced and confirmed through the violent reactions it generates.

In this new era of globalisation criminal justice, I will argue, has assumed a prioritised but problematic role in global governance. It is problematic when compared either with conventional expectations for the position of justice in liberal democracies (as the dominant global ideology would have it) and against wider measures of international human rights. Some commentators call on transitional justice to repair atrocities according to human rights and the rule of law (Gray 2005). But what form of rights, and which rule of law?

Criminal justice in the context of global governance imperatives, because of the politicality and relativity of that context, will never be *pure*. What I mean by this is that no single model of justice is the only model for global governance outcomes. In the concluding chapter I explore competing considerations of rights and their place in a more convincing notion of humanity. Why? Because both governance and justice are said to be concerned with human rights, and translated into the international situation, rights have no singular representation. This is only one component of justice and governance which demonstrates that cultural, or at least community relativity and relevance, will require regulatory strategies which respect difference. This is not a rejection of *best practice* approaches to global governance in favour of the irregularity of cultural relativity. Preferred justice and governance models can (and will here) be argued for. Yet in so doing, the analyst must be aware of competing claims to the context and conditions of governability which arise out of clashing cultures.

If law and criminal justice have a legitimate place in global governance then holism as a consequence of globalisation (or internationalism) will only convincingly grow as the dominant models of law and justice recognise the worth and potential of hybrid or alternative forms. A victim community focus for justice will eventually require this.

Despite my assertion that traditional (in terms of dominant and thereby conventional) criminal justice should not rigidly apply to one mechanic of global governance, the dominant political alliance today requires ascription to a singular notion of law and compliance to the law. Therefore the newly created institutions of formal criminal justice which are applied to global governance constrict the types of order which may best satisfy diverse victim communities (see Albrecht *et al.* 2006). The cultural location of crimes against humanity and their victims need close study if global justice and governance strategies are to develop to meet their particular challenges. Examining the unique conditions in societies capable of mass and institutional atrocities and the victim communities which result will stimulate a more multifaceted model of justice to inform global governance. Transformed international criminal justice (as described in Findlay and Henham 2005) is an attempt at this.

The social and legal environments which support abuse and atrocity on the scale of genocide and crimes against humanity may provide crucial clues for the construction of global governance strategies to counter such large-scale victimisation. The question remains: is legality alone sufficient to effectively anchor criminal justice within a wider fabric of regulatory governance (see Chapter 9)? Cassese (1996) recognises that international laws relating to terrorism are flawed and perverse but still provide a viable platform for advancing global security. Once legality is invoked as the regulatory framework then, it is argued, responses to terrorism can be peaceful or forceful (coercive) provided they accord with the law. Unfortunately this argument proceeds from a naive appreciation of the neutrality of the law and the impartial legitimacy of legal regulation. The current operation of the war crimes tribunals in translating international criminal law to advance victor's justice challenges such an interpretation. The next chapter will confront and confound the essentialist relationship between political and cultural dominion, good global governance and compromised ICJ. Victim-centred justice, I argue, will reposition global governance against commitments for access, inclusivity and interaction.

Notes

1 Jim Garamone (2007) *U.S.-U.K. Leaders Reaffirm Objectives in Terror War*, American Forces Press Service, Washington, 30 July.
2 Crimes against humanity, war crimes and genocide.
3 While the Chief Prosecutor of the ICC is cautious to identify peacemaking as a central aspiration for 'his' court, the prosecutorial commitment to victim communities and to neutralising violent threats against them means that restorative justice is directed to conflict resolution outcomes.
4 Stated in a speech to the Law Faculty, University of Sydney, 8 August 2007.
5 'In our war against terror I constantly remind our fellow citizens ... that we seek justices for victims. We seek justice for their families.'
6 ICC, Rule of Procedure and Evidence 85 (a) defining a victim as a natural person suffering harm.
7 Because of the abrogation of suspect's rights, and the reliance on and execution of violence in forms not condoned in formal justice agencies

and processes, it could be argued that these regulatory strategies should not share a classification of criminal justice. I contend that in light of the US Supreme Court's recognition of the limited procedural legality of some extraordinary justice forms they can be incorporated within new criminal justice/global governance relationships.

8 Perhaps such as the now defunct Human Rights Chamber of Bosnia and Herzegovina.

Chapter 8

The crucial place of crime and control within the transformation of globalised cultures

An international domestic tribunal that is grafted onto a weak domestic criminal justice system which cannot guarantee fundamental respect for human rights is unlikely to succeed in its task of bringing justice in accordance with international standards. International control of the process in such a situation is crucial, but it should not be assumed that the United Nations control of the process will guarantee that the process will accord with international standards. (Linton 2002: 114)

Introduction

In *The Globalisation of Crime* (Findlay 1999 b), cultures in transition were identified as crucial contexts in which the global crime/control nexus is revealed. At the time of writing that book, ICJ was nothing like the force for global governance which it is today. Transitional cultures have a special contemporary relevance for understanding the dynamics and development of ICJ in the present phase of globalisation. This relevance relates to the adaptation of justice traditions as they influence the procedures and practices of formal ICJ in particular. Transitional cultures, wherein criminal justice traditions have hybridised, may hold the key to resolving some of the central challenges for ICJ practice. This chapter identifies and explores several of these challenges and the cultural adaptations in criminal justice that offer models for change.

Globalisation also has a particular relationship with transitional cultures. I conclude in the final chapter that an interesting paradox of globalisation is its tendency to attack cultural pluralism through the application of a diverse range of regulatory strategies. Some significant world cultures, while being aggressively involved in the commercial arm of these strategies, have made the political decision to stay outside formal ICJ for the present. This being the case, the impact of the hybrid and transitional justice traditions is yet to be the influence which they otherwise might have on the evolution of ICJ in global governance.

Removing themselves from formal ICJ has not meant that transitional cultures have also eschewed indigenous justice resolutions to peacemaking and conflict resolution concerns. Transitional cultures offer valuable examples of where alternative justice mechanisms are even incorporated into the trial process so that its capacity for conflict resolution is localised and more flexible.

With the crime/control, risk/security relationship being even more central to globalisation than before 9/11, and ICJ now featuring in global regulatory strategies, governing through globalised crime should be evident worldwide. The effect is not so universal. Postcolonial cultures have imposed justice systems to reconcile before being confident to engage with ICJ. The justice traditions of resistant communities may form part of the 'risk' against which the dominant political alliance is waging the *war on terror.* The consequence of selective inclusion and differential engagement is that formal ICJ operates as an exclusive club, yet to sufficiently recognise (or be recognised by) some of the world's great legal traditions. Fundamantalist cultures have endorsed this separation by rejecting international criminal justice outreach and jurisdiction.

What hope then for a system of global governance in which ICJ can represent a pluralistic and riven global community? The place to start, I suggest in this chapter, is the generation of mutual interest between formal ICJ institutions and hybrid criminal justice traditions in transitional cultures. Greater engagement between ICJ and world justice traditions will better enable the justice transformation discussed throughout this text and detailed in the final chapter.

The structural and dynamic requirements for transformed institutions and processes of ICJ should demonstrate access, inclusivity and integration as primary motivations for justice service delivery. In establishing these commitments for ICJ, global governance strategies will be required to encounter and encourage human rights styles outside the individualised Western traditions. Communitarian justice protecting collective rights and social harmony should have equal claim as a global governance framework, next to the individual liberties promoted through Western justice ideologies.

Case studying the influence of hybrid jurisdictions – China and beyond

China remains outside the constitution of the International Criminal Court (ICC) and is not yet a State Party to the *Rome Statute*.[1] Even so, China is importantly positioned to influence international criminal justice (ICJ) in the future, and there are many aspects of ICJ (properly interpreted) where China can already have sway. To make this case it is necessary to reflect on the essentials of ICJ as featured in Chapter 5.

As we argue in *Transforming International Criminal Justice* (Findlay and Henham 2005), there is more that constitutes ICJ than just formal institutions and processes. What are misleadingly referred to as alternative justice paradigms, the *truth and reconciliation* pathways, have greater influence and coverage over victim communities[2] than can be claimed by the international criminal tribunals. International criminal justice is not merely a retributive framework. Restorative justice has also emerged as an important and legitimate expectation of victim communities (Albrecht *et al.* 2006). The communitarian control apparatus influential in China today[3] and the emphasis on *social harmony* as a primary motivator for Chinese criminal justice, suggest important cohesions with the development of restorative and less formal ICJ. The potential presented for China to influence the development of ICJ from this platform is critically evaluated in this chapter.

ICJ is increasingly employed, often following armed struggle, as a supplementary governance strategy for state reconstruction. Central to global governance in its current configuration is the nexus between crime and risk, control and security. Regional and international concerns over risk and security where dominant global alliances now determine to control international terrorism are features of ICJ from which China cannot exclude itself.

Finally, as with mercantilism and colonialism before it, globalisation is increasingly interested in crime and justice as discriminators for international alliances and hegemonies claiming dominance over political ideologies and economic agendas. China is actively involved in positioning itself with influence in such developments.[4]

This chapter builds on the earlier discussion of the different frameworks for ICJ in which China's influence can be measured or (we argue) should be present. From here we look specifically at the procedural traditions on which international criminal law and its procedural jurisprudence are said to be based. Seeing China as a hybrid tradition undergoing radical transformation in its criminal justice delivery, I suggest that recent Chinese legal traditions and experience should be significant in understanding where the synthesis of international criminal procedure may be heading. I take the example of tensions between individual and collective notions of liability to explore the importance of the hybrid traditions, away from narrow attempts to compromise common law and civil law.

From a more formalist consideration of ICJ, the chapter concludes by seeing what the *alternative* justice paradigms offer China and vice versa. This is a platform from which to speculate on the opportunities available to China in regional and international governance, through more constructive involvement with the ICJ discourse. As with China's active role in international commercial arbitration, there is potential for it to influence the development of international criminal justice beyond a formal institutional base. In some respects this allows engagement with themes like adversarial justice and human rights beyond rather narrow and irredentist normative debates, and enables some transition from constitutional legality to progressive practice. Throughout this examination of rights and international criminal justice I call for a wider consideration of the rights paradigms insofar as they recognise community interests as well as individual integrity. The tension between these priorities provides an insight into why certain nation-states such as China find it more difficult to administer domestic criminal justice in accordance with the rightful demands of international conventions.[5]

This chapter employs China as a significant representative of a *cohort* of Asian jurisdictions in particular that manage their domestic criminal justice within hybrid and dynamic procedural environments. Like Japan, China is experiencing rapid change within criminal justice and I argue these emerging traditions should assert greater influence over the development of international criminal justice if it is to be representative of important non-Western global communities.

China and the ICC[6]

Of the major global military and economic powers, the three states refusing to cooperate with the ICC (Russia, the USA and China) have the largest military capacity in their regions. Burns does not see this as a coincidence. Despite the domestic legal obligations required by the *Rome Statute* and concerns over the loss of autonomy which these may suggest;

> As an emerging military 'superpower', China has much in common with the United States in its wariness towards the ICC. In both cases these states have powerful military establishments that have developed their own military judicial systems that they will not easily give up any part of. (Burns 2005: 3)

However, Lu and Wang (2005) observe that, unlike the USA, China does not have extensive overseas military commitments and therefore it is not so concerned (as is the US) that its troops may one day come under the ICC jurisdiction. Also, China is not in the same international position as is the USA to pressure through economic sanction for the creation of bilateral agreements indemnifying troops against local prosecution.

When the *Rome Statute* was signed by an overwhelming number of UN member states, China was unexpectedly one of the seven countries to vote against it. China remains among the very few states not to sign, ratify or accede to the treaty.[7] What makes this all the more curious is that China was active in the plenary sessions of the Rome Conference and adopts a watching brief on the progress of the court's development, from the perspective of an observer state.

The reasons set out by the Chinese government for not joining the ICC are:

1 The *Rome Statute* is not a voluntary acceptance instrument and imposes obligations on nation-states and non-state parties without their consent, which violates the Vienna Convention on the Law on Treaties. Furthermore, the complementary jurisdiction principle gives the ICC the power to judge whether a state is willing or able to conduct proper trials of its own nationals.

2 War crimes committed in internal armed conflicts fall under the jurisdiction of the ICC. The definition of war crimes goes beyond that accepted under customary international law.

3 Contrary to the existing norms of customary international law, the definition of 'crimes against humanity' does not require that the state in which they are committed be at war. Many of the actions

listed under that heading should be covered by international human rights law and not criminal law.

4 The inclusion of the crime of aggression within the jurisdiction of the ICC weakens the power of the UN Security Council.

5 The power under Article 15 for the Prosecutor to initiate action *proprio motu* might make it difficult for the ICC to deal with the most serious crimes, and may tend to open up the court to political influence.

These arguments are the subject of wide-ranging and sometimes critical discussion among Chinese jurists and legal scholars.[8] Lu and Wang have presented detailed argument challenging the currency and cogency of each. They conclude that:

> Instead of opposing the ICC, China should participate in order to protect its national interests. (2005: 618–19)

Rather than deal with each of the arguments against China's reasons, it might therefore be useful to focus on those where its national self-interest is a clear motivation:

- The purpose of the ICC is to punish 'crimes against humanity'. There is no reason beyond the political why such a motive should be limited in its impact and direction to situations of war. *Crimes against humanity* do not take on their abhorrent characteristics from the theatre of war alone. The definition of war in international law may not cover those contexts of armed conflict internal to state sovereignty and transition wherein many of these atrocities are committed and which are exactly what the ICC was set up to prosecute.

- The doctrine of complementarity protects those states with the capacity to properly investigate and prosecute crimes which otherwise come to the attention of the ICC. This is the challenge. Judicial sovereignty is not an essential casualty of the limited submission of autonomy required by ICC membership: only where the states concerned have inadequate domestic criminal justice responses.

- It is only state parties to the *Rome Statute* that will be involved in the discussions determining the definition of crimes of aggression.

- Candidates for positions of judges and prosecutors with the court can only be drawn from state parties.

It is likely now that Japan has so recently signed up as a member state that the pressure on China to follow will intensify.

Procedural traditions for international criminal law – China's place?

In discussing the influences behind the development of international criminal law Martinez identifies:

1 international humanitarian law and the laws of war;
2 international human rights law;
3 domestic (national) criminal law and procedural traditions; and
4 transnational and regional justice.

> What we have ended up with is people coming from these different backgrounds, bringing with them different ideas about the role of law in protecting human rights. For example, criminal law is concerned with protecting the defendant's rights and individual guilt. International human rights law on the other hand is very victim focused … in contrast with the rule of lenity of criminal law, where you're going to construe prohibitions narrowly so that you're not catching people unawares as defendants, in human rights law the corresponding interpretative cannon is to interpret human rights more expansively to protect the rights of individuals. In international criminal law you can see the confluence of these two strands. Sometimes they move together in a positive direction, and other times there is tension.[9]

Zhang observes:

> The Chinese Criminal justice system is very different from Western justice systems. Influenced by Confucian communitarian ideology and communist philosophy, mass organisations at the grassroots level play a very important role in crime control.[10] Mediation committees and *bang jiao* groups exist in nearly every local community to deal with minor deviancies, resolve conflicts, and rehabilitate juvenile delinquents and released offenders. While the formal criminal justice system is used for

more serious offenders, mass participation in conflict resolution and crime prevention is an integral part of the Chinese criminal justice system. (2004: 2)

In imperial China the Tang and the Qing criminal codes were notable and sophisticated. The central purposes of these Codes were to punish those who violated the rule of order and to teach the value of good conduct. Leng and Chiu (1985) argue that these traditional codes paid less attention to the protection of individual interests than to the maintenance of social and political order. In this respect they were compatible in function to the more recent Chinese crime legislation. To some extent the Codes could be seen in conflict with Confucian legal theory which advocates ruling by moral education, with the law and its sanctions used only as the last resort. Punishment was still for the Confucianist the province of the state when moral education was rejected by the individual (Chen 2002).

The People's Republic of China was established as a socialist country in 1949. Since then, efforts have been made to enact basic laws concerning criminal justice administration. It was in 1979, after the anarchy of the Cultural Revolution, that the Criminal Law and Criminal Procedure Law were originally enacted. At the same time, laws concerning the organisation and function of the courts and public prosecution were also developed. Basic laws with regard to lawyers and the arrest and detention of suspects, have also been established. With the return of Hong Kong and then Macau as Special Administrative Regions within China, the criminal law now accepts to a limited extent the traditions of British and Portuguese criminal procedure and jurisprudence.

The Chinese criminal law takes the political ideologies of Marxism, Leninism and Mao Zedong as its guide. It proclaims that its tasks are to use criminal punishments to struggle against all counter-revolutionary and other criminal acts in order to safeguard the system of the people's democratic dictatorship and the smooth progress of the course of socialist reconstruction. In the early days of the Chinese soviet, the legal traditions of the USSR were heavily influential. Prior to that, western European civil law traditions had influence over the development of legal principle. The impact of the laws of imperial China has perhaps most clearly survived in the institutional structures of Chinese criminal justice.

It took 30 years for the People's Republic of China to enact its first laws. Until 1979 there were no legislative legal standards to guide judges to try criminals. The law takes the Constitution as its basis.

Article 28 of the Constitution stipulates that:

> The State maintains public order and suppresses treasonable and other counter-revolutionary activities; it penalises acts that endanger public security and disrupt the socialist economy and other criminal activities, and punishes and reforms criminals.

China's criminal justice system consists of police, procuracies, courts and correctional institutions. At the central level, the Ministry of Public Security and the Ministry of Justice administer China's police and correctional institutions, respectively. The Supreme People's Court is the highest judicial branch in the country. The Supreme People's Procuracy is the highest state branch of legal supervision, with prosecution as its main function. The police departments or public security bureaus, the justice departments or bureaus, procuracies and courts at various levels are established to fulfil their respective duties in their own jurisdictions.

The Chinese government revised the Criminal Procedure Law in 1996 and the Criminal Law in 1997.[11] The revisions promised increased protection for criminal suspects and defendants and a fairer trial process.[12] The amendments to the Criminal Procedure Law included an expansion of the right to counsel, a more meaningful role for defence attorneys during the pre-trial and trial stages, and other measures to address the problem of 'decision first, trial later' (*xian ding hou shen*). The amended Criminal Law abolished the provision on 'analogy' contained in the 1979 Criminal Law. Under this provision, a person could be punished for an act that was not explicitly prohibited by law at the time the act was committed by providing for punishment according to the closest analogous provision of the Criminal Law.[13] The revised Criminal Law also replaced *counter-revolutionary* crimes with 'crimes of endangering national security' as part of an effort to depoliticise criminal law, at least on paper.

A wide discrepancy often exists in China between the law on paper and the law in practice. Criminal suspects and defendants frequently do not enjoy the enhanced protections found in the revised laws. Excessive pre-trial detention has not been stamped out. Legal representation, widespread as it now may be, is compromised by regular instances where public security organs detain and punish active defence advocates. The presumptions of innocence and against self-incrimination constitutionally accorded and declared in the International Covenant of Civil and Political Rights (ICCPR), which

China has signed, are common casualties in criminal justice delivery. Torture remains a feature of policing practice.

Although the revisions to the Criminal Procedure Law and the Criminal Law reflect progress toward internationally recognised criminal justice standards as set forth in the Universal Declaration of Human Rights, the ICCPR and other international human rights documents, the administration of criminal justice in China has been criticised for falling far short of international standards.[14] These criticisms should be seen against the prominence given in China to communitarian over individual rights. In addition, the excesses of a one-party state and its functionaries with little regard for the law in practice should not be confused with an institutionalised commitment to subvert international rights conventions.

> Most legal scholars have not completely abandoned the idea of 'Chinese characteristics' or 'China's social situation' for explaining the actual discrepancies between the PRC's CPL and international standards, but they speak about it in quite flat and unconvincing tones. Moreover, they often identify China's retrograde legal mentality as one of the key factors that hinder legal progress and reforms ... (following on from the administration's recent denunciation of the excesses of public justice officials), the state demonstrates its benevolence in its willingness to defend individual rights and it makes obvious to its citizens that criminal justice reforms are an actual 'Chinese necessity' and not an imposition from abroad. On the other side, in promoting ideas of proceduralism and respect for human rights, it internationally shows its goodwill to adhere to international standards. (Nessossi 2007: 19–20)

However, as Nessossi rightly observes, criminal justice reform in China cannot be entirely explained as an effort to enhance state legitimacy, domestically and internationally. Pressures coming out of rapid changes in the Chinese social order, which in turn have increased the significance of crime and the fragility of conventional approaches to control, have required a reinterpretation of the relationship between the offender, the victim and state institutions. In addition, legal academics and professionals, as well as activists with a growing voice, are pushing for rights-based reforms. Above all this, the Chinese compromise of individual rights and social security prevails, negotiated as it will continue to be by the interests of the one-party state.

The debate about the compliance of Chinese criminal justice in practice with international human rights will be distorted if taken exclusively from perspectives outside Chinese legal and social traditions. Both Confucian and Chinese communist philosophies emphasise order over freedom, duty over rights and group interests over those of the individual (Leng and Chiu 1985: 171).

> The main objective of the Chinese criminal justice system is to protect, first of all, the socialist order, and next, the people's personal rights. (Leng and Chiu 1985: 123)

The challenge for a relevant 'rights and justice' debate in China is to recognise the political force of collective and state interests over the protection of the individual, while not sacrificing the sharp edge of international human rights conventions. This is in light of the invitation to emphasise the significance of criminal justice in protecting the individual as well as the collective through the Constitution's celebration of constitutional legality and the invocation of the rule of law.

Article 3 of the Chinese Criminal Law provides that '... offenders shall be convicted and punished in accordance with the law ...' Besides Article 33 of the Constitution, Article 4 of the Criminal Law states: 'The law shall be equally applied to anyone who commits a crime. No one shall have the privilege of transcending the law'. Article 5 equates punishment with the crime committed and 'the criminal responsibility to be borne by the offender'.

When this comes to pre-eminent considerations of individual rights such as that of the victim as an essential paradigm for international criminal justice, Chinese criminal law presents the rights of the individual (even victims) as subordinate to the public right to control crime when there is a conflict between the two. This is despite provisions allowing for civil claims along with criminal prosecution. Provisions for victim participation in mediation and the trial process, as well as the opportunities for compensation,[15] mean that the protection of victim interests are in keeping with the intentions of the *Rome Statute*, and the practice of the international criminal tribunals, and are consistent with international rights conventions. These are not merely symbolic balances against abuse of power and miscarriages of justice. For instance, the Supreme Peoples' Court President, Xiao Yang, recently indicated that legal action by the public against government officials had risen in the past six years, with an average of 100,000 cases now being heard each year.[16]

Echoing the concern of the Chinese Politburo Standing Committee about unjust official practice, a senior member said: 'The Party and the country have attached great importance to administrative trial work. Administrative litigation plays an indispensable function in realising the rule of law, building a lawful socialist country, and forging a harmonious society.'

Within the reform agenda there is retained and developed a range of unique substantive and procedural approaches to liability which unfortunately do not yet feature in the emerging jurisprudence of international criminal law. We would argue that hybrid and dynamic traditions such as that in China merit a more detailed engagement, particularly with those issues of international criminal justice principles which are most problematic.

Resolving the tensions between individual and collective criminal liability in international prosecutions

The *Rome Statute*[17] when determining *individual responsibility* states that the court shall have jurisdiction 'over *natural persons* pursuant to this Statute'.[18] However, during an address to the second assembly of State Parties, the first Chief Prosecutor of the ICC, Louis Moreno-Ocampo declared the intention to locate responsibility for crimes of genocide, war crimes and crimes against humanity in Ituri (Democratic Republic of Congo) in a wider arc.

> Different armed groups have taken advantage of the situation of generalised violence and have engaged in the illegal exploitation of key mineral resources ... according to information received crimes reportedly committed in Ituri appear to be directly linked to the control of resource extraction sites. Those who direct mining operations, sell diamonds or gold extracted in these conditions, launder the dirty money, or provide weapons could be authors of the crime, even if they are based in other countries.

No indictments have yet been laid by the ICC against corporations. Indeed, it has been argued (Eser 2002: 77) that both due to the significant evidentiary difficulties involved and on the principle of complementarity (if corporate criminal liability is not recognised in many national legal orders), it would then be inappropriate for the ICC to claim this jurisdiction.[19]

The ICC Prosecutor has signalled an interest to investigate beyond the immediate territory of local and regional armed conflict, and to extend narrower notions of criminal responsibility which have been accepted by the ad hoc tribunals. These courts have preferred to debate the nature of joint criminal enterprise,[20] common purpose and accessorial liability in international criminal law rather than embracing more collective concepts of responsibility which are at the heart of vicarious and corporate liability. The only ICC arrest warrant issued so far relating to the Congo conflict concerns the enlisting of children for the purposes of active participation in the hostilities.[21]

The UN Special Court for Sierra Leone (SCSL) has identified the unlawful international trade in diamonds as central to the funding of and motivation for conflict. In response the UN Security Council[22] expressed 'its concern at the role played by the illicit trade in diamonds in fuelling the conflict in Sierra Leone', and directed that steps be taken by certain states towards controlling the trade. Even so, the SCSL has not indicted any individual or organisation for trading in diamonds which then exacerbated military conflict.

Recently, the Max Plank Institute for Foreign and International Criminal Law (on behalf of the ICTY) conducted a global survey of national jurisdictions to understand and contrast the laws on joint criminal enterprise and collective liability. China provided a national report. The Chinese position exhibits certain unique interpretations of collective liability that, if influential on the development of ICC jurisprudence, might assist in the more creative and effective prosecution of collective liability beyond the limitations of common law and civil law principles:

- Under the section of the Criminal Law of the PRC dealing with criminal liability which examines 'joint crimes' (Ch. 2 s. 3) negligent commission will not substantiate inclusion in a joint criminal enterprise (Art. 25).

- Joint crimes are comprised of two or more persons in concert or *criminal groups*. A criminal group is organised and led by an individual in carrying out criminal activities.

- A criminal group is a relatively stable criminal organisation formed by three or more people for the purposes of committing crimes jointly (Art. 26).

- The punishment applied to members of a criminal organisation may vary depending on the nature and status of participation and whether coercion was present.

- More than this, any 'company, enterprise, institution, state organ, or organisation that commits an act that endangers society, which is prescribed by law as a crime committed by a unit, shall bear criminal responsibility' (Art. 30).

- If such a unit commits a crime, the unit and the individuals involved will be punished separately (Art. 31).

I am not suggesting that the general direction of the law relating to joint enterprise is unique in China. However, arguably original is the emphasis on the group and its organisation both as a locus and an entity for crime. In addition, considering criminal liability in terms of organisation opens up potential synergies with the determination of liability from 'criminal cultures' (ways of doing things and prevailing organisational ethics towards criminality) which are being explored in Australian law regarding corporate criminal liability. As is done commonly with the proscription of criminal societies in order to protect public order and national security, I consider the Chinese concentration on *criminal groups* a constructive paradigm for international criminal law to investigate in its search for an adequate method of prosecuting corporate liability.

The potential for substantive and procedural influence from the Chinese criminal procedural tradition over contentious concerns for international criminal liability, while significant, is in no way as potent as the traditional Chinese ways of mediation and communitarian intervention.

Alternative international criminal justice – the way forward for China?

As mentioned earlier, the alternative or non-formal justice paradigms are developing a significant dimension of international criminal justice. China is also heavily reliant on mediation-based communitarian criminal justice delivery at a local level. Despite the fact that this level of criminal justice is usually applied to less serious offending, it exhibits structures and processes of participation and of judicial creativity, from which both the formal and less formal international justice paradigms could learn.

The restorative justice paradigm is where unique Chinese socio-legal traditions can be meaningfully displayed. On this perspective and its relevance to the Chinese culture, Braithwaite laments:

> What a pity that so few Western intellectuals are engaged with the possibilities for recovering, understanding, and preserving the virtues of Chinese restorative justice while studying how to check its abuses with a liberalising rule of law.
>
> (Braithwaite 2002: 22)

As asserted earlier, there have been and still are powerful communitarian resolution practices operating across the peoples of China before and after the creation of the Communist Republic. These represent the Confucian and communist commitment to social order above the individual and in this regard may be both commended as restorative and yet criticised as outside the individualised rights environment of international human rights law. Braithwaite notes that while the traditions of mediation have survived translation into the 'mass line' strategies of Maoist communism, the dangerous patriarchal and hierarchic communitarianism of Confucian social order also has prevailed. Does this have to be so? Is it not possible to maximise the humanitarian and harmonising potentials of *bang-jiao* where real reintegration replaces stigmatising shaming, as mass mediation takes the place of formal punishment?

Another important consequence of interrogating Chinese communitarian traditions in contemporary criminal justice is the consequent reconfiguration of the rights debate. As noticed earlier, Chinese criminal justice has long been denigrated for failing to protect the individual rights of offenders in particular. As with international criminal justice, however, this concentration on the individual tends to diminish the other significant rights consideration in criminal justice, which restorative models re-emphasise. Collective or communitarian rights considerations, important in Chinese mediation environments, are also essential (if undervalued) in the confirmation of criminal justice internationally. The Chinese experience in recognising and protecting the rights of the community might add important understandings to victim interests in international criminal justice.

Zhong and Broadhurst (2007) argue that Chinese communitarian crime prevention has a rich tradition. In many respects it is the safety and social harmony of the neighbourhood which has motivated successful community crime prevention and social order programmes along with any consideration of victim protection or offender punishment. The crucial features of these programmes are their community organisational dimensions, the safety measures they incorporate (in collaboration with state organs) and their tendency to *civilise* communities through moral education, the promotion of harmonious relationships, building community culture and the purification of the environment.

Yet as is the case with so many societies experiencing rapid and radical socio-economic transformation, the nature of Chinese urban communities is fast-changing. The bonds of tradition which join community sentiment around the household and the family are strained through the itinerant migration which rages as a consequence of economic transition. Crime and the fear of crime accompany these changes. The conventional communitarian controls which were once sufficient to ensure social harmony and keep crime in check are as much at risk as are the communities they support, and the positive social consequences which they could claim. In this respect, the potential for the Chinese experience to inform the communitarian dimensions of international criminal justice goes beyond modelling or cultural convergence. The threats to communitarian control at work in China today, their consequences for the transformation of community crime control and the effective measures to minimise their negative intrusion give a critical case study from which much can be drawn.

Integrating hybrid traditions

China is playing a powerful role in regional and international relations. As with China's eventual entry into GATT and the WTO, we argue that a closer involvement in international criminal justice is a matter of advancing rather than risking national interest through more influential positioning within global governance trends. Such a move would benefit China on a number of levels:

- An important role for the ICC is to promote the improvement of domestic judicial systems. As a consequence of the new constitutional legality and its ascription to the rule of law voiced through China's present Constitution, recent legislative developments in China have indicated a genuine commitment to raise the domestic institutions of justice to prominence within China's national governance framework. For instance the Organic Law of the Peoples' Courts in China is an attempt to confront the paradox of judicial independence in a one-party state (Findlay 1999c). The new Criminal and Criminal Procedure Codes, and their particular influence over the development of the legal profession in China, and the rights and responsibilities of trial participants can be nurtured through a closer association with the development of international criminal justice process.

• The ICC should not run counter to UN rights charters to which China is a signatory. Particularly with the developing jurisdiction over crimes of aggression China would be wise to take a prominent role in this emerging jurisprudence.

However, beyond domestic concerns:

• China, as a developed exponent of restorative justice through mediation and an exponent of transformed trial adjudication, can critically inform similar developmental trends in international criminal justice.

• As a dynamic hybrid criminal procedural tradition, the Chinese experience of criminal law and process can assist in the formulation of a truly international and responsive criminal jurisprudence. This can be achieved, in our view, without the distraction of an overemphasis on the challenges to individual human rights in the Chinese delivery of domestic criminal justice.

In any case, China is not an island when it comes to the development of its contemporary criminal justice practice. China has benefited from mutual cooperation programmes in the area of criminal justice. For instance, the Canada-China Criminal Justice Cooperation Programme is claimed to have significantly developed the procuracy (Yang 2002). Internally, the 'Implementing International Standards for Criminal Justice in China Programme'[23] shows that academic lawyers from three recognised Chinese law schools are concerned to address the practical challenges of bringing domestic criminal justice in practice to a level of international comparability. It is argued that this bi-lateral capacity building will make the achievement of a *rule of law* context for criminal justice eventually attainable.

Essential for the achievement of reintegrative and communitarian justice aspirations in China and internationally is *participation*. From a victim perspective in particular, limited access to the formal institutions of international criminal justice and thereby a lack of genuine integration is a growing indictment of international criminal justice in practice. Certainly in terms of grassroots engagement with victim's interests there is much that international criminal justice could draw from contemporary Chinese experience, in particular the following:

1 The processes of mobilising people to resolve social conflicts through mediation as a central plank of communitarian justice.

2 Enshrined victim's rights to participate, such as to make accusations, attend court and give evidence regarding the nature and extent of victimisation, and to question defendants in court, argue the facts with the defendant and have some influence over the investigation. In the Chinese Criminal Procedure Law (CPL), however, these rights are based on retributive rather than restorative values.

3 Article 170 CPL enables victims to independently and individually prosecute crimes where their personal and property rights have been infringed. The court may also institute judicial mediation in instances of private prosecution. Under Article 172 the judge has both the role of facilitating the victim and the offender to reach resolution and reconciliation, and if the parties cannot resolve the matter, to act as an arbitrator and to issue a verdict. The importance of this merging of restorative and retributive justice within the discretion of the judge and in the setting of the courtroom cannot be overstated for the future of international criminal justice. While currently in China the discretion of the judge in such deliberations is more directed to avoid formal determinations of the offender's criminal liability rather than compensating the victim or rehabilitating the offender, there is no reason why the development of this model in the international justice setting could not re-emphasise these other legitimate victim concerns.

4 Article 77 CPL provides a formal opportunity for the victim to institute supplementary civil action against the perpetrator in parallel with the criminal proceedings. Interestingly, the same court will hear both the civil and criminal cases, and again may revert to mediation to resolve the compensation issue. If no agreement can be struck there from, the civil claim is formally heard after criminal liability is settled. There is no provision for mitigating the offender's criminal responsibility (and consequent sanction) if compensation is agreed to. Without this, certainly at the international level, there

may be insufficient effective inducement for adequate compensation to victim communities from state perpetrators in particular.

5 In addition to judicial facilitation through mediation, the offender can be incorporated into the facilitation process.

6 Crucially, in this cross-over of jurisdictional interests for the victim, the judge determines where his role as mediator ends and as adjudicator begins.

The *danwei* (work unit) system in China is transforming to take account of the new workforce landscape. Neighbourhood and residents committees remain in competition with the property management companies with their growing control over housing development in urban areas of China. Neighbourhood interests struggle against commercial priorities in order to maintain cohesive community-level control priorities. With the Chinese urban landscape transforming at an incredible rate over the past few decades, social control mechanisms such as mediation and *bang-jiao* are experiencing new and largely unexplored pressures. Even so, peoples' mediation (*tiao-jie*) is being supplemented by administrative and judicial mediation opportunities. The state and the community are being required to incorporate in a model which was once only a communitarian concern.

This unique case study of the exercise of judicial discretion over retributive and restorative process provides empirical foundation for some of our projections on transforming international trial decision-making (Findlay and Henham 2005; forthcoming). It also identifies the competing interests at work which may compromise the promise of mediation and other restorative forms within a rights framework that tries to respect individual and community interests.

Conclusion

The significance of victim community interests in legitimating ICJ and governance argues for a more conscious recognition of transitional cultures in global governance and hybrid traditions in the criminal justice component. Put simply, victim communities are often from transitional cultures, and might otherwise be left to the determinations of nation-states wherein hybrid or marginalised criminal justice systems operate problematically with little inter-national outreach. The problem identified and developed in the following chapter is that globalisation is tending to undermine legal and cultural pluralism. This in turn is reinforcing the intransigence and resistance of fundamentalist jurisdictions and isolated cultures to engage with ICJ and global governance.

How to stimulate engagement when globalisation works against the incorporation of transitional cultures within the regulatory frameworks of global governance is more than a matter of political realignment. Realistically the dominant political hegemony is unlikely to divest its dominion over global governance to facilitate this engagement unless its interests are shown to be served in so doing. Ironically, a key to this might be the risk/security focus of globalisation.

In Chapter 4, I suggested that violent justice responses to global terror carry with them the potential to exacerbate risk and endanger security. Non-violent justice responses to terror and other significant global crime risks are attractive at least in avoiding the violence spiral and promoting peacemaking and conflict resolution.

Globalisation is concerned with risk and security and employs international criminal justice as an important regulatory strategy. The national and regional divisions which often result in violent conflicts over state sovereignty and victimise innocent citizens caught up in the conflict are more effectively addressed through inclusive international criminal justice. Also, ICJ (formal and less formal) can provide adjudicatory and mediation environments where what separates terrorist and victim communities can be interrogated without violence.

Achieving a more universal and effective role for ICJ in the eyes of the dominant political alliance and its enemies will depend on enhanced legitimacy from victim communities. Victim communities, as a designated constituency of ICJ, also have the potential to endorse global governance in post-conflict settings. The legitimacy offered by the endorsement and involvement of victim communities in justice and governance will accompany a commitment from these frameworks to greater access, inclusivity and intervention.

The transformation of ICJ, as discussed in the chapter to follow, and its modifying and emancipating impact on global governance must have positive consequences for risk and security. If so, the focus for globalisation (with the assistance of ICJ as a central regulatory strategy) may eventually complement more concrete and credible directions in grounded global *good governance*.

Notes

1 This is the empowering legislation for the International Criminal Court (ICC) settled by the UN Diplomatic Conference of Plenipotentiaries on the Establishment of an International Criminal Court (17 July 1998).

2 This notion is explored in chapter 8 of Findlay and Henham (2005). It invites consideration of international crime victimisation beyond individual harm or even generic notions of 'humanity'.

3 See Zhong and Broadhurst (2007), for a discussion of the pressures at work on communitarian control in the cities as China transforms economically and the Chinese workforce breaks free of the household registration system.

4 For instance, note the efforts employed to position China within the WTO.

5 Evidence of these tensions in the Chinese context, against instances of individual and institutional abuses of power and miscarriages of justice, are described in great detail in Nesossi (2007).

6 See Lu and Wang (2005: n.23).

7 Even the US has reluctantly signed on.

8 Lu and Wang (2005: n.9).

9 Martinez, in Stanford Lawyer (2005).

10 For example, in the control of gambling see Findlay and Zvekic (1988) (1993).

11 Criminal Procedure Law of the People's Republic of China [*Zhonghua renmin gongheguo xingshi susongfa*], adopted 1 July 1979, amended 17 March 1996 [hereinafter 'Criminal Procedure Law']; Criminal Law of the People's Republic of China [*Zhonghua renmin gongheguo xingfa*], adopted 1 July 1979, amended 14 March 1997 [here in after 'Criminal Law'].

12 See generally Lawyers Committee for Human Rights, Opening to Reform? An Analysis of China's Revised Criminal Procedure Law, October 1996 [hereinafter, 'LCHR, Opening to Reform?']; Lawyers Committee for Human Rights, Wrongs and Rights: A Human Rights Analysis of China's Revised Criminal Law, December 1998 [hereinafter 'LCHR, Wrongs and Rights'].

13 In theory, the abolition of analogy brings the Criminal Law into conformance with the principle of *nullum crimen sine lege* (no crime without law making it so), which is expressed in Article 11 of the Universal Declaration of Human Rights: 'No one shall be held guilty of any penal offence on account of any act or omission which did not constitute a penal offence, under national or international law, at the time when it was committed.'

14 Congressional Executive Committee on China Annual Report 2002 – http://www.cecc.gov/pages/virtualAcad/crimjustice/crimeannrept02.php

15 Article 14(6) of the ICCPR creates a right to compensation for miscarriages of justice. According to Art. 15 of the PRC State Compensation Law, victims can claim compensation if an investigative, procuratorial, judicial or prison organ infringes their rights by, among other things, wrongful detention or arrest without substantiated strong suspicion or sufficient incriminating facts.

16 Wang, I. (2007) 'People's legal action on the rise', *South China Morning Post*, 30 March.

17 Article 25:1, *Rome Statute for the International Criminal Court* (Rome Statute).

18 In commenting on this Article, Albin Eser observes that '... there can be no doubt that by limiting criminal responsibility to individual natural persons, the Rome Statute implicitly negates – at least for its own jurisdiction – the punishability of corporations and other legal entities' (Eser 2002: 778). The same is the case for the International Criminal Tribunal for the Former Yugoslavia (ICTY) and the International Tribunal for Rwanda (ICTR) (Article 6, *ICTY Statute*; Articles 1 and 5, *ICTR Statute*).

19 The success rate for prosecutions at the Nuremberg Tribunal (and cases following) of persons playing an economic role in crime was poor (Eser 2002: 307–10).

20 For instance before the ICTY see *Prosecutor* v. *Tadic*, Case No. IT-94-1-T, TC Judgement 7.5.97; *Prosecutor* v. *Tadic*, Case No. IT-94-1-A, AC Judgement 17.7.99.

21 See *Prosecutor* v. *Dylio*, Case No. ICC-01/04-01/06. Warrant of Arrest 10.02.06.

22 Security Council Resolution 1306 (2000).

23 http://www.icclr.law.ubc.ca/china_iiscj/index.html

Chapter 9

Global governance and the future of international criminal justice transformed

This means rethinking politics. We need to take our established ideas about political equality, social justice and liberty and refashion these into a coherent political project robust enough for a world where power is exercised on a transnational scale and where risks are shared by peoples across the world. And we need to think about what institutions will allow us to tackle these global problems while responding to the aspirations of the people they are meant to serve. (Held *et al.* 1999: 495–6)

Introduction

This final chapter I intend to be unconventional as a conclusion. Usually, the end of a work such as this draws together in summary the central themes of analysis and attempts a coalescence of thought which leaves the reader satisfied that the argument has been contained. I may not leave you so satisfied.

In part this is a consequence of the futurism that pervades this section. It is challenging enough to be definitive about the current state of international criminal law and international criminal justice. Both are in formative states, with unstable and contested foundations, immature jurisprudence and a development plagued by the burden of politicisation. International criminal law claims lineage from international customary law, far from a settled legal tradition in itself (Cryer *et al.* 2007). The human rights predisposition of international public law has not been convincingly taken up in international

215

criminal justice, certainly not when considering second-generation rights. The institutions of ICJ are yet to be fully installed or, like the international criminal tribunals and the special criminal courts, may have a shelf life dependent on the interest of the UN Security Council. All this does not instil confidence in the smooth and rich evolution of a new and vital formal legal tradition.

Then there is the *alternative* justice paradigm. It is clear that informal, transitional and grassroots justice institutions and processes are contesting precedence with the retributive and more politically endorsed formal ICJ structures (see Findlay and Henham 2005). This leaves even the common or perhaps cohesive representation of ICJ and its distinct responsibility to process international criminal law in a state of flux.

Necessarily in the earlier chapters some important tangential themes are left undeveloped, and definitional issues have not always been run to ground. To pause and fully explore each conjecture would have fragmented a central argument, drawing as it does on certain general and contingent assertions. I delayed unpacking a number of these assertions and challenge their constructive effect on the future of international criminal justice. However, like deeply problematic concerns such as the relative risk represented by global terror, the analysis has worked with political and popular conceptualisation in order to explain important causal connections. Here it is time to interrogate these popular wisdoms and their roots.

Another difficulty with this analysis so far has been the relentless need to range across broad disciplines in order to engage with grand themes like globalisation, global governance and international political hegemony. Issues such as culture, custom, community, the state and political dominion have had to receive general treatment in a work such as this. Deep and more critical interrogation within the framework of independent analytical and regulatory traditions would not have permitted the central consideration of nexus and transformation to receive convincing dynamic treatment. To achieve the purposes of testing important structural and functional connections, the analysis has constantly been required to accept priorities and procedural boundaries inherent in the nature of globalisation and its predisposition to justice in limited form as governance. Outside these constraints, as the literature on globalisation demonstrates, there is much work which challenges the integrity of these assumptions. I am more interested in their interconnection rather than their inconsistencies for the purposes of global governance, symbolic and actual.

Having recently enjoyed a lecture by Brian Tamanaha[1] in which he pierced the mysteries of legal pluralism I am encouraged to advance some critical reflections which my analysis so far has been skirting. By repositioning his take on pluralism, the discussion that follows will address and engage some of the more open questions that the context of the *new* globalisation necessitates for global governance and, within it, justice regulations.

My concluding thoughts are around the notion of dialectic and how it enables a critical evaluation of relationships between crime, risk, security and governance. In addition, the paradox of globalisation to which I referred ten years back (Findlay 1999b) is now recurrent in the justice/governance dialectic. Using this analytical model I will show how an extant purpose of the new globalisation, what I call the *war on pluralism*, supports why crime and justice are crucially located within international governance. This anti-pluralist push will also reveal the connection between globalisation and a dominant neo-liberal political culture.

From here, the dialectic will be refined. A *war on pluralism* is ongoing in the context of specific pluralist regulation on the rise. The chapter will move beyond the fragmentation of formal politics, justice and governance to consider how victim communities and *communities of justice* (see Chapter 7) exist and survive in a contrary direction and movement in global governance that celebrates pluralism in many normative and process contexts.

Returning to law and justice as global governance tools the dialectical directions of globalisation will be examined in the context of legal pluralism and models of regulation. More particularly, international criminal law and ICJ as a central model of global regulation (somewhat artificially distanced from administrative and commercial regulation) (see Dorn, forthcoming) are returned to in order to test my original crime and global governance assumptions.

To be clear, the focus on international criminal justice as a regulatory model discussed to this point consciously avoids other related legal or normative regimes of regulation where this intolerance of pluralism is not so apparent, if at all. For instance, global commercial ordering, the formal and informal frameworks of *lex mercatori*, has conjoined to advance international capitalism. This novel regulatory model clearly establishes a mutual relationship between globalisation and pluralism in a market context. Even so, if my arguments about the dialectic situation of international criminal justice and governance are sustained, they are not diminished by failing to translate into a grand theory of globalisation and governance. That was never the intention. On the contrary, a particular risk/security social location for global regulatory options places ICJ and governance, post-military intervention, in a unique contemporary position when governance is at issue.

The governance project within globalisation is as diverse as the cultures it confronts. I say that ICJ is essential for global governance where the risk of terror is the identified challenge and militarism has conceded to justice as a regulatory model. This does not mean that administrative or commercial regulatory frameworks more pluralistic in their operations may not exist alongside ICJ in the wider global governance project (Dorn, forthcoming). ICJ can be employed to counter violent challenges to state integrity, and in so doing may work from pre-existing administrative regulation and rely on consequent commercial consolidation. As Tamanaha observes of global regulation more generally (2007), its hybridity and fluidity at once expresses the distinctions from which globalisation proceeds and at the same time challenges essential indicators of traditional identity. Law, justice and crime are three such indicators under challenge.

The concluding speculation of this chapter on *where to international criminal justice?*, provokes the global justice regulatory model towards to a more conventional purpose in making governance accountable while at the same time transforming its institutions and processes so that they better represent new victim constituencies.

Before returning to the *new* globalisation project and its influence on regulatory pluralism, it is worthwhile recounting the reasons for this book.

Restating the thesis

Put simply the argument in this book advances from two directions. First is to say that formal ICJ has become a key element of post-military global governance. The *justice* frameworks influencing global governance are both conventional institutions and processes such as courts and tribunals and the *para-justice* distortions that now feature as an important control mechanism of the dominant political alliance (see Chapter 3). The other direction indicates that the current phase of globalisation, with its risk/security focus, has politicised ICJ in the governance spectrum. This in turn challenges the legitimacy of ICJ in conflict resolution and accountable global governance more generally. The challenge I propose is through a radically trans-formed ICJ to return it to a more communitarian, inclusive and accountable practice of justice which then can keep global governance *honest*.

The crucial stakeholders in this analysis are the dominant political alliance and victim communities whether they are legitimated through global citizenship or excluded through criminalisation and military might. The new globalisation is committed to endorsing the dominant political alliance against cultural challenge and violent resistance. Global governance directed against risk and security is intolerant of normative and *value* pluralism (see Chapter 2). The war against polarised risk marginalises resistant cultures and valorises victim/citizen communities. Therefore global governance secures the interest of a global citizen community and criminalises resistant communities and contrary cultures (see Chapter 7).

But to achieve security aims against risk as determined in global governance, justice so modelled has become complicit and thereby a victim in its own terms. The proliferation of para-justice distortions is testament to their political instrumentality which endangers the conventional features of formal criminal justice as a governance accountability framework. Para-justice at least recognises the need from the dominant political alliance to work outside the minimal due process restrictions of ICJ, while at the same time claiming their legitimacy within wider frameworks of global governance. But both ICJ and global governance institutions and processes have not been able to successfully challenge and overturn the para-justice distortions of the dominant alliance. In fact they have been compromised by sharing a common preoccupation with risk and security designated through a narrow and exclusionist political/cultural lens (see Chapter 5). The political and cultural hegemony preferred in globalisation, and so influential over contemporary global governance, strongly dictates the styles of ICJ on offer.

Pluralism within globalisation

Tamanaha, not content to deconstruct legal pluralism in the various phases of globalisation (feudal land tenure, European colonisation, industrialisation and early capitalism, and the modern), suggests the significance of competing normative systems and what happens for global governance when inevitable clashes between these arise. I am principally interested in an international criminal justice regulatory model for global governance. But when it fits within *new* globalisation, the interface with other regulatory frameworks reveals the idiosyncratic impact of a regulatory strategy intolerant of competing forms.

At a time when he was convinced about its actuality Griffiths (1997) said of legal pluralism that it represented a fundamental 'characteristic of social affairs'. As such pluralism was central to the operation of social ordering. Legal pluralism, in his view, comprised an agglomeration of governmental and non-governmental norms.

Legal pluralism is one normative style and one regulatory option in governance with a capacity to engage with cultural diversity. ICJ, with its preference for a compromise of Western procedural traditions, has been employed to control the risk of global terror and impose the security of a dominant legal order. As such, a sympathetic combination in competing styles of regulation is unlikely to feature in global governance crime/control, risk/security considerations.

The globalisation project to modernise the world economy has undermined cultural integrity and diversity (Findlay 1999b). The new globalisation and its *war on terror* have tended to reject regulatory strategies that appreciate cultural diversity and recognise the signifi-cance of pluralist security priorities.

The globalisation project in context

For me the hurdle in this analysis is to adequately reconcile the dialectic which is the new globalisation. I hinted at this in the conclusion to *The Globalisation of Crime* (1999) by suggesting a paradox waiting to be resolved. The paradox as I saw it then was between the *one culture/many cultures* audience for globalisation. Cultural harmonisation through economic modernisation was then the assignment and the outcome for globalisation. However, a materialist economic model centred on artificial divisions of labour and capitalist market dynamics relies on mass movements of workers across the globe to drive production. In addition, some degree of consumer market diversity favours consumerism. For the sake of economic profit at least, a mixing of different and dependent cultures in a singular industrial and economic environment is essential for modernisation. The wealth generated for some is at the expense of others and cultures would continue to divide, rich and poor.

The identity offered through economic opportunity is at the same time denied through constant uprooting from communities of origin. The paradox is between cultural harmony, economic conformity, and community difference. It has not been resolved in this new phase of globalisation. My impression is that this paradox over cultural strain will not be capable of resolution, so long as the theme of regulatory pluralism remains vulnerable to contextual negotiation where risk/security plays a central role.

Working my way to the determination of crime and global governance, I have avoided so far a detailed interrogation of pluralism and the challenge to it which new globalisation represents. Globalisation as a process of change epitomises hybridity and fluidity. However, the mission of the new globalisation is a confined governing regulatory strategy in the face of terror. The focus of my analysis is criminal justice regulation and as such what I have to say concerning globalisation and regulation has up until now been constrained within that concern.

In order not to distort the relative significance of criminal justice governance for globalisation, it is necessary to consider alternative normative frameworks of control and discuss the clashes which arise through their competing application. Analysing some of these clashes will highlight the artificiality of risk/security as a global governance priority. The preferred military, then justice responses to violent terror risks, struggle against cultural and regulatory pluralism otherwise tolerated in globalisation. The application of formal ICJ to the regulation of global terrorism exemplifies this. Prioritising the risk of global terror and neutralising the meaning of violent resistance through military incursion, and next through justice segregation, has tended to de-legitimate cultural diversity where it cannot be denied.

The hybridity and fluidity of globalisation exposes the resilience of cultural difference in the face of impressive and intrusive political domination internationally and challenges traditional identity. Inside this process of cultural colonisation, denial and resistance simmer the tensions that ultranationalism and religious fundamentalism foster in confronting globalisation and its universal ideals for governance and economic advancement.

Tamanaha suggests that in clashes over difference and commonality might emerge some central insights into the nature and development of globalisation. I have already spent some time disentangling these as they relate to the risk/security nexus. Now it is useful to go outside the narrow regulatory conundrum created through the threat of global terror and examine risk and security for the modernisation project at large. In so doing, regulatory pluralism in other important contexts of globalisation challenges the essence of a narrow formalist ICJ regulatory model facing international terror.

Clashes in regulatory strategies, normative frameworks for law and ultimately over cultural integrity are not the sole consequences of criminal justice reaching a crucial position of influence in global governance. In fact if ICJ were operating for the benefit of *humanity* rather than for communities in the victor's domain, then it should act to resolve rather than exacerbate conflict. Until ICJ can adequately recognise as its constituency the diverse culture of *humanity* then it will be unable to impartially scrutinise the cultural tension which globalisation tries to repress.

The cultural paradox of globalisation is not an inevitable invitation to *chaos theory*. *Chaos theory* which employs clash or conflict scenarios is reliant on the existence of difference and strains to manage that difference. Globalisation is in the business of strain management, through denial *and* through exploitation. The current incarnation of ICJ in global governance is active in cultural diminution while purporting to protect humanity. This is another tension within globalisation as it stimulates the evolution of an international criminal justice worthy of its mission. To understand the dynamics of managing the tensions within globalisation, pluralism (and legal pluralism in particular) offers much for the management of cultural conflict, violent and otherwise. Hegemony is the first enemy of pluralism as it operates to deliver global governance against a particular terror and for a delimited security.

The dialectic of global hegemony

I have already suggested that the monocultural push in globalisation is paradoxical (Findlay 1999b). Modernisation may be the preferred cultural context for globalisation, but the reaction to modernisation in many instances has been a reassertion of nationalism and a reformulation of economic development within particular customary and cultural settings. Even so, the trappings of modernisation are seductive particularly to those constituents of transitional societies where materialism and its aspirations bite hardest.

Free market economics and liberal democratic governance structures accompany the global march of modernisation. Here too the hegemony required by dominant political alliances in order to secure the preferred economic model is necessarily culturally elitist and exclusionary (see Chapter 8). This is *hegemony* through economic rather than political dominion, offering a discourse of inclusion and democracy for any and all who commit to the modernisation project.

Governance becomes an issue of global hegemony into which ICJ is now crucially incorporated. This is so despite more communitarian neo-liberal aspirations for criminal justice regionally and domestically, and bearing in mind the absence of credible and culturally inclusive forms of global democracy (see Chapter 7). Endorsing and largely endorsed by this hegemony is a style of contemporary global governance set in a risk/security commitment.

One could argue that the predominant regulatory frameworks of global governance are concerned with the control of economic resources through the advancement of the modernisation project. However, the risk/security focus of globalisation sporadically redirects regulation priorities along a militarist/justice push. Released from this risk/security focus and its attendant influence over global regulation strategies, globalisation would have remained dedicated to economic modernisation. As such, value pluralism and cultural differentiation could have continued to be employed in the advancement of a common commercial agenda (see Chapter 1). Risk/security has fractured this tolerance.

So where does the risk/security focus for globalisation come from? It is not only a consequence of 9/11 terror. Risk and security, featuring in global governance still tied to the modernisation project and sharpening their regulatory relevance as routes and resources essential for materialist profit, came under terrorist threat. When materialist economy, stability, prosperity, and ultimately the life of the globalised market are violently endangered through cultural resistance and normative contradiction then contained and politically contingent regulatory strategies are trained against such an outcome.

In earlier phases of globalisation regulatory strategies engaged with cultural diversity and sometimes adapted to a variety of cultural contexts (Findlay 1999b). Risk/security as a contemporary global governance priority has globalisation at war with cultural diversity and regulatory pluralism. The socio-economic divide as a by-product of modernisation further differentiates states, regions and cultures. Compared with terrorism which may be fostered by it, socio-economic disparity fails to be recognised as an equivalent influence over risk/security and their global resolution.

On this level, ICJ is wedged. Its interests in crimes against humanity and genocide cannot be contained within hard legalist parameters of individual liability. The demand from governance that ICJ should be effective in state reconstruction has seen to that. ICJ (formal and informal) now legitimately crosses over from legality to conflict resolution and peacemaking as important competing priorities (Braithwaite 2002).

The connection between poverty, crime and inhumanity is clear (Braithwaite 1979). As such this link should be (and is) at the heart of ICJ dedicated as it is to protect humanity against criminal harm. But ICJ is now so aligned to the cause of victor's justice that poverty and social inequality are sidelined to contextualising crimes against humanity rather than as crucial conditions for individual and collective liability. The rejection of state terrorism as a central concern for formal ICJ is vivid evidence of the potential to ignore political and economic discrimination in determining global crime.

A neo-liberal value structure as the preferred normative framework for the new globalisation passes over this poverty/humanity link as the core threat to world order, in preference for apprehending the dangers demonstrated by terrorism (see Chapter 2). The critique of equitable global governance (if ever so defined) is not therefore simply about real and measurable risks to security, but their selective prioritisation against wider and more prevailing *crimes* against humanity. For global governance to reflect a more humanitarian justice focus it should confront the political reasons why risk threats and security responses are ranked against political and economic rather than humanitarian concerns.

The dialectic of global hegemony is so posed. The dominant political alliance has long set economic priorities for globalisation. Despite the discriminatory consequences of these priorities, they are explained in terms of opportunity enhancement for the global community. Any challenge to the security of this economic model and the communities that benefit from it and enjoy it are identified as risks worthy of harsh and immediate security intervention. Along the way, crimes against humanity, ethnic cleansing, genocide and war crimes victimise poor and underdeveloped cultures. Global terror attacks the rich West. At the same time it decimates innocent victim communities in places like Iraq in order to foment further violent opposition to the dominant political alliance. These outrages in part may be seen as the *inhumane* downside of globalisation both generating and confronting violent and resistant communities. This is the *thesis and antithesis* of hegemonic global governance moulded as it is by modernist economics and the exclusive cultural/political alliance best benefited by it.

International criminal justice becomes important in the governance mix as the potential agent for synthesis. The injection of ICJ within global governance frameworks can result in selective and discriminatory law enforcement and criminal justice service delivery. However, in a different fashion from bald political domination and military intervention, ICJ is mediated and universalised through resonant ideologies such as the rule of law. Apparently insulated from cultural relativity, ICJ rests its powers to select and discriminate in authority idealised above political parties and military adventurism. The constituency for ICJ may also be objectified as worthy or valorised victim communities than more obvious relationships of political patronage. The hegemony of global governance gains from ICJ a mantle of legitimacy in the resolution of the conflicts which may have arisen as a direct result of globalising the preferred global economic and cultural model.

If this dialectic (and its synthesis) is a fact of contemporary globalisation, then the global governance by powerful states and alliances is, for the time being, inevitable. Humanitarian values increasingly become contingent when only powerful elites can meaningfully assert humanity's value and status. Formal trial-centred ICJ has come to confirm this process through a culturally narrow brand of justice regulation protecting a privileged citizen/victim community. Criminalisation distinctions available through ICJ litigation offer legitimacy to a system which excludes the poor, the resistant and their contrary cultures.

The dialectic of ICJ and global governance

Beyond its broad neutralising function, why is ICJ so important in contemporary global governance? The answer lies in the capacity of ICJ to legitimate *the truth* as determined through a dominant political *and* legal culture.

The role of *alternative* ICJ mechanisms in the negotiation of *truth* is well documented (see Chapter 5). In fact, those who advance restorative or transitional justice have warned that the burden imposed on reconciliation mechanisms to market *truth* for the primary purposes of state reconstruction and political conflict resolution risks the capacity of informal mechanisms of crime control satisfying the restorative interests of victim communities (Findlay and Henham 2005). Even so, the potential of ICJ to construct and confirm wider political and cultural *truths* is more evident in the role of institutionalised ICJ within global governance, and just as problematic.

Like globalisation and its current economic monotheism, ICJ advances a preferred style of justice delivery which diminishes resistance as inconsistent with an individualised rights model and thereby unjust, or at worst criminal. The normative and procedural core is order through the rule of law and punishment as a consequence of liability. Resistance to a liberal, sectarian, Western justice model not only challenges the governance which it supports, but also the authority and integrity of the justice it administers.

Synthesising tensions of this nature between a culturally preferred justice model, and resistance to it, is contained in ICJ's potential to protect *humanity* (above sovereignty and citizenship). In this lies the seed to critique the real place of ICJ within global governance: the failure to realise this potential except in a selective and partisan fashion.

As noted in the previous chapter, an explanation for the fit between international trial justice and the individualised ideology of neo-liberalism is the almost exclusive influence of the Western criminal justice procedural traditions in ICJ. This fit makes the marketing of a particular political culture more compatible through trial procedures and professionals familiar with the rules and practice of Western trial cultures. As Simon strongly establishes in a domestic setting (2007), criminal justice institutions and processes are critically important to Western styles of governance. In the domestic example it is obvious that the justice traditions in theory will sit within the political culture of a particular state. The Western democratic ascription to *separation of powers* for good governance and the supervisory role of the judiciary on which it relies, is a case in point. For single party states or nations and jurisdictions where religion and the state are one, such a governance model will be confusing and culturally incompatible.

Flowing from a *separation of powers* governance tradition, con-stitutional legality (and ICJ within it) retains important supervisory capacities in global governance. World courts more than international representative bodies are empowered to make work key themes in international law and governance, such as human rights and peaceful coexistence. Consequentially this translates globally because the global governance style presently exercised through the institutions of the UN (and confirmed by world courts) mirrors Western neo-liberal democracy. Compatible with this correlation, formal ICJ has been crafted in the image of Western trial traditions (military and civil). Whether states and cultures outside these governance traditions like it or not, global governance will require their acquiescence or will treat their resistance as a threat.[2]

Globalisation comfortably exports and expands that prevailing global culture (political and legal). The contemporary cultural predisposition of globalisation is ensured through its overwhelming commitment to modernisation and free market capitalism as cultural unifiers. The political and legal dimensions of global governance are compatible with the globalised economic imperative. As such, the *truth* essential in globalisation is political, legal and economic. Such truth is confirmed through modes of regulation which in the domestic setting would ensure those truths through similar styles of governance to that employed globally. This is the prevailing *hegemony of truth* in global governance.

The *hegemony of truth* in ICJ, or other elements of global governance, is not about legality alone. Manifest in the decisions of world courts and tribunals this hegemony seems largely concerned with ways of ordering the world (religious or secular) and asserting those values regarded as necessary for the essence of humanity to be realised.

And what future (if any) is there for cultural (and thereby legal) pluralism represented in global governance? Very little if justice, a central concern for the *rule of law*, remains compromised in its utility to dominant political cultures, advanced as these are through globalisation.

The dialectic of regulatory pluralism and globalised economy

A regulatory dialectic in all of this is revealed unlike that operating as responses to terror. Here globalisation draws from a pluralistic control agenda to advance free market economy and modernisation. I mentioned previously that world commercial order is sustained through a mix of global regulatory strategies. These include:

- ignoring or tolerating transgressions;
- permitting degrees of flexible or deregulated commercial relationships and transactions;
- absorbing variations in commercial practice into wider conventions or institutional frameworks;
- controlling the scope of aberrant commercial behaviours; and
- proscribing and prohibiting.

Within the proscriptive option a variety of methods are available and practised by international financial and regulatory agencies:

- legal rules;
- administrative sanctions;

- collaborative inclusion/exclusion (such as with the WTO and GATT);
- access to capital and markets (through world financial institutions as well as competition);
- internal compliance;
- registration and licensing;
- contractual arrangements and trade preferencing;
- resource access.

Legal regulation is simply one regulatory option, and perhaps a blunt and limited one. In world economic relations, an agglomeration of governmental and non-governmental rules proliferate. The normative framework of the globalised economy is singular and catholic, while its surrounding regulatory framework is pluralist and contingent.

If on the other hand regulatory pluralism is not a feature of the risk/security nexus in global governance, this may not make pluralism an inevitable casualty of globalisation. The fate of regulatory pluralism as a feature of global governance can be determined by:

- the strength and resilience of the risk/security nexus as a focus for globalisation;
- the predominance of terror as the risk to global order against which military intervention and then ICJ will be directed;
- the extent to which violent challenges to the dominant political/cultural order are interpreted as having economic consequences;
- the need for international commerce to be transacted in a peaceful environment;
- the extent to which the economic benefits of militarism and violent conflict are maintained;
- the continued disassociation between commercial exploitation, socio-economic disadvantage and global terror;
- the continued coexistence within global governance of policies promoting economic deregulation on the one hand, and cultural/political regulation on the other.

Regulatory pluralism is not a feature of risk/security globalisation where crime and not commerce is to be controlled. The dialectic in regulation as a mission for global governance is that ICJ is not providing uniform boundaries of permission within which peaceful civil and commercial coexistence is maintained. The synthesis will be a move back towards regulatory pluralism covering civil and commercial relations for the benefit of *humanity*, and not just for the selective enrichment and protection of the valorised citizen/victim, and designated market participant.

Even legal regulation in its original form as a *folk concept* suggests pluralistic manifestations. However, the symbiotic relationship between the law and the state has tended to see law move away from social more towards scientific construction. With international legality it might be anticipated that the recognition of *customary* foundations would return legal regulation to more pluralist sympathies (see Bantekas and Nash 2007: ch. 1). The institutional rigidity of formal ICJ and the strict focus on individual liability in a narrow frame of criminal conduct has meant, on the other hand, that international criminal law does not countenance a pluralist regulatory regime.

The tension between narrow and rigid regulation through formal ICJ and the considerably more pluralist regulatory opportunities in the *alternative* ICJ paradigm is ripe for resolution through the transformation argued for below. Victim communities demonstrate a range of legitimate justice interests which cannot be satisfied through retributive justice alone (Findlay and Henham 2005; Weitekamp *et al.* 2006). A crucial communitarian focus in the transformation of ICJ will necessarily stimulate a reconsideration of pluralism in regulatory choices, along with a new normative framework which fosters diversity in the protection of *humanity*.

Resolving clashes

A rehabilitation of regulatory pluralism within global governance is one route for resolving the clashes and tensions which feature in the governance imposed through global hegemony. In microcosm, some of the clashes and tensions identified in the application of formal ICJ to the risk/security nexus may also find reconciliation through greater engagement with the heterogeneous expectations of victim communities.

The clashes:

- within and beyond vulnerable social arenas;
- between and over confrontational normative orders;
- around power differentials between warring normative systems and;
- over individualised and collective difference.

cannot be sustainably resolved through the autocratic imposition of a singular and culturally dependent justice model. The violent consequences of this imposition in the *war on terror,* have become the almost predictable results of a politically directed formal justice unable to address the competing interests of victim communities.

As I asserted at the outset of my argument, the conflict resolution and peacemaking potential of ICJ is largely dependent on a reformulation of its central morality. Currently ICJ struggles to reconcile competing value systems within a narrow retributive project. Such clashes of values primarily identify as:

- capitalist vs. cultural norms (played out over issues such as individual and collective property rights);
- public vs. private domain;
- rule-based vs. consensual regulatory systems;
- liberal vs. dogmatic governance, and so on.

These clashing values exist within and contest the same governance spaces. For instance, the suicide bomber and the opposing religious fundamentalist in Iraq inhabit a common spatial, temporal, cultural and political landscape. This makes it easy for one to morph from the victim to the aggressor and back again while retaining a common life experience. Externally imposed regulatory enterprises, rooted in foreign and further clashing value structures, have little prospect of permanent risk reduction and security enhancement.

ICJ has become part of a global governance strategy of distant, indirect rule and intrusive economic manipulation. Administrative sanctions and military intervention designate a form of order which ICJ is left to police with the dubious benefit of a dislocated and culturally equivocal legality. In situations of greatest conflict and violence ICJ is unable to even rely on stable state legal systems and consequent social controls that are consensually grounded, not dictated and opposed.

Law has become an uncertain weapon for resolving the fundamental clashes endangering world order (Bikundo, forthcoming). The force-based foundations of legal authority have become globally aligned with military intervention as problematic regulatory strategies putting civil order in jeopardy.

In terms of international humanitarian law it is argued that rights protection is a pathway through which to bolster the weakness of formal regulatory structures. In the case of ICJ and its formal dedication to individualised liability and punishment, the narrow conceptualisation of human rights protection leaves communitarian cultures largely out in the cold. Self-regulation or compliance as the alternative to harsh legal intervention is not an option when violence is a dominant reaction to conflict and cultural clashes.

Does this therefore mean that ICJ cannot play an effective role in conflict minimisation and cultural harmony in the face of violent clashes and retaliation? An over-concentration on formal justice instrumentalities and processes might lead to that conclusion. However, a significant imperative in the evolution of *truth-based* indigenous or transitional justice enterprises confronting similar conflict and mass crime victimisation has been to engage with diverse community aspirations for justice. One telling aspiration which reconciliation and amnesty focused strategies have advanced is accountability through revelation rather than retribution. Genuine accountability through justice for governance will be crucial in the rehabilitation of formal ICJ as a critical governance element.

Dialectics of accountability and politicised justice

As formal ICJ currently sits within global governance it is substantially and procedurally accountable primarily to instruments derived from the UN Security Council. This is not a representative body beyond its significant reflection of the dominant political alliance. True it is that the membership of Russia and China and rotational states may mean that the views of the Council in total may not be an automatic reflection of Western culture. However, as the most recent invasion of Iraq clearly demonstrates, when the Security Council is not seen by the dominant alliance as reflecting its views then the Council is bypassed and vilified.

The war crimes tribunals have always been a feature of victor's justice. In form they reflect the laws and procedures of Western military justice (Cockayne 2005). The selection of defendants to be prosecuted and the manner in which these individuals are compelled before the court reflect and rely on the victor's considerations of victimisation and resultant liability.

Accountability as a feature of ICJ is not even a significant feature of the less formal and alternative justice paradigm. Chapter 5 suggests the debate around amnesty as the trade-off for truth-telling has left many victim communities wondering whether criminals can be brought to justice, if the truth is to be told. Victims are forced into a *Sophie's Choice* situation, where retributive justice outcomes are off the agenda if they participate in mediation or reconciliation enterprises for the purpose of conflict resolution and truth-telling. As we have argued (Findlay and Henham 2005), for international trial justice to be transformed, embracing responsibility for a wider range of legitimate victim community interests, stratified justice should not be the inevitable lot of those left out of the tribunal experience.

The other attraction of drawing victim communities into the international trial structure is that those who have been exposed to witness in community court settings would be expected to receive greater protections through due process. Aligned to this is the reality that higher-profile trial justice, publicly portrayed and managed through independent professionals, may offer to victim communities a more transparent and accountable engagement in justice decision-making. The judicial management of mediation in China (see Chapter 8), with all its limitations and suggestions of judicial overbearance, at least provides a public forum for the resolution of difficult victim interests.

Accountability within ICJ should also encompass how justice can better hold governance responsible to the community over which it holds sway. That ICJ can take on a role in effectively delivering accountability frameworks (something approaching a separation of powers paradigm) for global governance necessitates the reduction of its political patronage. A move away from the service of the dominant political alliance towards *communities of justice* will help. Preceding this repositioning, and for it to take hold long-term, the normative location of ICJ within the service of *humanity* needs to be practically declared.

The moral dialectic – governance in the name of humanity

A possible redirection in the *moral* foundations of global governance (as mentioned in the introduction) is premised on a tolerance of community identity. Even the most homogeneous communities demonstrate pluralism and diversity. *Communities of justice,* and their victim community constituents require the type of governance (and criminal justice) that respects cultural diversity beyond political dominion and criminalised opposition.

The moral dilemma of justice for some in the name of governance for all seems overlooked when formal ICJ is responsible to a dominant culture.[3] While broadcasting a commitment to the security of humanity, retributive justice institutions and individual liability processes are failing to engage with legitimate victim community interests. This is a normative and an active stimulus to the development of *communities of justice.*

The task for governance (including ICJ) remains one of asserting acceptable forms of moral dominion over resistant as well as compliant communities. If there is ever to be an achievable world order more consensual than compelled, then an integrated, inclusive and accessible criminal justice will be essential for its maintenance.

Communities of justice are not much more than a syllogism without a complementary normative framework governing formal ICJ. *Communities of justice* will fail to be constructive influences over global governance if they are confined within the alternative and informal realms of ICJ. Communitarian justice in theory and in practice can infiltrate the structures and formal procedures of ICJ (as I suggested in Chapter 8) through an encounter with procedural traditions which have to date largely remained outside international trial practice. Were this to become a feature of formal ICJ then a more pluralist community engagement would follow. As a result, the influence of the dominant political culture over the development of ICJ will be lessened.

With the US and several other key Security Council players prevaricating over recognising the ICC, the court has some breathing space in which to experiment with legal pluralism and cultural diversity, not available to the war crimes tribunals and the special courts. The ICC will also need to reflect a more communitarian normative commitment if it is to work as an agent of *humanity* rather than as an offshoot of the Security Council.

Partial and politically partisan global governance is the reality of international relations in the foreseeable future. Even so, the transformation of ICJ (and its foundational morality) towards a real engagement with *communities of justice* can start now.

Transforming global governance – paths yet to be taken

This conclusion moves on from the conviction that ICJ is crucial to global governance in the *new* globalisation. Reflecting on the way this relationship attacks pluralism and community diversity exposes the repressive and recursive influences on global governance which otherwise should be obliged to the global community in all its forms.

I am not the first to comment on the cultural paradox of globalisation (Findlay 1999b). In his exploration of 'Disjuncture and difference in the global cultural economy', Arjun Appadurai (1996: ch. 2) explains the tensions at work in 'global cultural flows'. Appadurai identifies that the 'central problem of today's global interactions is the tension between cultural homogenisation and cultural heterogenisation' (1996: 32). The fear of cultural absorption has been exploited by separatist religious fundamentalists and nationalists among their minorities 'by posing global commoditisation (or capitalism, or some other such external enemy) as more real than the threat of its own hegemonic structures' (1996: 32).

> The new global cultural economy has to be seen as a complex, overlapping, disjunctive order that cannot any longer be understood in terms of existing centre-periphery models ... nor is it susceptible to simple models of push and pull ... or of surpluses and deficits ... or of consumers and producers ... the complexity of the current economy has to do with certain fundamental disjunctures between, economy, culture and politics that we have only begun to theorise.
>
> (Appadurai 1996: 32–3)

Global governance is failing to reconcile these disjunctures. International criminal justice, now declared a crucial component of global conflict resolution, is in fact exacerbating cultural divisions through its narrow and partial progress in criminalising resistant or opposed communities.

It is realistic to highlight the capacity in globalisation both to gloss over cultural difference if it stands in the way of modernisation and to differentiate cultures in terms of terror and violent justice responses (see Chapter 4). When it comes to risk determination and security policy, globalisation configures cultural forms as fractured, not due to violence but over the authority for its exercise. Unfortunately, this fracturing of culture in terms of legitimacy overlooks the disturbing similarities in the nature of the violence on both sides of the risk/ security divide. The 'overlaps and resemblences' (as Appadurai sees them) in the exercise of violence culture to culture, if better recognised, can offer a new vision for risk management and security maintenance on a global scale:

> Thus we need to combine a fractual metaphor for the shape of cultures ... with a polythetic account of their overlaps and resemblances. Without this latter step, we remain mired in comparative work that relies on the clear separation of the

entities to be compared before serious comparison can begin. (Appadurai 1996: 46)

And we need a convincing political reason for that comparison to begin. It is a more uniform application of justice for all which provides that reason. The political reward in a realistic appreciation of contesting violence within the context of risk and security should be a much more convincing reiteration of world order. To get there:

> ... we will need to ask not how these complex overlapping, fractual shapes constitute a simple, stable (even if large scale) system, but to ask what the dynamics are: Why do ethnic riots occur when and where they do? Why do states wither at greater rates in some places and times than others? Why do some countries flout conventions of international debt replacement with so much less apparent worry than others? How are international arms flows driving ethnic battles and genocides? Why are some states exiting the global stage while others are clamouring to get in? Why do key events occur at a certain point in a certain place rather than others? These are, of course, great traditional questions of causality, contingency and prediction in the human sciences, but in a world of disjunctive flows, it is perhaps important to start asking them in a way that relies on images of flow and uncertainty, hence chaos, rather than the older images of order, stability and systematicness.
>
> (Appadurai 1996: 46–7)

International criminal justice is complicit in a style of global governance which seeks an *illusion of order* against threats of terror met with terrible violence. Coming on as it does to follow massive military intervention, formal ICJ is not easily able to disengage from an atmosphere of violent security responses. In actioning a process of criminalisation against some genocides and not others, some crimes against humanity and not others, global governance through formal ICJ struggles to convincingly impose order on a world that is so transparently volatile. In so doing, the discrimination in criminal justice is divisive in failing equally to prosecute the violence of victor and vanquished.

In Appadurai's 'five dimensions of global cultural flows' employed to explore globalisation's tensions and disjunctures, law and justice considerations feature little. This might be a result of his fascination for the creation of *imagined worlds* in which much of modernisation is played out. The landscapes of these worlds and their inhabitants 'are able to contest and sometimes subvert the imagined worlds of the official mind and the entrepreneurial mentality that surrounded them' (1996: 33). In the age before 9/11 where globalisation was clearly a modernisation project, Appadurai would not prioritise the landscape of criminal justice as a change agent in global governance beyond its location within a more complex *ideoscape*. The risk/security repositioning of globalisation would no doubt adjust that analysis. Even so, the *ideoscape* of ICJ is:

> Composed of elements of the Enlightenment worldview, which consists of a chain of ideas, terms and images, including *freedom, welfare, rights, sovereignty, representation* and the master term *democracy* ... constructed with a certain internal logic and presupposing a certain relationship between reading, representation and the public sphere ... but the diaspora of these terms and images across the world, especially since the nineteenth century, has loosened the internal coherence that held them together in the Euro-American master narrative and provided instead a loosely constructed synopticon of politics, in which different nation-states, as part of their evolution, have organised their political cultures around different keywords.
>
> (Appadurai 1996: 36)

Such a keyword for today is *terror*.

A path away from imagined world order and on to encompassing global security is transformed ICJ. A genuine attempt to engage the legitimacy of victim communities will shift ICJ from imagined to actual justice outcomes.

It seems dangerous to declare this so definitively when there prevails much controversy surrounding the place of victims in domestic criminal justice. In a domestic, state-centred, jurisdictionally bound setting I would be reluctant to rely on this connection. Partisan inclusions of individual victims into the trial process, consequentially diminishing the protection of the offender, have produced regrettable distortions of fundamental principles on which criminal justice has for centuries relied. The recent *level playing field* argument in common-law justice traditions has in particular justified the denial of conventions against self-incrimination, presumptions of innocence in bail, contested trial and sentence setting with worrying regularity. Then why should the international location of criminal justice necessarily remove these concerns?

Two reasons. First, the premise on which the need for international criminal justice has been advanced is urgently required to protect victim communities that represent *humanity*. Unlike domestic criminal law, it is not the state or even representative international bodies who stand proxy for the victim in ICJ. Even where states take responsibility for the prosecution of genocide and crimes against humanity (as the ICC statutes envisage) it is victim communities and not the state that drive the liability process.

Second, in international criminal justice deliberations (formal and alternative) victim status is truly communitarian. In this respect the interests of victims are not simply the interests of an aggrieved individual. They are interests which require mediation and negotiation against wider cultural and collective considerations. They are interests which can be governed by truly communitarian rights. They are interests that are tested and thereby invigorated through the bonds that make and break communities. They can be moulded into the interests of *humanity*.

Without wishing to diminish that controversy surrounding problematic individualised victims' interests (and their inclusion in criminal justice), I would argue that global crimes are so centrally directed against the collective notion of humanity as to stand apart from domestic criminal justice concerns. In ICJ, perpetrators and victims are more likely to be a collective. As such, from a victim perspective, the influence of victim interests is made more significant not just by the number of victims covered, but that the victim may be the community or a culture in a complex sense (see Chapter 7).

The victim focus in a communitarian form is itself far from simple. Just to distil a victim community so that it might form a tangible justice focus is challenging.

- How can victimisation be removed from the individual harm?
- How are communities (in all their diversity) to be conceived so that some convincing notion of victimisation can emerge?
- And if it does, what are legitimate interests in a community context?
- How are such interests to be revealed, and how is a community to be given access to, and voice within criminal justice determinations?
- What particular impact should the voice of victim communities be accorded against the conventional protections for the accused in due process?

ICJ will have a crucial role to play in the decades to come, formulating and materialising victim communities as a force in justice regulation. The formal institutions of ICJ will come to prosecute on behalf of and in protection of humanity. As such, victim constituencies will exceed the authorising agencies of the ICC as essential legitimators, beyond the victors who give perspective to the war crimes tribunals and beyond the indigenous sponsors of truth and reconciliation alternatives. But this requires transformation from perceived to actual, exclusive to inclusive justice.

Transformation proposed here is unlike transitional justice arguments which demand a move away from formal institutional justice in order to remedy the failings of ICJ from a victim perspective. Transformed ICJ as I see it encapsulates all that trial justice has to offer, promising a better deal for victim communities. Detailing the nature and mechanics of this transformation is for another project (Findlay and Henham, forthcoming). And a new style of international criminal justice will not of itself guarantee good global governance.

The history of globalisation demonstrates that its central concerns are transient and contingent on the political priorities of dominant hegemonies. Risk/security as the driving focus for globalisation will have its day. However, from the earliest mercantile eras, market economics and modernisation have prevailed as the critical contexts within which globalisation has sponsored cultural change. This being the case, as the risk/security emphasis recycles, ICJ will return to a less instrumental relationship within global governance. This should also see a reduction in the political utility of ICJ for the forces of global dominion in achieving their partial governance interests.

How will this impact on a world where, for the sake of the victims in *humanity as a whole*, global cultural flows need to be towards diversity and integrity rather than homogeneity and domination?

Before this restoration of global regulatory dynamics, ICJ has a powerful opportunity to impose on global governance a normative influence and a victim sensitivity which will determine the measure of *best practice*. For the sake of accountable governance, to the measurable benefit of *humanity* which ICJ arose to serve, it is an opportunity not to be missed.

The transformed international trial holds out a vastly improved capacity to satisfy legitimate victim community interests (Findlay and Henham 2005). Beyond this, and as a consequence of the deep mutuality of formal ICJ and global governance in the new globalisation, it will be a transformation that challenges the foundations and future of the regulatory world order.

In the current era of globalisation Weber's predictions about modernity are coming true. Intimate social and cultural forms are disintegrating and being replaced by more regimented bureaucratic legal orders (Weber 1964). This is happening on both sides of the terror divide. Weber saw these new orders as being regimented by procedures and predictability. Political and religious fundamentalism challenge West, Middle East, East and South world orders. At the same time they are offering a reconfigured order as the fruits of violence.

International criminal law and its formal institutions aspire to achieve a secure and predictable governance framework, away from fundamentalist arenas of violence. Less formal ICJ also endeavours through reconciliation and truth-telling to give a sense of certainty in post-conflict communities.

For the sake of humanity and its diverse victim communities, ICJ must tackle violence in all its forms. It must break free of the cycle in which victor's violence is confirmed and the violence of the vanquished is criminalised. This transformation requires a keen commitment to a vision of world order which is tolerant of cultural diversity. The counterbalance is a vigilant resistance to hegemony through economic exploitation.

International criminal justice can thereby grow to require accountability from global governance as it pursues its modernisation project. The first step is to help reformulate the risk/security nexus in globalisation. With legitimacy regrounded in victim communities, global governance can move its risk focus away from politicised terror towards violence at large. Global security strategies will be empowered in so doing by attacking cycles of violence: the 'memory and countermemory, where one remembered atrocity becomes the basis of another' (Appadurai 1998: 917).

Globalisation does not produce one road to violence and terror. Globalisation is not responsible for the risk or the security that other roads to violence and terror represent. When the cultural *other* is violently opposed it is for criminal justice, wherever and however located, to offer a safe and sustainable catharsis.

Notes

1 Tamanaha, B. (2007) *Contemporary Legal Pluralism*, Julius Stone Lecture, University of Sydney, 6 July 2007.
2 It might be said that in its opposition to the International Criminal Court the dominant global political force, the USA, is resisting a central

element within global governance. It is certainly not this simple. The US has supported other important trial structures in ICJ. Further, by exerting pressure on the ICC to intervene in the Sudan conflict, the US has confirmed its willingness to employ the ICC when it suits American global interests.

3 In suggesting this I recognise that the ICC and the war crimes tribunals in particular are accountable to the Security Council and to member states. At this level it might be said that there is an accountability framework beyond that dominant political alliance. However, as previously argued, the influence of the dominant political alliance, militarily and diplomatically, over the UN and over member states through bilateral arrangements diminishes the representativeness and independence of this framework.

Bibliography

Abbott, C., Rogers, P. and Sloboda, J. (2006) *Global Response to Global Threats*. Oxford: Oxford Research Group.

Abrams, J. and Hayner, P. (2002) 'Documenting, acknowledging and publicizing the truth', in M. Bassiouni (ed.), *Post Conflict Justice*. New York: Transnational Publishers, pp. 459–86.

Agnew, J. (2003) *A World That Knows No Boundaries? The Geopolitics of Globalization and the Myth of a Borderless World*, CIBR Working Papers in Border Studies 2003.

Akhavan, P. (2001) 'Beyond impunity: can international criminal justice prevent future atrocities?', *American Journal of International Law*, 95 (7): 7–31.

Aksu, E. and Camilleri, J. (eds) (2002) *Democratising Global Governance*. Basingstoke: Palgrave Macmillan.

Albrecht, H.G., Simon, J., Rezaei, H., Rohne, H.C. and Kiza, E. (2006) *Conflict and Conflict Resolution in Middle Eastern Societies – Between Tradition and Modernity*. Berlin: Duncker & Humblot.

Amnesty International (2006) 'Stop Torture and Ill Treatment in the War on Terror', March (online unpublished).

Amnesty International (2007) *Amnesty International Says International Criminal Court Action against Sudanese Minister and Militia Commander in Darfur is 'A Step Toward Justice for Millions'*, Public Statement, 7 February.

Andreas, P. and Price, R. (2001) 'From war fighting to crime fighting: transforming the American National Security State', *International Studies Review*, 3 (3): 31–52.

Appadurai, A. (1996) *Modernity at Large: Cultural Dimensions of Globalization*. Minneapolis, MN: University of Minnesota Press.

Appadurai, A. (1998) 'Dead certainty: ethnic violence in an era of globalization', *Development and Change*, 29 (4): 905–2005.

Appadurai, A. (ed.) (2001) *Globalisation*. Durham, NC: Duke University Press.

Arbour, L. (1997) 'Progress and challenges in international criminal justice', *Fordham International Law Journal*, 21: 531–241.

Arendt, H. (1994) *Eichmann in Jerusalem: A Report on the Banality of Evil*. Harmondsworth: Penguin.

Arts, K. and Popovski, V. (2007) *International Criminal Accountability and the Rights of Children*. Hague: Hague Academic Coalition.

Baeza, E. (2006) 'The creation of the International Court for Cambodia', *Chicago Global*, 18 April. Blog post online at: http://chicagoglobal.typepad.com/chicago_global_commentary/2006/04/the_internation.html

Bagaric, M. (2005) 'A case for torture', *Sydney Morning Herald*, 17 May.

Bakken, B. (2000) *The Exemplary Society: Human Improvement, Social Control, and the Dangers of Modernity in China*. Oxford: Oxford University Press.

Ball, H. (1999) *Prosecuting War Crimes and Genocide: The Twentieth Century Experience*. Lawrence, KS: University Press of Kansas.

Ball, H. (2004) 'Terrorism, human rights, social justice, freedom and democracy: some considerations for the legal and justice professionals of the "Coalition of the Willing"', *QUT Law and Justice Journal*, 14 (2): 199–218.

Bantekas, I. (2003) 'Current developments: the international law of terrorist financing', *American Journal of International Law*, 97 (2): 315–33.

Bantekas, I. and Nash, S. (2007) *International Criminal Law*. London: Routledge.

Barker, T. and Simon, J. (2002) *Embracing Risk: The Changing Culture of Insurance and Responsibility*. Chicago: Chicago University Press.

Bass, G. J. (2000) *Stay the Hand of Vengeance: The Politics of War Crimes Tribunals*. Princeton, NJ: Princeton University Press.

Baumann, Z. (1998) *Globalisation: The Human Consequences*. Cambridge: Polity Press.

Baxi, U. (2007) *Revisiting Social Dimensions of Law and Justice in a Post-human Era*. Keynote Address, Julius Stone Centenary Conference, University of Sydney.

Beck, U. (1992) *Risk Society: Towards a New Modernity*. London: Sage.

Beigbeder, Y. (1999) *Judging War Criminals: The Politics of International Justice*. New York: St. Martin's Press.

Berger, M. (forthcoming 2008) 'Development', entry in H. Fagan and R. Monk (eds), *Globalization and Security: An Encyclopedia*. New York: Praeger.

Bibes, P. (2001) 'Transnational organized crime and terrorism: Columbia, a case study', *Journal of Contemporary Criminal Justice*, 17 (3): 243–58.

Bierne, P. (1983) 'Cultural relativism and comparative criminology', *Crime, Law and Social Change*, 7 (4): 371–91.

Bierrnatzki, W. (2002) 'Definition: what is terrorism? Terrorism and the mass media', *Communication Research Trends*, 21 (1): 3–6.

Bikundo, E. (forthcoming) 'Crimes of Aggression and the Abuse of Power in International Criminal Law', LLD thesis. Sydney: Law Faculty, University of Sydney.

Block, A. A. (ed.) (1991) *Perspectives on Organising Crime: Essays in Opposition.* Dordrecht: Kluwer.

Block, A. A. and Chambliss, W. (1981) *Organizing Crime.* New York: Elsevier.

Booth, C. (2003) 'Prospects and issues for the International Criminal Court: lessons from Yugoslavia and Rwanda', in P. Sands (ed.), *From Nuremberg to The Hague: The Future of International Criminal Justice.* Cambridge: Cambridge University Press, pp. 157–210.

Boraine, A. (2004) *Transitional Justice as an Emerging Field.* Presented at the Repairing the Past: Reparations and Transitions to Democracy Symposium, Ottawa, Canada, 11 March.

Bordier, P. and Wacquant, L. (1992) *An Invitation to Reflexive Sociology.* Chicago: University of Chicago Press.

Bork, E. (2005) 'Men without a country', *Weekly Standard*, 15 August, pp. 13–14.

Bormann, T. (2004) 'Travellers tales: stories', *ABC's Foreign Correspondents.* Sydney: ABC Books, p. 122.

Box, S. (1983) *Power, Crime and Mystification.* London: Tavistock.

Braithwaite, J. (1979) *Inequality, Crime and Public Policy.* London: Routledge & Kegan Paul.

Braithwaite, J. (1989) *Crime Shame and Re-integration.* Oxford: Oxford University Press.

Braithwaite, J. (2002) *Restorative Justice and Responsive Regulation.* Oxford: Oxford University Press.

Braithwaite, J. (2005) 'Pre-empting terrorism', *Current Issues in Criminal Justice*, 17 (1): 96–114.

Braithwaite, J. and Pettit, P. (1990) *Not Just Deserts: A Republican Theory of Criminal Justice.* Oxford: Clarendon.

Brandt, W. *et al.* (1980) *North-South, A Programme for Survival: Report of the Independent Commission on International Development Issues.* London: Pan Books.

Brownsword, R. (2004) *Global Governance and the Quest for Justice*, Vol. 4: *Human Rights.* Oxford: Hart.

Brzezinski, Z. (1883) *Power and Principle: Memoirs of the National Security Advisor 1977–1981.* London: Weidenfeld & Nicolson.

Burchfield, K. (1978) 'The economic organisation of crime: a study of the development of criminal enterprise', *Criminal Law Quarterly*, 20 (4): 478–512.

Burgenthal, T. (1994) 'The United Nations Truth Commission for El Salvador', *Vanderbilt Journal of Transnational Law*, 27: 488–510.

Burns, P. (2005) 'Some features of the International Criminal Court', (Unpublished conference paper).

Bush, G. W. (2002) 'President calls for crime victims' rights amendment', Speech at US Justice Department, 16 April.

Butler, P. (2003) 'Foreword: terrorism and utilitarianism: lessons from and for the criminal law', *Journal of Criminal Law and Criminology*, 93 (1): 1–22.

Cardoso, F. (1979) *Dependency and Development in Latin America*. Berkeley, CA: University of California Press.

Cassese, A. (1989) 'The international community's "legal" response to terrorism', *International and Comparative Law Quarterly*, 38 (3): 589–608.

Cassese, A. (1998) 'Reflections on international criminal justice', *Modern Law Review*, 61 (1): 1–10.

Chadwick, E. (2003) 'It's war Jim, but not as we know it: a "reality-check" for international laws of war?', *Crime Law and Social Change*, 39 (3): 233–62.

Chambliss, W. (1989) 'State organised crime', *Criminology*, 27 (2): 103–208.

Cheema, S. *et al.* (2006) 'Strengthening accountability and transparency in Timor-Leste', Report of the Alkatiri Initiative Review, United Nations Office in Timor-Leste, 27 January.

Chemerinsky, E. (2005) 'Detainees (wartime security and constitutional liberty)', *Albany Law Review*, 68 (4): 1119.

Chen, X. (2002) 'Community and policing strategies: a Chinese approach to crime control', *Policing and Society*, 12 (1): 1–13.

Chirot, D. (1977) *Social Change in the Twentieth Century*. New York: Harcourt Brace Jovanovic.

Chomsky, N. (2002) 'International terrorism: image and reality (1989)', in N. Chomsky (ed.), *Pirates and Emperors, Old and New: International Terrorism and the Real World*. Cambridge, MA: South End Press, pp. 119–44.

Christie, N. (1993) *Crime Control as Industry: Towards Gulags Western Style*. London: Routledge.

Clapham, A. (2003) 'Issues of complexity, complicity and complementarity: from the Nuremberg trials to the dawn of the new International Criminal Court', in P. Sands (ed.), *From Nuremberg to The Hague: The Future of International Criminal Justice*. Cambridge: Cambridge University Press, pp. 30–68.

Clark, G. J. (2002) *Military Tribunals and the Separation of Powers*, Suffolk University Law School Faculty Publications, Paper 111.

Clarke, D. C. and Feinerman, J. V. (1995) 'Agnostic contradictions, criminal law and human rights in China', *China Quarterly*, 141: 135–54.

Coakley, V. (2001) 'Towards justice and reconciliation in East Timor', *Alternative Law Journal*, 26 (5): 229–35.

Cockayne, J. (2004) *Operation Helpem Fren: Solomon Islands, Transitional Justice and the Silence of Contemporary Legal Pathologies on Questions of Distributive Justice*, Center for Human Rights and Global Justice Working Paper, Transitional Justice Series, No. 3.

Cockayne, J. (2005) 'The fraying shoestring: rethinking hybrid war crimes tribunals', *Fordham International Law Journal*, 28 (2): 635–46.

Cockayne, J. (2006) 'Commercial security in the humanitarian space'. Online at: http://web.gc.cuny.edu/ralphbuncheinstitute/IUCSHA/fellows/ Cockayne-paper-final.pdf (unpublished).

Cockayne, J. and Huckerby, J. (2004) 'Special Court for Sierra Leone: Truth and Reconciliation Commission applications for hearings with Samuel Hinga Norman and Augustine Gbao' (unpublished briefing paper).

Cohen, S. (1985) *Visions of Social Control*. Cambridge: Polity Press.

Colson, A. J. (2000) 'The logic of peace and the logic of justice', *International Relations*, 15 (1): 51–62.

Commission of Inquiry for the International War Crimes Tribunal (1992) *War Crimes: A Report on United States War Crimes against Iraq*. New York: Maisonneuve Press.

Conte, A. (2002) 'Terror meets tyranny? The interface between counter terrorism and human rights', *Murdoch University Electronic Journal of Law*, 9 (3): 38.

Crawford, J. (2003) 'The drafting of the Rome Statute', in P. Sands (ed.), *From Nuremberg to The Hague: The Future of International Criminal Justice*. Cambridge: Cambridge University Press, pp. 109–57.

Crenshaw, M. (1983) *Terrorism, Legitimacy and Power*. Middletown, CT: Wesleyan University Press.

Crenshaw, M. (ed.) (1994) *Terrorism in Context*. Pittsburgh: Penn State Press.

Cressey, D. (1969) *Theft of a Nation*. New York: Harper & Row.

Cryer, R., Friman, H. Robinson, D. and Wilmshurst, E. (2007) *International Criminal Law and Procedure*. Cambridge: Cambridge University Press.

Czarnota, A. (2001) 'A few reflections on globalisation and the constitution of society', *University of NSW Law Journal*, 24 (3): 809–17.

Danner, A and Martinez, J. S. (2004) *Guilty Associations: Joint Criminal Enterprise, Command Responsibility and the Development of International Criminal Law*, Vanderbilt Public Law Research Paper No. 04-09; Stanford Public Law Working Paper No. 87.

Dauvergne, P. (ed.) (1998) *Weak and Strong States in Asia-Pacific Societies*. Canberra: Department of International Relations, ANU.

De Feyter, K., Parmentier, S., Bossuyt, M. and Lemmens, P. (eds) (2005) *Out of the Ashes. Reparation for Victims of Gross and Systematic Human Rights Violations*. Antwerp: Intersentia.

Delmas-Marty, M. (2002) 'Global crime calls for global justice', *European Journal of Crime, Criminal Law and Criminal Justice*, 10 (4): 286–93.

Delmas-Marty, M. (2003) 'The contribution of comparative law to a pluralist conception of international criminal law', *Journal of International Criminal Justice*, 1 (1): 13–25.

Department of Foreign Affairs and Trade (1999) *International Convention for the Suppression of Financing of Terrorism*, New York, 9 December.

Der Derian, J. (1990) 'The (s)pace of international relations: simulation, surveillance, and speed', *International Studies Quarterly*, 34 (3): 295–310.

Dershowitz, A. (2006) 'Should we fight war with torture?', *The Independent*, 3 July.

Devetak, R. and True, J. (2006) 'Diplomatic divergence in the Antipodes: globalisation, foreign policy and state identity in Australia and New Zealand', *Australian Journal of Political Science*, 41 (2): 241–56.

Dickie, P. (1994) 'Organised crime: towards a research-regulatory approach to organised crime', in D. Chappell and P. Wilson (eds), *The Australian Criminal Justice System: The mid 1990s*. Sydney: Butterworths, pp. 106–20.

Dinnen, S. and Ley, A. (2000) *Reflections on Violence in Melanesia*. Sydney: Hawkins Press.

Dorn, N. (forthcoming) 'Contrasting the dynamics of global administrative measures and the international criminal courts: Cosmopolitanism, Militarism, state interests,' in M. Findlay and R. Henham (eds), *Exploring the Boundaries of International Criminal Justice*, Aldershot: Ashgate.

Duffy, H. (2005) 'Case study: Guantanamo Bay detentions under International Human Rights and Humanitarian Law in H. Duffy, *The 'War on Terror' and the Framework of International Law'*. Cambridge: Cambridge University Press, pp.379-442.

DuPont, B., Grabosky, P. and Shearing, C. (2003) 'The governance of security in weak and failing states', *Criminal Justice*, 3 (4): 331–49, at p. 348.

Dutton, M. (1992) *Policing and Punishment in China: From Patriarchy to 'The People'*. Cambridge: Cambridge University Press.

Dutton, M. and Xu, Z. (1998) 'Facing differences: relations, change and the prison sector in contemporary China', in R. Weiss and N. South (eds), *Comparing Prison Systems: Towards a Comparative International Penology*. Amsterdam: Gordon & Breach, pp. 289–336.

Dyzenhaus, D. (2003) 'Judicial independence, transitional justice and the rule of law', *Otago Law Review*, 34 (4): 345.

Eastman, J. (2002) 'Moral equivalency in international law', *Los Angeles Daily Journal*, 28 January.

Elsea, J. K. and Thomas, K. (2005) *Guantanamo Detainees: Habeas Corpus Challenges in Federal Court*, CRS Report for Congress, Congressional Research Service, December.

Erez, E. and Rogers, L. (1999) 'Victim impact statements and sentencing outcomes and processes: the perspectives of legal professionals', *British Journal of Criminology*, 39 (2): 216–39.

Eser, A. (2002) 'Individual Criminal Responsibility', in A. Cassese, P. Gaeta and J. Jones (eds), *The Rome Statute of the International Criminal Court: A Commentary*. Oxford: Oxford University Press, Chapter 20.

Eser, A. (2007) 'The nature and rationale of punishment', *Cardozo Law Review* 28(6): 2427–37.

Evans, P. (1979) *Dependency Development*. Princeton, NJ: Princeton University Press.

Feldman, D. (2006) 'Human rights, terrorism and risk: the roles of politicians and judges', *Public Law*, 50 (2): 364–84.

Ferencz, B. (2003) 'The International Criminal Court: the first year and future prospects', *American Society of International Law Proceedings*, 97: 259.

Findlay, M. (1986) 'Organised crime as terrorism', *Australian Quarterly*, pp. 286–96.

Findlay, M. (1992) 'The Mafia menace', *Criminal Organisations Journal*, 7 (3): 3–17.

Findlay, M. (1994) 'Breaking the crime/control nexus: market models of corruption and opportunity', in D. Chappell and P. Wilson (eds), *Australian Criminal Justice System: the Mid 1990s*. Sydney: Butterworths, pp. 100–11.

Findlay, M. (1995) 'Criminal tendencies: the international breakdown of law and order', *States of Disarray: The Social Effects of Globalisation*. Geneva: UNRISD, Ch. 4.

Findlay, M. (1997) 'Crime, community penalty and integration with legal formalism in the South Pacific', *Journal of Pacific Studies*, 21: 145.

Findlay, M. (1998) 'Crime as a force in globalisation', *Journal of Financial Crime*, 6 (2): 100.

Findlay, M. (1999a) 'Relating crime and globalisation', *Australian Quarterly*, 71 (4): 23–7.

Findlay, M. (1999b) *The Globalisation of Crime: Understanding Transitional Relationships in Context*. Cambridge: Cambridge University Press.

Findlay, M. (1999c) 'Independence and the judiciary in the PRC: expectations for constitutional legality in China', in K. Jayasuriya (ed.), *Law, Capitalism and Power in Asia*. London: Routledge, pp. 281–99.

Findlay, M. (2000) 'Decolonising restoration and justice: restoration in transitional cultures', in H. Strang and J. Braithwaite (eds), *Restorative Justice: Philosophy to Practice*. Aldershot: Ashgate Dartmouth, pp. 185–202.

Findlay, M. (2001a) 'Synthesis in trial procedures? The experience of the international criminal tribunals', *International and Comparative Law Quarterly*, 50 (1): 26–53.

Findlay, M. (2001b) 'The cost of globalised crime: new levels of control', *International Journal of Comparative Criminology*, 1 (2): 109–31.

Findlay, M. (2002a) 'Decolonising restoration and justice: restoration in transitional cultures', in H. Strang and J. Braithwaite (eds), *Restorative Justice: Philosophy to Practice*. Dartmouth and Aldershot: Ashgate.

Findlay, M. (2002b) 'Internationalised criminal trial and access to justice', *International Criminal Law Review*, 2 (3): 237.

Findlay, M. (2002c) 'The international and comparative criminal trial project', *International Criminal Law Review*, 2: 47–78.

Findlay, M. (2003) 'The Pacific', in Transparency International (eds), *Global Corruption Report 2003*. Berlin: Transparency International, pp. 115–28.

Findlay, M. (2004) 'Crime, terror and transitional cultures in a contracting globe', in P. Dauvergne (ed.), *Jurisprudence for an Interconnected Globe*. Burlington, VT: Ashgate, pp. 231–48.

Findlay, M. (2007a) *Governing through Globalised Crime*. Pluto Press, in press.

Findlay, M. (2007b) 'China's Place in International Criminal Justice?' Unpublished conference paper.

Findlay, M. (2007c) 'Terrorism and relative justice', *Crime Law and Social Change*, 47 (1): 57–68.

Findlay, M. and Bohlander, M. (2003) 'The use of domestic sources as a basis for international criminal law principle', in Z. Capaldo (ed.), *Yearbook of International Law and Jurisprudence 2002*. New York: Oceana.

Findlay, M. and Henham, R. (2002) 'Criminal justice modelling and the comparative contextual analysis of trial process', *International Journal of Comparative Criminology*, 2 (2): 162–86.

Findlay, M. and Henham, R. (2005) *Transforming International Criminal Justice: Retributive and Restorative Justice in the Trial Process*. Cullompton: Willan.

Findlay, M. and Henham, R. (2007) 'Integrating theory and method in comparative contextual analysis', in M. McConville *et al.* (eds), *Research Methods for the Arts and Humanities*. Edinburgh: Edinburgh University Press, pp. 104–32.

Findlay, M. and Zvekic, U. (1988) *Informal Mechanisms of Crime Control*. Rome: UNSDRI.

Findlay, M. and Zvekic, U. (1993) *Alternative Policing Styles: Cross Cultural Perspectives*. Deventer: Kluwer.

Findlay, M., Odgers, S. and Yeo, S. (1995) *Australian Criminal Justice*. Melbourne: Oxford University Press.

Finger, M. (2005) 'Global governance through the institutional lens', in M. Lederer and P. Muller (eds), *Criticizing Global Governance*. New York: Palgrave Macmillan, pp. 145–60.

Fiorentini, G. and Pelzman, S. (1995) *The Economics of Organised Crime*. Cambridge: Cambridge University Press.

Floud, J. and Young, W. (1981) *Dangerousness and Criminal Justice*. London: Heinemann.

Fogarty, G. P. (2005) 'Is Guantanamo Bay undermining the global war on terror?', *Parameters*, 35 (3): 59–67.

Foreign Languages Press (1984) *The Criminal Law and the Criminal Procedure Law of the Peoples' Republic of China*. Beijing: FLP.

Forman, S. and Segaar, D. (2006) 'New coalitions for global governance: the changing dynamics of multilateralism', *Global Governance*, 12 (4): 523–6.

Foucault, M. (1975) *Discipline and Punish*. London: Peregrine.

Foucault, M. (1997) 'Governmentality', in J. Faubion and R. Hurley (eds), *Essential Works of Foucault 1965–1984*. New York: New Press.

Freeman, M. (2007) *Truth Commissions and Procedural Fairness*. New York: Cambridge University Press.

Friedman, L. (2004) 'Frontiers: national and transnational order', in K. Heinz-Lader (ed.), *Public Governance in the Age of Globalisation*. Aldershot: Ashgate, pp. 25–51.

Friedman, T. (2002) 'Globalization, alive and well', *New York Times*, 22 September, p. 13.

Friedrichs, J. (2005) 'Global governance as the hegemonic project of transatlantic civil society', in M. Lederer and P. Muller (eds), *Criticizing Global Governance*. New York: Palgrave Macmillan, pp. 45–68.

Fukyama, F. (2006) *Nation Building: Beyond Afghanistan and Iraq*. Baltimore, MD: John Hopkins University Press.

Gaita, R. (2001) 'Terror and justice', in P. Craven (ed.), *The Best Australian Essays 2001*. Melbourne: Black, pp. 19–36.

Galtung, J. (1995) *On the Social Costs of Modernization: Social Disintegration, Atomie/Anomie and Social Development*, United Nations Research Institute for Social Development (UNRISD) Discussion Paper, Geneva.

Gamble, A. and Payne, A. (eds) (1993) *Regionalism and World Order*. Basingstoke: Macmillan.

Garland, D. (1990) *Punishment and Modern Society*. Oxford: Clarendon Press.

Garland, D. (1996) 'The limits of the sovereign state', *British Journal of Criminology*, 36 (4): 445–71.

Garland, D. (2001) *The Culture of Control: Crime and Social Order in Contemporary Society*. Oxford: Oxford University Press.

Gearty, C. (ed.) (1996) *Terrorism*. Aldershot: Dartmouth, pp. 73–92.

Giddens, A. (1991) *Modernity and Self-Identity*. Cambridge: Polity Press.

Giddens, A. (1996/97) 'Anthony Giddens on globalization: excerpts from a keynote address at the UNRISD conference on Globalization and Citizenship', *UNRISD News* (United Nations Research Institute for Social Development Bulletin), 15: 4–5.

Giddens, A. (1999) 'Runaway world: the Reith Lectures revisited', *The Director's Lectures*, Lecture 1: 10 November.

Gilligan, G. and Pratt, J. (eds) (2003) *Crime, Truth and Justice: Official Inquiry, Discourse, Knowledge*. Cullompton: Willan.

Gillespie, J. (2001) 'Globalization and legal transplantation: lessons from the past', *Deakin Law Review*, 6 (2): 286–311.

Gilpin, R. (1987) *The Political Economy of International Relations*. Princeton, NJ: Princeton University Press.

Goddard, L. (2000) 'The globalisation of criminal justice: will the international criminal court become a reality?', *Canterbury Law Review*, 7: 452–64.

Goh, B. C. (2002) *Law Without Lawyers, Justice Without Courts: On Traditional Chinese Mediation*. Hampshire: Ashgate.

Grabosky, P. and Smith, R. (1990) *Crime in the Digital Age: Controlling Telecommunications and Cyberspace Illegalities*. Sydney: Federation Press.

Gray, D. (2005) *An Excuse-Centered Approach to Transitional Justice*, Duke Law School Working Paper Series, Paper 27 [51].

Greer, S. and Lim, T. P. (1998) 'Confucianism: natural law Chinese style', *Ratio Juris 11/1*. Oxford: Blackwell.

Griffiths, D. (1997) 'The Case for Theoretical Pluralism', *Educational Management Administration and Leadership*, 25(4): 371–80.

Gross, E. (2002) 'Trying terrorists – justification for differing trial rules: the balance between security considerations and human rights', *Indiana International and Comparative Law Review*, 13 (1): 1–98.

Hague Academy of International Law (1961) *Collected Courses, 1960-II*. Leyden: Sijthoff A W.

Hall, R. B. (2005) 'Private authority – non-state actors and global governance', *Harvard International Review*, 27 (2): 66–70.

Harvey, D. (1989) *The Conditions of Postmodernity*. Oxford: Blackwell.

Hay, D., Linebaugh, P. and Thompson, E. P. (1975) *Albion's Fatal Tree*. London: Allen & Lane.

Hazan, P. (2000) *La Justice Face à la Guerre: de Nuremberg à la Haye*. Paris: Stock.

He, B. S. (1992) 'Crime control in China', in H. Heiland, L. Shelley and H. Katoh (eds), *Crime Control in Comparative Perspectives*. New York: Walter de Gruyter.

Head, M. (2000) 'Sydney Olympics used as a catalyst for permanent military powers over civilian unrest', *Alternative Law Journal*, 25: 192–5.

Heffelfinger, C. (2005) *Unmasking Terror: A Global Review of Terrorist Activities*. Washington, DC: Jamestown Foundation.

Hegel, G. (1955, 1983) *Grundlinien der Philosophie des Rechts* (*Elements of the Philosophy of Right*). Frankfurt am Main: Surkamp.

Heinz-Ladeur, K. (2004) 'Globalisation and public governance – a contradiction?', in K. Heinz-Lader (ed.), *Public Governance in the Age of Globalisation*. Aldershot: Ashgate, pp. 1–21.

Held, D. (2004a) 'Economic globalisation', in D. Held (ed.), *Global Covenant – The Social Democratic Alternative to the Washington Consensus*. Cambridge: Polity Press, pp. 21–33.

Held, D. (2004b) 'Political globalisation', in D. Held (ed.), *Global Covenant – The Social Democratic Alternative to the Washington Consensus*. Cambridge: Polity Press, pp. 73–87.

Held, D., McGrew, A., Goldblatt, D. and Perraton, J. (1999) *Global Transformations, Politics, Economics and Culture*. Stanford, CA: Stanford University Press.

Henham, R. (1997) 'Protective sentencing: ethics, rights and sentencing policy', *International Journal of the Sociology of Law*, 25: 45.

Henham, R. (2003) 'Some issues for sentencing in the International Criminal Court', *International and Comparative Law Quarterly*, 52 (1): 81–114.

Henham, R. (2004) 'Theorising the penalty of sentencing in international criminal trials', *Theoretical Criminology*, 8 (4): 429.

Henham, R. and Mannozzi, G. (2003) 'Victim participation and sentencing in England and Italy: a legal and policy analysis', *European Journal of Crime, Criminal Law and Criminal Justice*, 11 (3): 278.

Herbert, S. (1999) 'The end of the territorially-sovereign state? The case of crime control in the United States', *Political Geography*, 18 (2): 149–72.

Hester, S. and Elgin P. (1992) *A Sociology of Crime*. London: Routledge.

Hinkson, J. (2005) 'After the London bombings: an exercise in avoiding the truth', *Areana Magazine*, 78: 34.

Hocking, J. (1993) 'Constructing "terrorism"', in J. Hocking (ed.), *Beyond Terrorism – The Development of the Australian Security State*. Sydney: Allen & Unwin, pp. 1–16.

Hodgson, J. (2000) 'Comparing legal cultures: the comparativist as participant observer', in D. Nelken (ed.), *Contrasting Criminal Justice: Getting from Here to There*. Aldershot: Ashgate.

Hogg, R. (1988) 'Criminal justice and social control: contemporary developments in Australia', *Journal of Studies in Justice*, 2: 98–121.

Hogg, R. and Brown, D. (1998) *Rethinking Law and Order*. Melbourne: Pluto.

Hsu, L. S. (1932) *Political Philosophy of Confucianism*. London: George Routledge & Sons.

Huang, Z. and Luo, J. (1997) 'Preliminary exploration of the new characteristics of the management of public sector work in Schenzen: reflections on the Schenzen BLSCC', *Schenzen Political and Legal Yearbook*. Schenzen: Haitian Press, pp. 5–7.

Ignatieff, M. (1978) *A Just Measure of Pain: The Penitentiary in the Industrial Revolution*. London: Macmillan.

Ignatieff, M. (2003) 'The burden', *New York Times*, 5 January, pp. 22–31.

International Peace Research Institute Oslo (2006) *Report from the Conference 9/11 Five Years After: Values, Risk and Identity in the War on Terror*. Oslo: PRIO.

Jaber, H. (1999) 'Consequences of imperialism: Hezbollah and the West', *Brown Journal of World Affairs*, 6 (1): 163–75.

Johnson, R. (2005) 'Reconstructing the Balkans: a global governance construct?', in M. Lederer and P. Muller (eds), *Criticizing Global Governance*. New York: Palgrave Macmillan, pp. 177–95.

Jones, J. (2004) 'Human security and social development', *Denver Journal of International Law and Policy*, 33 (1): 92–103.

Katzenstein, P. (1996) *The Culture of National Security: Norms and Identity in World Politics*. New York: Columbia University Press [66].

Kay, J. (2004) 'Redefining the terrorist', *The National Interest*, 7 (Spring): 87.

Keith, R. (1994) *China's Struggle for the Rule of Law*. London: St. Martin's Press.

Kelsen, H. (1944) *Peace Through Law*. Chapel Hill, NC: University of North Carolina Press.

Kemshall, H. (2003) *Understanding Risk Through Criminal Justice*. Milton Keynes: Open University Press.

Keohane, R. (2001) 'Governance in a partially globalized world: presidential address, American Political Science Association', *American Political Science Review*, 95 (1): 1–13.

Kiss, C. (2006) 'The misuses of manipulation: the failure of transitional justice in post-conflict Hungary', Europe-Asia Studies, 58 (6): 925–40.

Koch, H. G. (2006) *Comparative Analysis of Case Scenarios*. Freiburg: MPI.

Krasner, S. (2001) 'Think again: sovereignty', *Foreign Policy*, 122 (Jan./Feb.): 20.

Kritz, N. (2002) 'Progress and humility: the ongoing search for post-conflict justice', in M. Bassiouni (ed.), *Post Conflict Justice*. New York: Transnational Publishers, pp. 55–89.

Lake, A. (1993) 'From containment to enlargement', *US Department of State Dispatch*, vol. 4, no. 39, 27 September.

Lederer, M. and Muller, P. (2005) *Criticizing Global Governance*. New York: Palgrave.

Leng, S. C. and Chiu, H. (1985) *Criminal Justice in Post Mao China: Analysis and Documents*. Albany, NY: State University of New York Press.

Levi, M. (1997) *Consent, Dissent and Patriotism*. Cambridge: Cambridge University Press.

Levi, M. (ed.) (1998) *The Howard Journal of Criminal Justice – Reflections on Organised Crime: Patterns and Control*, 37 (4): 335–45.

Linton, S. (2001) 'Cambodia, East Timor and Sierra Leone: experiments in international justice', *Criminal Law Forum*, 12: 185–246.

Linton, S. (2002) 'New approaches to international justice in Cambodia and East Timor', IRRC 84/845: 93–119.

Logan, W. (2008) 'Confronting evil: victims' rights in an age of terror', *Georgetown Law Journal*, 96 (3).

Lomasky, L. (1991) 'The political significance of terrorism' in R. Frey and C. Morris (eds), *Violence, Terrorism and Justice*. Cambridge: Cambridge University Press, pp. 86–115.

Lu, H. (1999) 'Bang jiao and re-integrative shaming in China's urban neighbourhoods', *International Journal of Comparative and Applied Criminal Justice*, 23 (1): 115–23.

Lu, J. and Wang, Z. (2005) 'China's attitude towards the ICC', *Journal of International Criminal Justice*, 3 (3): 608–20.

Lubman, S. (1997) 'Dispute resolution in China after Deng Xioping: "Mao and mediation" revisited', *Columbia Journal of Asian Law*, 11 (2): 229–31.

McBarnet, D. J. (1978) 'False dichotomies in criminal justice research', in J. Baldwin and A. K. Bottomley (eds), *Criminal Justice: Selected Readings*. London: Martin Robertson.

McCabe, E. (1989) 'Structural elements of contemporary criminal justice in the People's Republic of China', in R. Troyer, J. Clark and D. Rojek (eds), *Social Control in the People's Republic of China*. New York: Praeger.

McCauley, C. (ed.) (1991) *Terrorist Research and Public Policy*. London: Frank Cass.

McCauley, C. (2005) *The Psychology of Terrorism*. New York: SSRC.

McCoy, A. (2006) 'Invisible Industry: Jueteng Gambling and Philippine Politics'. Unpublished conference paper.

McCulloch, J. (2003) 'Counter-terrorism, human security and globalisation – from welfare state to warfare state?', *Current Issues in Criminal Justice*, 14 (3): 283–98.

McCulloch, J. *et al.* (2004) 'Suppressing the financing of terrorism', *Current Issues in Criminal Justice*, 16 (1): 71–8.

MacDonald, M. (2005) 'Constructing insecurity: Australian security discourse and policy post 2001', *International Relations*, 19 (3): 297–320.

McGeary, K. (1996) 'Face to face with evil', *Time*, 13 May, pp. 22–7.

McGregor, P. (1998) 'Telling My Lais: war crimes and reconciliation', *Human Rights Defender*, 7 (3): 4.

McKay, A. (forthcoming) 'Free Will, Genetic Pre-disposition and Sentencing'. PhD thesis, Law Faculty, University of Sydney.

McLuhan, M. (1964) *Understanding Media*. London: Routledge.

McRae, H. (1994) *The World in 2020: Power, Culture and Prosperity A Vision of the Future*. London: HarperCollins.

Mandal, M. (2001) 'NATO's bombing of Kosovo under international law/ politics and human rights in international criminal law: our case against NATO and the lessons to be learned from it', *Fordham International Law Journal*, 25: 95–128. [66]

Mann, M. (1986) *The Sources of Social Power, Vol. 1*. Cambridge: Cambridge University Press.

Marks, J. (2006) '9/11 + 3/11 + 7/7 = ? – What counts in counterterrorism', *Columbia Human Rights Law Review*, 37: 101–61.

Marx, G. (1980) 'The new police undercover work', *Urban Life*, 8 (4): 30–42.

Massicotte, M. (1999) 'Global governance and the global political economy: three texts in search of synthesis', *Global Governance*, 5 (1): 127–48.

Matwijkiw, A. (2002) 'A philosophical perspective on rights, accountability and post-conflict justice: setting up the premises', in M. Bassiouni (ed.), *Post Conflict Justice*. New York: Transnational Publishers, pp. 155–202.

Matza, D. (1964) *Delinquency and Drift*. New York: John Wiley.

Megret, F. (2002) 'The politics of international criminal justice', *Emory Journal of International Law*, 13: 1261.

Meister, R. (2004) *The Supreme Court, Guantanamo Bay and Justice Fix-It*, Cornell Law School Berger International Speaker Series, Paper 4.

Mendez, J. E. (1997) 'In defense of transitional justice', in A. J. McAdams (ed.), *Transitional Justice and the Rule of Law in New Democracies*. Notre Dame, IN: University of Notre Dame Press.

Michaelson, C. (2003) 'International human rights on trial – the United Kingdom's and Australia's legal response to 9/11', *Sydney Law Review*, 21 (3): 275–303.

Milanovic, B. (2006) 'Global Income Inequality: What is it and why it matters', *World Economics*, 7(1): 71–94.

Milanovic, M. (2006) 'State Responsibility for Genocide', *European Journal of International Law*, 17(3): 553–604.

Miller, L. (1999) 'The idea and the reality of collective security', *Global Governance*, 5 (3): 303–32.

Miller, T. (2005) 'Blurring the boundaries between immigration and crime control after September 11th', *Third World Law Journal*, 25 (1): 81–124.

Mintrom, M. and Wanna, J. (2006) 'Innovative state strategies in the antipodes. Enhancing the ability of governments to govern in the global context', *Australian Journal of Political Science*, 41 (2): 161–76.

Mittelman, J. and Johnston, R. (1999) 'The globalization of organized crime, the courtesan states, and the corruption of civil society', *Global Governance*, 5: 103–26.

Mythen, G. and Walklate, S. (2006) 'Which thesis? Risk society or governmentality?', *British Journal of Criminology*, 46 (3): 379–98.

Naim, M. (2003) 'The five wars of globalisation', *Foreign Policy*, 134: 28.

Napoleoni, L. (2005) *Terror Incorporated: Tracing the Dollars Behind the Terror Networks*. New York: Seven Stories Press.

Narveson, J. (2001) 'Terrorism and morality', in R. Frey and C. Morris (eds), *Violence, Terrorism and Justice*. Cambridge: Cambridge University Press, pp. 116–70.

Nelken, D. (ed.) (1995) 'Legal culture, diversity and globalisation', *Social and Legal Studies*, 4 (4) (Special Issue).

Nelken, D. (1997) 'The globalisation of crime and criminal justice: prospects and problems', in M. D. A. Freeman (ed.), *Law and Opinion at the End of the Twentieth Century*. Oxford: Oxford University Press, pp. 439–64.

Nelken, D. (1998) 'The globalisation of criminal justice', in M. Freeman (ed.), *Law at the Turn of the Century*. Oxford: Oxford University Press. N.1.

Nessossi, E. (2007) 'Limits to the Protection of Suspect's Rights at the Pre-trial Stage: The PRC's Application of Criminal Justice and Human Rights Standards'. Unpublished conference paper.

Newman, D. (2006) 'Borders and bordering – towards an interdisciplinary dialogue', *European Journal of Social Theory*, 9 (2): 171–86.

Nina, D. (1997) 'Panel beating for the smashed nation? The Truth and Reconciliation Commission, nation building and the construction of a privileged history in South Africa', *Australian Journal of Law and Society*, 13: 55–71.

O'Malley, P. (1992) 'Risk, power and crime prevention', *Economy and Society*, 21: 252–75.

O'Malley, P. (2002) 'Globalising risk? Distinguishing styles of "neo-liberal" criminal justice in Australia and the USA', *Criminal Justice*, 2 (2): 205–22.

O'Malley, P. (2007) 'Neo-liberalism and risk in criminology', in C. Cunneen and T. Anthony (eds), *New Essays in Critical Criminology*. Sydney: Federation Press.

O'Neil, A. (2005) 'The evolving nature of international terrorism and Australia's response', in D. Chappell and P. Wilson (eds), *Issues in Australian Crime and Criminal Justice*. Sydney: Butterworths, pp. 377–91.

Oliver, W. (2005) 'The era of Homeland Security: September 11, to ...', *Crime and Justice International*, 40 (3): 19–29.

Onwudiwe, I. (2001a) 'Terrorism: definitional problems', in I. D. Onwudiwe (ed.), *The Globalisation of Terrorism*. Aldershot: Ashgate, pp. 28–50.

Onwudiwe, I. D. (2001b) 'World systems theory', in I. D. Onwudiwe (ed.), *The Globalisation of Terrorism*. Aldershot: Ashgate, pp. 1–27.

Ozoren, S. (2004) 'Turkish Hizbollah: a case study of radical terrorism', *Journal of Turkish Weekly*, Wednesday, 1 December.

Paoli, L., Rabkov, I. and Reuter, P. (2006) 'Heroin Trafficking in Tajikistan: A Case-study in the Interaction of Weak Government and Illegal Markets'. Unpublished conference paper.

Parachini, J. (2001) 'Religion isn't the sole motivation of terror', *LA Times*, 16 September: M7.

Passas, N. and Nelken, D. (1993) 'The thin blue line between legitimate and criminal enterprises: subsidy frauds in the European Community', *Crime, Law and Social Change*, 19 (3): 223–44.

Patomaki, H. (2005) 'Democratizing global governance: beyond the domestic analogy', in M. Lederer and P. Muller (eds), *Criticising Global Governance*. New York: Palgrave Macmillan.

Paye, J. (2005) 'Guantanamo Bay and the new legal order', *Monthly Review*, 57 (1): 45.

Pendleton, M. (1999) 'Our allegiance – Australians or global citizens?', *Murdoch University Electronic Journal of Law*, 6 (3) (see: http://www.murdoch.edu.au/elaw/issues/vgn3/pendleton63.html).

Peng Er, Lam (2006) 'Japan's human security role in Southeast Asia', *Contemporary Southeast Asia*, 28 (1): 141–59.

Perez, A. F. (2000) 'The perils of Pinochet: problems for transitional justice and a supranational governance solution', *Denver Journal of International Law and Policy*, 28: 175.

Phelan, L. (2003) 'The war on terror's other front: The Philippines', *Human Rights Defender*, 12 (1): 7.

Pierson, C. (1996) *The Modern State*. London: Routledge.

Piotrowicz, R. (1998) 'International focus', *Australian Law Journal*, 72: 844.

Player, T., Skipper, H. and Lambert, J. (2002) 'A global definition of terrorism', *Risk Management*, 49 (9): 60.

Popovski, V. (2000) 'The International Criminal Court: a synthesis of retributive and restorative justice', *International Relations*, 15 (3): 1–10.

Posner, E. (2002) 'Fear and the regulatory model of counter-terrorism', *Harvard Journal of Law and Public Policy*, 25 (2): 681–98.

Poynting, S. *et al.* (2004) *Bin Laden in the Suburbs: Criminalising the Arab Other*, Institute of Criminology Monograph Series. Sydney: Institute of Criminology.

Pratt, J. (2000) 'Emotive and ostentatious punishment: its decline and resurgence in modern society', *Punishment and Society*, 2: 417.

Proulx, V. (2005) 'Babysitting terrorists: should states be strictly liable for failing to prevent transborder attacks?', *Berkley Journal of International Law*, 23: 615–68.

Pye, L. (1996) 'The state and the individual: an overview interpretation', in B. Hook (ed.), *The Individual and the State in China*. Oxford: Clarendon.

Rasmussen, M. (2002) 'A parallel globalization of terror: 9/11, security and globalization', *Cooperation and Conflict: Journal of the Nordic International Studies Association*, 37 (3): 323–49.

Rees, S. and Blanchard, L.-A. (1999) 'Security through international citizenship', in M. Tehranian (ed.), *Worlds Apart: Human Security and Global Governance*. New York: I. B. Tauris, pp. 168–77.

Rehman, J. (2002) 'The influence of international human rights law upon criminal justice systems', *Journal of Criminal Law*, 66 (6): 505–23.

Reiner, R. (2000) *The Politics of the Police*. New York: Oxford University Press.

Reno, W. (2006) 'Redefining Statehood in the Global Periphery'. Unpublished conference paper.

Robb, P. (1996) *Midnight in Sicily*. Sydney: Duffy & Snellgrove.

Roberts, P. (2002) 'On method: the ascent of comparative criminal justice', *Oxford Journal of Legal Studies*, 22: 539.

Roberts, S. (2005) 'After government? On representing law without the state', *Modern Law Review*, 68 (1): 1.

Robertson, R. (1992) *Globalization*. London: Sage.

Roche, D. (2003) *Accountability and Restorative Justice*. Oxford: Oxford University Press.

Roling, B. V. A. (1961) 'The law of war and the national jurisdiction since 1945', in Hague Academy of International Law, *Collected Courses, 1960-II*. Leyden: Sijthoff A W, pp. 323–456.

Rosenfeld, S. (2004) 'Gitmo justice', *The American Prospect*, 15 (10): 8.

Rotman, E. (2000–1) 'The globalisation of criminal violence', *Cornell Journal of Law and Public Policy*, 10 (1): 1–43.

Roznovschi, M. (2003) 'Book review: Sadat, L. N., *The International Criminal Court and the Transformation of International Law: Justice for the New*

Millennium (International and Comparative Criminal Law Series)', *International Journal of Legal Information*, 3 (1): 120–3.

Rusche, G. and Kirchheimer, O. (1935) *Punishment and Social Structure*. New York: Columbia University Press.

Sands, P. (ed.) (2003) *From Nuremberg to The Hague: The Future of International Criminal Justice*. Cambridge: Cambridge University Press.

Sarkin, J. (1997) 'The Truth and Reconciliation Commission in South Africa', *Commonwealth Law Bulletin*, 23 (1 & 2): 528–42.

Saul, B. (2006) 'Legal response of the League of Nations to terrorism', *Journal of International Criminal Justice Advance Access* (online), 19 January.

Scharf, M. P. (1997) *Balkan Justice: The Story Behind the First International War Crimes Trial since Nuremberg*. Durham, NC: Carolina Academic Press.

Scharf, M. P. (1999) 'The amnesty exception to the jurisdiction of the International Criminal Court', *Cornell International Law Journal*, 32: 507–29.

Scharf, M. P. (2000) 'The tools for enforcing international criminal justice in the new millenium: lessons from the Yugoslavia Tribunal', *International Criminal Justice*, 49: 925–80.

Schmid, A. (2004) *Terrorism – The Definitional Problem*. Paper presented at the 'War Crimes Research Symposium: Terrorism on Trial' at Case Western Reserve University School of Law, sponsored by the Frederick K. Cox International Law Center, on 8 October.

Schorr, D. (2005) 'Quaint premises: prisoners of war held under rigorous conditions at Guantanamo Bay', *The New Leader*, 88 (2): 5.

Scratton, P. (2007) *Power, Conflict and Criminalization*. London: Routledge.

Seneviratne, K. (2006) *Australia – Peacekeeper or Petroleum Predator?*, Inter Press Service, 22 June (http://www.globalpolicy.org).

Shearing, C. (1992) 'The relationship between public and private policing', in M. Tonry and N. Morris (eds), *Modern Policing*. Chicago: University of Chicago Press, pp. 399–433.

Shearing, C. and Johnston, L. (2005) 'Justice in the risk society', *Australian and New Zealand Journal of Criminology*, 38 (1): 25–38.

Shearing, C. and Leman-Langois, S. (2004) 'Repairing the future: the South African Truth and Reconciliation Commission at work', in G. Giligan and J. Pratt (ed.), *Crime, Truth and Justice: Official Enquiry, Discourse, Knowledge*. Cullompton: Willan, pp. 222–43.

Shearing, C. and Stenning, P. (1981) 'Modern private security: its growth and implications' in M. Tonry and N. Morris (eds), *Crime and Justice – A Review of Current Research, Vol. 3*. Chicago: University of Chicago Press.

Sheptycki, J. W. E. (1996) 'Law enforcement, justice and democracy in the transnational arena: reflections on the war on drugs', *International Journal of the Sociology of Law*, 24 (1): 61–75.

Sheptycki, J. W. E. (2003) 'Global law enforcement as a protection racket: some sceptical notes on transnational organized crime as an object of global governance', in A. Edwards and P. Gill (eds), *Transnational Organised Crime: Perspectives on Global Security*. London: Routledge, pp. 42–59.

Silke, A. (2003a) 'Retaliating against terrorism', in A. Silke (ed.), *Terrorists, Victims and Society: Psychological Perspectives on Terrorism and Its Consequences*. Chichester: Wiley, pp. 215–31.

Silke, A. (2003b) 'Fire of Iolaus: the role of state counter-measures in causing terrorism and what needs to be done', in T. Bjorgo (ed.), *Root Causes of Terrorism: Proceedings from an International Expert Meeting in Oslo*. Oslo: Norwegian Institute of International Affairs, pp. 179–93.

Silke, A. (ed.) (2003c) *Terrorists, Victims and Society: Psychological Perspectives on Terrorism and Its Consequences*. Chichester: Wiley.

Silke, A. (2004) 'The road less travelled: trends in terrorism research', in A. Silke (ed.), *Research on Terrorism: Trends, Achievements and Failures*. London: Frank Cass, pp. 186–214.

Silove, D., Zwi, A. and le Touze, D. (2006) 'Do truth commissions heal? The East Timor experience', *The Lancet*, 367 (9518): 1222–4.

Simon, J. (2001–2) 'Governing through crime metaphors', *Brook Law Review*, 67 (4): 1035–70.

Simon, J. (2007) *Governing Through Crime: How the War on Crime Transformed American Democracy and Created a Culture of Fear*. New York: Oxford University Press.

Slaughter, A. and Burke-White, W. (2006) 'The future of international law is domestic (or, the European way of law)', *Harvard Law Review*, 47 (2): 327–51.

Smith, D. (1975) *The Mafia Mystique*. New York: Basic Books.

Steele, J. (2005) 'Annan attacks erosion of rights in war on terror – US and Britain in UN Secretary General's sights', *Guardian*, 11 March.

Stenson, K. (2001) 'The new politics of crime control', in K. Stenson and R. Sullivan (eds), *Crime, Risk and Justice: The Politics of Crime Control in Liberal Democracies*. Cullompton: Willan.

Strang, H. (2002) *Repair and Revenge: Victims and Restorative Justice*. Oxford: Oxford University Press.

Tamanaha, B. (1997) *Realistic Socio-legal Theory: Pragmatism and a Social Theory of Law*. Oxford: Clarendon Press.

Tamanaha, B. (2007) *Contemporary Legal Pluralism*, Julius Stone Lecture, University of Sydney, 6 July.

Tan, M. (2003) 'Money laundering and the financing of terrorism', *Journal of Banking and Finance Law and Practice*, 14 (2): 81–107.

Taylor, L. (1984) *In the Underworld*. London: Basil Blackwell.

Teitel, R. (1999) 'The universal and the particular in international criminal justice', *Columbia Human Rights Law Review*, 30: 285–305.

Teixeira, P. (2004) 'Public governance and the co-operative law of transnational markets: the case of financial regulation', in K. Heinz-Lader (ed.), *Public Governance in the Age of Globalisation*. Aldershot: Ashgate, pp. 305–35.

Thatcher, D. (2005) 'The local role in homeland security', *Law and Society Review*, 39 (3): 635–376.

Thompson, E. P. (1975) *Whigs and Hunters: The Origins of the Black Acts*. Harmondsworth: Peregrine.

Thorup, M. and Sorrenson, M. (2004) 'Inescapably side by side: an interview with David Held', *Polity*, February (see: http://globalpolicy.icg.org/globalize/define/2004/04heldinterview.htm).

Tochilovsky, V. (2002) 'Proceedings in the International Criminal Court: some lessons to learn from ICTY experience', *European Journal of Crime, Criminal Law and Criminal Justice*, 10 (4): 268–75.

Troyer, R. (1989) 'Chinese thinking about crime and social control', in R. Troyer, J. Clarke and D. Rojek (eds), *Social Control in the People's Republic of China*, Westport: Greenwood Publishing Group.

Tunander, O. (1997) *Geo-politics in Post Wall Europe: Security, Territory and Identity*. London: Sage.

Tunander, O. (2006) 'Democratic State vs Deep State Approaching the Dual State of the West'. Upublished conference paper.

Turk, A. (1982) 'Social dynamics of terrorism', in *Annals of the American Academy of Political and Social Science*, Vol. 463: International Terrorism, pp. 119–28.

UN Security Council Resolution 1377, 12 November 2001, Colin Powell's Response to UN.

UN Security Council Resolution 757 (1992).

UN Security Council Resolution 955 (994).

UN Security Council Resolution 965 (1994).

Van Creveld, M. (2004) 'On globalisation: the military dimension', in K. Heinz-Lader (ed.), *Public Governance in the Age of Globalisation*. Aldershot: Ashgate, pp. 197–210.

Van der Vyver, J. D. (2001) 'American exceptionalism: human rights, international criminal justice, and national self-righteousness', *Emory Law Journal*, 50 (3): 775–832.

Van Duyne, P. (1993) 'Organised crime and business-crime enterprises in the Netherlands', *Crime, Law and Social Change*, 19 (2): 103–42.

Van Duyne, P. (1996) 'The phantom and threat of organised crime', *Crime, Law and Social Change*, 24 (3): 341–77.

Viano, E. (ed.) (1999) *Global Organised Crime and International Security*. Aldershot: Ashgate.

Vogler, R. (2006) *A World View of Criminal Justice*. Aldershot: Ashgate.

Vold, G. (2005) *Theoretical Criminology*. New York: Oxford University Press.

Volkov, V. (2002) *Violent Entrepreneurs: The Use of Force in the Making of Russian Capitalism*. Ithaca, NY: Cornell University Press.

259

Wainwright, E. *et al.* (2002) *New Neighbour, New Challenge – Australia and the Security of East Timor*, Australian Strategic Policy Institute Report. Canberra: Australian Strategic Policy Institute.

Walace, D. and Kreisel, B. (2003) 'Martial law as a counter-terrorism response to terrorist attacks: domestic and international legal dimensions', *International Criminal Justice Review*, 13 (1): 50–74.

Walker, C. (1992) *The Prevention of Terrorism in British Law*. Manchester: Manchester University Press.

Walker, C. and Starmer, K. (1999) *Miscarriages of Justice: A Review of Justice in Error*. Oxford: Blackstone.

Wallerstein, I. (1979) *The Capitalist World Economies: Essays*. New York: Cambridge University Press.

Wang, J. (2003) 'Eastern Turkistan Islamic Movement: a case study of a new terrorist organisation in China', *International Journal of Offender Therapy and Comparative Criminology*, 47 (5): 568–84.

Ward, P. and Dobinson, I. (1988) 'Heroin: a considered response', in M. Findlay and R. Hogg (eds), *Understanding Crime and Criminal Justice*. Sydney: Law Book Co., pp. 128–48.

Waters, M. (1995) *Globalization*. London: Routledge.

Weaver, G. and Wittekind, J. (2002) 'Categorizing September 11: casualties as acts of terrorism', *Homicide Studies*, 6 (4): 372–6.

Weber, M. (1964) *The Theory of Social and Economic Organisation*. New York: Free Press.

Weitekamp, E. G. M., Parmentier, S., Weinkamp, W., Vanspauwen, K., Valiñas, M. and Gerits, R. (2006) 'How to deal with mass victimisation and gross human rights violations: a restorative justice approach', in U. Ewald and K. Turkovic (eds), *Large-scale Victimisation as a Potential Source of Terrorist Activities. Importance of Regaining Security in Post-Conflict Societies*, NATO Programme for Security through Science Series, Vol. 13. Amsterdam: IOS Press, pp. 217–41.

Werle, G. and Jessberger, F. (2002) 'International criminal justice is coming home: the new German Code of Crimes Against International Law', *Criminal Law Forum*, 13: 191–223.

Wessel, J. (2006) 'Judicial policy-making and the International Criminal Court: an institutional guide to analyzing international adjudication', *Columbia Journal of Transnational Law*, 44 (2): 377–452.

West, R. (1999) 'Taking moral argument seriously', *Chicago Kent Law Review*, 74 (2): 499–562.

Wheeler, N. and Dunne, T. (2001) 'East Timor and the new humanitarian interventionism', *Journal of International Affairs*, 77 (4): 805–27.

White, T. (2006) 'Non-proliferation and counter-terrorism cooperation in Southeast Asia: meeting global obligations through regional security architectures?', *Contemporary Southeast Asia*, 28 (1): 1–26.

Wilson, R. (2001) *The Politics of Truth and Reconciliation in South Africa: Legitimizing the Post-Apartheid State*. Cambridge: Cambridge University Press.

Winter, S. (1988) 'The metaphor of standing and the problem of self-governance', *Stanford Law Review*, 40 (6): 1371–516.

Wippman, D. (1999) 'Atrocities, deterrence, and the limits of international justice', *Fordham International Law Journal*, 23: 473–89.

Wong, D. (1999) 'Delinquency control and juvenile justice in China', *ANZ Journal of Criminology*, 32 (1): 27–41.

Wu, Z., Chen, Z., Ye, D. and Ma, X. (2003) *Research on Non-custodial Sentences*. Beijing: People's Public Security University Publishing House of China.

Yang, J. (1998) 'The situation and developmental paradigm of mass prevention and mass management team in Shanghai,' *Juvenile Delinquency Research*, 188(2): 16–25.

Yang, V. (2002) 'Working with Chinese Prosecutors: Sixth Year of the Canada-China Criminal Justice Co-operation Program'

Zahar, A. and Sluiter, G. (2007) *International Criminal Law: A Critical Restatement*. Oxford: Oxford University Press.

Zhang, X. (2004) 'A Restorative Justice Audit of the Chinese Criminal Justice System'. Unpublished MSc thesis.

Zher, H. (1990) *Changing Lenses*. Ontario: Herald Press.

Zhong, L. and Broadhurst, R. (2007) 'Building little safe and civilised communities: community crime prevention with Chinese characteristics?', *International Journal of Offender Therapy and Comparative Criminology*, 51 (1): 52–67.

Zhu, Y. and Zhang, G. (2003) 'Re-integrating the criminals into society: a report on the experiment of community rehabilitation in Shanghai', *Legal Daily*, 24 June.

Films and documentaries

Between Joyce and Remembrance, Bullfrog Films, dir. Mark Kaplan (2005).

The Accused, BBC, Panorama documentary (2001).

A Licence to Kill, BBC, Panorama documentary.

State of Fear – The Truth About Terrorism, Skylight Pictures, dir. Pamela Yates (2006).

Campaign Against Terror, PBS Frontline documentary, from the 'Age of Terror' series.

Global Security, Watson Institute, Brown University, dir. James Der Derian.

The Power of Nightmares, Special Broadcasting Service, Australia (2007).

Electronic references

Discussion of the International Military Tribunal for the Far East: http://www.arts.cuhk.edu.hk/NanjingMassacre/NMTT.html

Full text of the Geneva Conventions (1949) and the 1977 Protocols:
http://www.icrc.org/ihl.nsf/WebCONVFULL?OpenView
For the full text of the Special Court Agreement (Ratification) Act 2002 follow
the links from:
http://www.sc-sl.org/
Agreement between the UN and Cambodia concerning the Prosecution under
Cambodian Law of Crimes Committed during the Period of Democratic
Kampuchea (6 June 2003). Outline at:
http://www.asil.org/ilib/ilib0611.htm#a1
Widespread dissatisfaction with Indonesia's Ad Hoc Human Rights Tribunal
on East Timor has repeatedly led to calls for the creation of an independent
international tribunal. For example:
http://www.globalpolicy.org/intljustice/tribunals/timor/2003/
0818renew.htm
Full text of the Rome Statute of the International Criminal Court:
http://www.un.org/law/icc/statute/romefra.htm
The 1992 media reports of Bosnian concentration-camps were unfounded:
http:/www.terravista.pt/guincho/2104/199810/deichmann_9701.html
and
http://www.balkan-archive.org.yu/politics/conc_camps/html/Kenney.
html
Scharf's comments in *The Washington Post* (3 October 1999):
http: //www.fair.org/reports/post-war-crimes.html
Full text of the International Covenant on Civil and Political Rights
(ICCPR):
http://www.unhchr.ch/html/menu3/b/a_ccpr.htm
Full text of the European Convention for the Protection of Human Rights
and Fundamental Freedoms (ECHR):
http://www.echr.coe.int/Eng/BasicTexts.htm
Full text of the Rules of Procedure and Evidence of the International Criminal
Court:
http://www1.umn.edu/humanrts/instree/iccrulesofprocedure.html
Full text of the Draft Legislation, Enacted Legislation and Debates relating to
the implementation of the Rome Statute into national law:
http://www.iccnow.org/resourcestools/ratimptoolkit/
nationalregionaltools/legislationdebates.html
Full text of the Statute of the International Tribunal (Adopted 25 May
1993):
http://www.un.org/icty/basic/statut/statute.htm
Human Rights Committee:
http://www.unhchr.ch/html/menu2/6/hrc.htm
Committee against Torture:
http://www.unhchr.ch/html/menu2/6/cat.htm

Index

Added to a page number 'n' denotes notes.